The Peaceful Uses
of Military Forces

PRAEGER SPECIAL STUDIES IN
INTERNATIONAL POLITICS AND PUBLIC AFFAIRS

The Peaceful Uses of Military Forces

Hugh Hanning

Published in cooperation with
the World Veterans Federation

FREDERICK A. PRAEGER, Publishers
New York · Washington · London

The purpose of the Praeger Special Studies is to make specialized research monographs in U.S. and international economics and politics
available to the academic, business, and government communities. For
further information, write to the Special Projects Division, Frederick
A. Praeger, Publishers, 111 Fourth Avenue, New York, N.Y. 10003.

FREDERICK A. PRAEGER, PUBLISHERS
111 Fourth Avenue, New York, N.Y. 10003, U.S.A.
77-79 Charlotte Street, London W.1, England

Published in the United States of America in 1967
by Frederick A. Praeger, Inc., Publishers

© 1967 by Frederick A. Praeger, Inc.

Library of Congress Catalog Card Number: 67-22282

Printed in the United States of America

FOREWORD

Hugh Hanning's study of the peaceful uses of military forces was sponsored by the World Veterans Federation as an expression of several of the organization's fields of interest. As the international body speaking for the community of veterans and war victims, the WVF and the more than twenty million persons it represents constitute the world's greatest organized reservoir of experience in military service. From this experience stems a knowledge of the potentialities and the limitations of military service as an element in the lives of individuals and as a prerequisite of national survival in a world not yet governed by law and reason.

From the point of view of the individual, the Federation and its member associations in forty-nine countries have seen that the training and experience of military service can provide an important preparation for post-service employment. Having recognized this factor, a number of governments have included specific programmes to give vocational training aimed at post-service careers to personnel terminating or having already terminated military life. In any case, the character of modern military forces requires a level of literacy and mechanical skill that makes it necessary to include in the training programme instruction that is also relevant to civilian pursuits such as civil engineering, public health, communications, transportation, teaching, and administration.

Thus, as an organization concerned with the post-service resettlement of veterans, the WVF is interested in encouraging and expanding the vocational training and placement facilities that may be provided by the military establishments of the various nations. That is one element of this study.

From the point of view of the nation, we recognize that-- while we hope and work for the day when it will be less so--the facts of modern life require the maintenance of military forces. Happily, these forces are not usually engaged in combat or even in operations more onerous than required to maintain a reasonable degree of readiness. Consequently, the existence of a military force in peacetime usually means that there is a reservoir of people, of equipment, and of capabilities for both leadership and training that can be employed for constructive purposes. In a number of countries, these resources have been applied to development projects ranging from literacy training to road building, to emergency relief actions, and to other social requirements that supplement the normal civilian instrumentalities. Such experience has proved invaluable in the development of some of the presently industrialized nations and is being employed in several of the newly developing countries.

To encourage and expand such constructive uses of military forces is consistent with the aims of the WVF in the field of economic and social development. The organization is of course aware of the necessity of establishing and observing standards that will ensure that neither fair labour standards nor the rights of civilian enterprise are violated.

As progress in communications and transportation shrinks the world and as the employment of international institutions to mobilize and coordinate multi-national action gains acceptance in functions ranging from United Nations peace-keeping missions to relief services in cases of major catastrophe, the need for trained and ready resources in the various countries increases. An organization dedicated to the peaceful settlement of international disputes and to support of the United Nations, the WVF has been one of the pioneers in studying the problems of international peace-keeping and in advocating measures to improve the resources of the world community for this purpose. Reserves of trained individuals organized in military units prepared and equipped for these types of international service are an element in what the WVF believes to be the necessary congregation of facilities to help ensure progress towards a peaceful world.

For these reasons, the World Veterans Federation decided to examine experience in the peaceful uses of military forces, to facilitate communication among officials engaged in such work in the various countries, and to offer a compendium of information and, if possible, generally accepted principles for the planning and conduct of related activities. Mr. Hanning's study is the result.

A veteran of the British Navy in World War II, an experienced journalist and observer, and a recognized commentator on subjects related to war and peace, Mr. Hanning travelled thousands of miles to observe peaceful uses projects in sixteen countries and to interview governmental officials and others responsible for their planning and implementation. During the course of his work, he developed and made known the new word "PUMF," which has rapidly come into use among the professionals active in the field.

Both Mr. Hanning and the WVF regretted that it was not possible to visit PUMF projects in many more countries and to obtain the advice of many more of the officers and others who have accumulated first-hand experience in this field. The limitations of time and resources made it necessary to select a group of projects, of countries, and of people who would provide a cross-section of the various situations and types of experience that exist. Thus Mr. Hanning's study includes reports on the experiences in Belgium, Brazil, Colombia, France, India, Iran, Israel, Ivory Coast, Morocco, Nigeria, the Netherlands, Pakistan, Peru, Thailand, the United Kingdom, and the United States of America.

When the study was in draft form, the Federation then convened at its Paris headquarters an expert committee to review the material and to give advice on the drafting of a set of general principles that could be applied to activity for the peaceful uses of military forces. The WVF is deeply grateful to the individuals who gave their time and effort to the work of that committee. They are: Col. Gilles Baudoin, Commission Armées-Jeunesse, Paris; Mr. Robert Black, Agency for International Development, Department of State, Washington, D.C.; Mr. Wynne James, Assistant for Civic Action, Office of the Assistant Secretary of Defense, Washington, D.C.; Lt-Col. M. Gulzar Khan, Secretary, Pakistan Armed Services Board, Ministry of Defence, Rawalpindi; Lt-Col. Olufemi Olutoye, Chief Education Officer, Ministry of Defence, Lagos; Mr. C. Rossillion, International Labour Office, Geneva; Brigadier K.C. Sharma, Director General of Resettlement, Ministry of Defence, New Delhi.

It should be emphasized that the general principles which have been prepared by the WVF Secretariat with the advice of the above group remain the sole responsibility of the World

Veterans Federation.   The contents of Mr. Hanning's study have been modified somewhat in consultation with the above expert group and the WVF Secretariat, but the opinions expressed remain those of Mr. Hanning and have not been the subject of either approval or disapproval by either the statutory bodies of the WVF or the individuals listed above.

Moreover, it is not intended to imply that the kinds of action described in the study are the only ones that constitute "peaceful uses" of military forces. Differences of opinion as to what can be defined as "peaceful" as contrasted to "non-peaceful" utilization of military forces have produced an as yet unresolved international controversy into which this survey has not entered. It is our conviction that the activities described by Mr. Hanning will fall within the scope of any objective definition of "peaceful uses."

Finally,   the World Veterans Federation expresses its sincere appreciation to all who have helped to make this project possible: to the governments and their officials who have cooperated in it, to the International Labour Office for its interest and assistance, to the WVF member associations in the countries studied which have greatly facilitated Mr. Hanning's work, to the experts listed above and, with a special note of gratitude and esteem, to Mr. Hanning himself.

> Norman Acton
> Secretary General
> World Veterans Federation

PREFACE

The foundations of this book were laid by the World Veterans Federation in the form of a detailed questionnaire to member organizations around the world relating to resettlement practices and civic action programmes. The resulting unique body of information enabled me to probe much deeper into the achievements of these countries than anyone could possibly have done without such backing; for the amount of written material available is extremely limited. While there is a growing corpus of excellent literature on armies in the developing world, I am aware of only one published book explicitly on civic action--though it is an excellent panorama of the subject: Harry F. Walterhouse's A Time to Build.

During my tour, I travelled more than 100,000 miles--to each of the countries dealt with in individual chapters. My first-hand experience covered a very wide area, ranging from civic action projects in the field to technical training centres in almost every country.

I spoke mainly to senior officers, particularly directors of education and resettlement, and to heads of service departments; where heads of government were particularly interested--President Ayub Khan of Pakistan, for example, and Mr. Shastri of India--I talked with them, too. I also sought out individual officers whom I knew were particularly experienced in the subject, among them the Engineer-in-Chief of the Pakistan Army, the Commander-in-Chief of the Nigerian Army, and Colonel Valencia, the leading civic action expert in the Colombian Army.

In Washington, I had long discussions with Mr. Wynne James, the Defense Department's Assistant for Civic Action, and was similarly much helped by officials of the State Department, notably Mr. Robert Smith and Mr. Robert Black.

Everywhere there was total cooperation--a reflection partly, I think, of the prestige of the World Veterans Federation, and partly also of the pride of these governments in the work they were doing, and the knowledge that they had valuable experience to impart to others.

The opinions in this book, and any errors that may be contained in it, are entirely the responsibility of the author. It does not claim to be exhaustive--on the contrary, it is highly selective in seeking to highlight the particular form of activity that particular countries are doing best. But it does attempt to grapple with some of the underlying issues of a complex, important, and novel subject that bears directly on the problems of nearly all governments today, particularly those of developing countries.

The whole conception of the study, and its organization, was that of the World Veterans Federation. Whatever credit attaches to it, therefore, belongs to the officers of the Federation, notably Secretary General Norman Acton and Director of Programmes James Knott, and to its representatives, particularly those in the United Kingdom, France, Belgium, the Netherlands, Israel, Pakistàn, India, Thailand, Malaysia, Nigeria, the Ivory Coast, Morocco, the U.S.A., Colombia, and Brazil. Without the active helpfulness of these representatives, the considerable amount of information in this study could not possibly have been accumulated. The author would like to extend his gratitude to them, and to hope that in this book he has gone some way to justifying the efforts that they put into promoting this study.

                                        Hugh Hanning

CONTENTS

CONTENTS   xiii

Chapter   Page

GENERAL PRINCIPLES ON THE
PEACEFUL USES OF MILITARY FORCES

INTRODUCTION

The primary purpose of military forces must be recognized as being to provide for the external and internal security of their countries. However, in a world of sizable standing military forces, the concept of the supplementary peaceful use of such forces along constructive lines of benefit to the community at large deserves exploration and definition. Indeed, in many countries, such use is an integral part of attaining national security and not a pure supplement. There are skills required in modern military structures that are capable of being used for non-military purposes, skills that in some areas of the world are in short supply. To be found in military forces today are individuals and units skilled in engineering, medicine, communications, transportation, procurement and distribution techniques, and adult training and education. Further, the period of military service provides an opportunity for general education and for training, or the basis for further training upon release, in such skills.

Probably in every country, such peaceful uses of military forces (PUMF) are conducted in a variety of forms by ground, naval, and air forces. It should also be mentioned that they are organized internationally in the case of some natural disasters and in the course of peace-keeping operations--which indeed themselves embody PUMF action. Our main focus, however, is on the national level and we seek to determine whether, from the experience gained, certain general principles can be established for the successful conduct of PUMF activities. The following are offered as such general principles, always allowing that in widely varying circumstances there will be some exceptions and that it is essential that there be a continuing process of objective evaluation of successes and failures to guide such present and planned activities.

DISASTER OR EMERGENCY RELIEF

The use of military forces in situations of disaster or emergency relief is a generally accepted and most often invaluable PUMF action. Without subjecting this over-all category of PUMF action to detailed scrutiny, a few general principles are worth stating:

1. The utilization of military capabilities in these situations should be the prerogative of the political leadership of the country.

2. Contingency plans should be drawn up and should provide an instant assessment of the skills and supplies available to assist in the emergency relief action and their mobility to reach the scene.

3. As soon as possible, one "focal point" must be established on the scene to arrive at a clear definition of the men and material needed.

4. If there is to be an appeal for international assistance, there should be an international "focal point" working in the closest possible liaison with the national authority directing the operation.

5. There should be an advance stand-by arrangement for the civil-military supervisory mechanism to be utilized in such a situation so that channels of authority are swiftly determined.

6. If at all possible, the military part of the operation should be structured geographically and functionally to correspond to the relevant civilian authorities.

7. Realistic exercises should be staged to improve military and civilian capabilities for emergency relief on both the national and international levels.

Note: The use of military forces to ensure the continuation of essential civil services when these are disrupted during strikes and labour strife is sometimes treated as falling within this category of emergency relief action. Such use should generally be avoided where it damages over-all civilian-military relationships.

EDUCATION AND TRAINING

Governments often recognize the obligation to re-establish productively veterans or ex-servicemen (both officer and enlisted personnel) and the economic and social value of doing so. At the international level, one even finds such guidelines as ILO Recommendation No. 71 Concerning Employment Organization in the Transition from War to Peace and many other standards applicable to this field. Some governments have further recognized the utility of service-connected training as a means of combating illiteracy, providing direction toward skills needed by the country, and instilling a sense of national consciousness. The provision of such training opportunities can also be of assistance to recruitment. The general principles that appear to apply to this category of PUMF action are:

1. Training should include the instilling of self-discipline and self-reliance and the encouragement of a sense of national consciousness and citizenship responsibility.

2. The level of skill to be aimed at for such pre- or post-release training programmes obviously depends upon the amount of training time available. Where the training is not directly related to the specific military functions of the trainee, the length of service is a particularly determining factor as to training opportunities offered and the level of skill that can realistically be achieved. A military service training programme should aim at the encouragement of post-release continuation of education and training.

3. An equally important determining factor is an evaluation of the existing levels of education, skill, aptitude, and interest of the servicemen to whom such training might be made available. Elementary education is an obvious prerequisite for many vocational skills. Testing and evaluation techniques must be matched to the age levels and national culture of the individuals involved.

4. The selection of fields in which supplementary training might be given should be made on the basis of national manpower forecasts and plans as to the types of skills

to be most needed, combined with assessment of the potentials and numbers of servicemen to be released. A national interdepartment coordinating mechanism is essential to coordinate the resulting plans as a part of the national training programme.

5. Before a training programme is undertaken, there must be assurance that the appropriate facilities, equipment, and instructors will be available. Adequate provision for these has sometimes been overlooked. It should be mentioned, however, that trainees have on occasion constructed their own facilities. It is recommended that separate pre- or post-release training facilities or courses be established for servicemen where applicable, due to age and background differences with regular civilian students. Nevertheless, maximum utilization should be made of existing facilities to avoid duplication and extra costs. For military conducted programmes, the special training of instructors in civilian schools may be desirable to upgrade the teaching competence of military personnel. The utilization of leadership and instruction capabilities among the participants in the training programmes, especially in off-duty voluntary courses, has proved very valuable.

6. Experience has shown that greater attention needs to be devoted to equipment maintenance, not only at training installations but for that equipment which the trainee will be using following graduation.

7. For training on any considerable scale, pre- and post-release instruction recommends itself for the attainment of primary and middle level technical skills. Most particularly in the developing countries, this PUMF action can help meet the great need for such skills, especially in agriculture and mechanics.

8. In areas of extreme shortage of technical skills, the potential of PUMF action to provide primary level instructors is particularly important.

9. In connection with such service-connected programmes, a thoroughgoing system must be established of informing the serviceman of what instruction is available, testing

his aptitudes and current abilities, counselling him on his opportunities, and providing demonstration of successful results. Where training facilities are limited, a careful selection process of those interested must be maintained. The close cooperation and participation of unit commanders and non-commissioned officers in such programmes are necessary.

10. Both pre-release and post-release training programmes are valuable. However, for the attainment of primary and middle level technical skills, the system of pre-release training is more effective and is recommended. A combination of both on- and off-duty training periods in pre-release systems is also recommended.

11. Where one of the objectives of a training programme is the resettlement of the ex-serviceman in a new location, the method that has proved most effective is to provide the training and practical application of training at such a new location. Resettlement programmes require carefully designed incentives if they are to succeed, and special attention should be given to the provision of proper schooling facilities for the children of those being resettled. For rural resettlement, a continuing ex-service pension rather than a lump sum release payment has appeared more effective in encouraging the ex-serviceman to stay on the land, which he appears inclined to do.

12. No programme will attain its full potential unless it is accompanied by a placement programme for the graduates of the programme. A system of issuing certificates attesting to levels of proficiency, with the positive participation of trade unions in such a system, is to be highly recommended. Rigorous attention to rating on strict merit on such certification is absolutely essential. In addition, where re-establishment involves an initial investment by the graduate in equipment, stock, land, or buildings, the provision of these by the government or the availability of a government-provided credit scheme is urged.

13. Particular attention in these programmes might be paid to the officer and non-commissioned officer personnel

not only due to specialized skills they may possess
but also to their continuing potential for leadership following their years of service. Training periods in civilian institutions during the course of their service can
increase their service and post-service utility.

ECONOMIC AND SOCIAL PROJECTS

This type of PUMF action is more controversial than the
others. It is, however, widely pursued, and, in areas facing
enormous problems of development, recommends itself to the
governments concerned. In many cases, it is directly related
to the maintenance of internal security. By consideration of
this type of PUMF action, it is not intended to condone its use
by régimes attempting to retain themselves in power where a
clearly workable alternative national consensus for government
exists, although this PUMF action is obviously preferable to
non-productive repression. It can help in economic and social
betterment under any conditions, although as a technique to be
used it may be considered most appropriate where rapid development is essential. Some of the general principles that appear to apply to this category of PUMF action are:

1. Economic and social development activities undertaken
   by military forces must be seen largely as a complementary and not a primary means of development that util-
   izes for constructive purposes resources existing in military forces. In some cases, their contribution will constitute a very important element--particularly as a means
   of demonstrating and promoting innovation--but primary
   means of development must be civil.

2. The military forces may provide a temporary framework
   and discipline for crash programmes to meet such problems as serious under-employment or unemployment, but
   their replacement by civilian mechanisms should be foreseen. In general, new military units should not be created
   specifically for PUMF purposes, but the revamping of
   presently justifiable units to engage at least part-time
   in PUMF can be beneficial on a continuing basis. An
   organization aiming mainly at training and use of conscripts in economic development should generally be separate from the regular armed forces.

3. In view of the necessary mobility of the military forces
    and their primary mission of security, such activities by
    military forces should in general concentrate on short-
    term impact projects. Long-term major developmental
    projects are appropriate for military units whose con-
    tinued presence in a particular geographic area is not
    detrimental to national security.

4. These activities should form a part of the over-all na-
    tional development plan and should accordingly be planned
    by interdepartmental coordination involving the civ-
    ilian organizations responsible for the sector of the econ-
    omy concerned. They should be financed under the over-
    all plan consistent with its timing and priorities. Where
    justifiable on economic grounds, the civilian sector, both
    public and private, should participate and support par-
    ticular projects with funds, materials, and labour. Proj-
    ects undertaken for a primarily security-related justi-
    fication require some flexibility within the defence
    budget.

5. Civil-military cooperation in developing these projects
    is essential to ensure that the results achieved will be
    followed up and maintained by the civilian authorities
    after the military forces have completed their tasks.

6. Preference should be given to projects that are re-
    quested by the local community, that develop local re-
    sourcefulness and capacities, and that involve collab-
    oration between the military forces and civilians.

7. The question of "follow-up" by either military forces or
    civilian authorities to the next stage of development is
    essential. The progress made must be consolidated and
    capacities to meet the resulting "rising expectation" must
    be developed.

8. An information programme, based upon results   that
    can be demonstrated, must communicate the objectives
    of and reasons for the particular projects, from the date
    of military-civilian agreement through the initiating and
    conducting of the projects to the period following com-
    pletion.

9. Economic and social betterment must be accompanied by the current and continued maintenance of law and order in the area of the activity.

10. While certain geographical areas of concentration must be chosen, economic conditions of need and not just political criteria for choosing these areas must be used. These operations should be conducted in furtherance of establishing or reinforcing the basis for democratic institutions giving freedom of citizen choice. Under multi-party governmental systems, these operations' continued effectiveness will depend upon their having multi-party support and being clearly under the control of the national civil authority and in the service of the nation.

11. The strong central backing of these programmes at the highest levels of government should be clear and well known. This, combined with well-defined goals allowing latitude to local cadres in which the central authorities have confidence, can help strengthen and improve local government and the channels of civilian authority, which should continue to be used in implementing the programmes.

12. Whenever possible, and particularly where these activities are undertaken by conscript forces, the concept of permitting the serviceman to volunteer for such activities should be followed. It is recognized, however, that in some cases where these activities are needed for essential national development, justification may exist for incentives, such as the prospect of free land, awards of recognition, and special attention to working conditions and welfare.

13. The servicemen chosen for these community development programmes must be carefully trained and oriented. They must possess the qualities needed to inspire cooperative action, initiative, a sense of service, and discipline. Their task is facilitated when their living conditions are essentially equivalent to those of the people among whom they are working.

14. These activities should have as their objective both the accomplishment of certain development projects and the

increase in the talents and future productivity of the individual serviceman.

15. During the course of a PUMF project, on-the-job training of associated civilians by the military unit should be encouraged, primarily by demonstration, but possibly by informal training sessions as well. The benefits include helping guarantee the maintenance of the project, as well as increasing individual skills, sanitary standards, and confidence in the government and the security forces.

16. The utilization of a technical capacity within the military forces that is under-employed and that can provide a service expected of government--such as mapping, surveying, meteorological work, fisheries, river and air transport to areas not served by civilian facilities--should give rise to little controversy. There are, however, certain fields within which such military capacities exist that are normally accomplished by civilian agencies, and the utilization and particularly the expansion of military facilities to fill such functions can and should be questioned if it impedes the development of competent and economic private or public civilian capacities. There exist, however, conditions of scarce resources where the direct relation of such activities to military training needs and the relative costliness of a civilian undertaking in comparison with the cost of a military undertaking (with proper regard to human conditions of work) would justify the use of military forces. Military personnel are being paid anyway, and if an under-employed potential exists within force levels properly based on security needs, there can be strong economic justification for its use. There are also conditions of disturbed national security and hostilities involving dangers that can make these development activities more appropriate for a military force than a civilian work force.

17. These activities should be of a nature to enhance and not damage the serviceman's morale, which is so essential to his primary security functions and his future civic role. They should give the individual serviceman a sense of participation in his country's development effort.

18. In countries that have adopted a system of national service, and in particular where the State directly supports individuals attaining higher education, the utilization of such graduates for a period of developmental work should be most seriously considered.

The Peaceful Uses
of Military Forces

1

The purpose of this book is to show what a selected number of countries have done to harness their military potential for non-military purposes and to draw conclusions from this experience. It should be said at once that, though novel, this is not a negligible or marginal field of activity; it is of great potential consequence to any country struggling with the problems of development while weighed down with a burden of armaments. The fact that this is the first international survey of the subject does not mean that it is in any way an intellectual by-road or cul-de-sac. On the contrary, it is hoped here to explain that the field, though hitherto largely unexplored, is of such importance that it should soon occupy the attention of a large number of experts in the problems not only of development but also of defence and politics.

A comparison with disarmament may help to put the subject into focus. In that field, theory has outrun practice. The subject has attracted eminent thinkers from all parts of the world, and their work has ensured that, when governments eventually decide that the time has come to disarm, they will not be wanting in suggestions about how to do it. With "peaceful uses," on the other hand, the practitioners have far outstripped analysis. Remarkable development programmes have been undertaken by the military, particularly in the last three years, but little attempt has been made to evaluate them.

As to the scope of the subject, the non-military uses of armed forces strictly speaking embrace a wide range of ad hoc activities such as the loan of brass bands to village fêtes and of whole regiments to film companies; but these do not concern us here. What concerns us is the systematic application of military expertise and resources to the betterment of man's estate. This falls mainly into three categories:

I. At the national level, there are currently many instances of units of military forces being employed in functions not primarily military. In the newly developing countries, this may

1

be a means of advancing essential economic and social projects. In the developed countries, the armed forces are often a vital reserve of skill and manpower in natural disaster. In either case, such uses of units of the armed forces are closely related to the training of individuals in vocations that also have a non-military potential.

II. At the level of the individual soldier, sailor, or airman, this is a matter of procedures which are taken during the period of service to facilitate employment and vocational success after release. Governments often recognize the obligation to re-establish ex-servicemen productively, and the economic and social value of doing so. In areas where there are shortages of required skills, the provision of pre- and post-release training in accordance with planned manpower needs is a constructive method of fulfilling this obligation. Several countries have established such service-connected programmes, and others have expressed interest in the idea.

III. At the international level, there are a growing number of situations that have called into being United Nations Emergency Forces. In such cases, there are often related needs of a civic nature that appropriately trained military units have fulfilled. Experienced observers have remarked that the prompt meeting of such needs can avert much bloodshed, confusion, and suffering and greatly facilitate the U.N. objectives.

As between Categories I and II, each activity could play an important role in an emergent country's development. Just which is the more important has been the subject of a developing debate; in the past, the Americans have tended to place more emphasis on Category I (development projects), while the Israelis have strongly favoured Category II (vocational training). For the purposes of this book, however, it should be noted that the problems raised by Category II projects tend to be mainly administrative and technical. Those of Category I will be seen to be more consequential politically and, therefore, more controversial.

As to Category III, this is, for practical governmental purposes, in essence an extension of Category I. A private soldier who has been engaged in his home country in any sort of aid to the civil power, whether it be police work or the establishment of communications or hygiene enforcement, is to that extent already qualified to undertake these same tasks as they arise in a United Nations peace-keeping operation. Aside from instruction in the local languages and customs, the service-man who has been effectively engaged in Category I will need no extra training for Category III; the critical factor lies in the word "effectively."

Hence, while each of these three categories is of consid-erable importance in terms of the benefits it may provide, the one that raises the most issues is unquestionably Category I; for this reason, it merits investigation at some length.

Before embarking on this analysis, however, it may be opportune to descend from generalities and cite some con-crete examples of the peaceful uses of military force (PUMF) around the world today. It will immediately be seen that this is no visionary, Utopian subject, but a philosophy of action that is gathering momentum. It is worth noting, in pass-ing, that those sceptics encountered by the author invariably tended to be those remotest from the practical needs of devel-oping countries. Those in a position to make decisions, on the other hand, always took the subject extremely seriously.

Brazil   The armed services have for many years made a big contribution to the colossal task of surveying the country and of uniting it with highways and railroads. In December, 1965, the Air Force bought three C 130's purely for use as civilian transports.

Chile   An important feature here, lacking in most develop-ing countries, is pre-release training in agriculture and the maintenance of farm machinery--a practice that has been going on for many years. During training periods, agricul-tural and minor engineering jobs are done. The Army's Engi-neer Work Corps is also conducting an extensive public works programme in co-operation with the Ministry of the Interior.

Colombia   Here, even the most cautious observers agree, PUMF has played an absolutely vital part in enlisting the loy-alty of the campesinos in a struggle with the guerrillas that has cost more than 200,000 lives since 1948, but which is now on the decline, at least in the countryside.

Guatemala   Though small in size, this country has been one
of the leaders in this field, concentrating particularly on literacy. The Army produces textbooks with a double objective:
to teach both literacy and hygiene. At any one time, more than
4,000 civilians and 5,000 soldiers are being instructed in this
manner at around 100 centres. The Army is also active in the
medical field through its mobile medical unit, which has done
much to keep down tuberculosis.

India   Considerable post-release training facilities exist.
Within the Army recently, the most urgent need has been for
military training; however, the emergency work performed by
the Indian Armed Services in a country constantly stricken by
floods and drought has been on a prodigious scale. At the end
of 1965, a radical innovation was announced: the call-up of
10,000 university graduates whose functions seemed likely to
be partly military and partly civilian-economic.

Iran   Several thousand high school graduates are conscripted
into the Education Corps every year, where after three months
of both military and civic training they are sent out to the villages to teach children and adults to read and write, to initiate
communal development schemes, and to advise on agricultural
techniques. Following the success of this scheme, a Health
Corps was set up in 1964. This has stopped the drain of first-
class doctors from the cities to foreign lands and reversed it
from cities to the countryside, where they are needed most.
In addition, Iran runs an impressive pre-release vocational
training programme.

Israel   This country is, in a sense, the founder of PUMF, preceding even classical Rome. (In his instructions for rebuilding Jerusalem, Nehemiah ordered the Israelites to carry a
sword in one hand and their implements in the other.) In this
century, Israel not only developed the concept of the farmer-
soldier, but its experts overseas are currently advising on the
training of servicemen in civilian skills in a wide range of
countries from South America via West Africa to Burma.   In
the Nahal (Pioneer Fighting Youth), young men and girls are
taught both to fight and to farm, operating frontier settlements.
The Army is expressly used as an instrument of integration,
its civil education programme being among the most intensive
in the world.

<u>Ivory Coast</u>   With several other African countries, a form of mixed military-civil service has been adopted. The <u>Service Civique</u> trains men to be farmers under military discipline. Originally, this was a conscript system, but it has been found to work well with volunteers.

<u>Morocco</u>   The Army has played a large part in <u>Promotion Nationale</u>, the King's strategy for harnessing the large numbers of unemployed to economic projects. Among the Army's more spectacular achievements was an important part in the building of 1,200 schools in one summer.

<u>Pakistan</u>   During the 1950's, the Army provided one of the most dramatic examples of action in the economic sphere by crushing the smuggling of jute out of East Pakistan, which was disastrously affecting the country's economy. Particularly since the military take-over in 1958, the Army has engaged in an extremely intensive programme of PUMF. Apart from the construction of dams and major road works, one of its most outstanding features has been the facilities offered to ex-servicemen, under the Post War Services Reconstruction Fund, to train themselves for civilian life.

<u>Peru</u>   A large part of the Peruvian Army is engaged in one form of civic action or another. President Belaunde is using it as a cutting edge to drive roads through the Andes into the Amazon Basin, where he plans to set up colonies in whose construction servicemen will play a vital part, and where it is hoped that ex-servicemen will in due course live. Both Colombia and Peru, in addition, have some of the most impressive pre-release training facilities in the world.

<u>Philippines</u>   The success of President Magsaysay in defeating the Communist-led guerrillas in 1950-53 owed much to PUMF-- or, as the Americans call it, civic action. Magsaysay was able to win over the disgruntled peasant population, many of whom had legitimate grievances against landlords and against the military who they felt were protecting them. This involved using troop labour to build schools, wells, and other public works and, not least, the introduction of stricter discipline in the Army. A particularly popular feature was the loan to tenant farmers of Judge Advocate officers to appear in court in civilian clothes and represent them in their disputes against landlords.

Thailand   The Mobile Development Units, launched entirely on the initiative of the Thai Government, are proving so successful that the formula is being closely studied with a view to its adaptation to other areas of the world with similar problems.

Turkey   An outstanding feature has been the Armed Forces Literacy Training Project, aimed at eliminating illiteracy in the military services. An important element is the employment of school-teachers as instructors in lieu of their national service. Since most servicemen return to their villages on release, the effects on the country's economy are considerable. Another innovation has been the call-up of thousands of reserve officers for six months' active duty to teach children in primary schools.

THE BACKGROUND

What lies behind this outbreak of PUMF action? The answer is that it is a response to the needs of both development and defence.

This problem is basically that of guns v. butter. This is present in some form in virtually every country in the world. At the most affluent level, America cancels the RS 70, and Britain cancels the TSR2, because further such indulgence would injure the economy. In poorer countries, the conflict is even more acute. In Asia, it is no exaggeration to say that, for one reason or another, an arms race is in full swing from the Mediterranean to the China Sea. In Africa, armies are small by comparison and there is as yet little indication of anything that could be called a real arms race. The proportion of gross national product devoted to defence rarely exceeds 5 per cent.   Yet defence expansion is the order of the day in most of these countries. It is a process which few African governments evidently relish, conscious as they are of the inevitable withdrawal of resources and expert manpower from their already indigent economies which it entails.

In Latin America, the likelihood of international war is low--even more so than in Africa; there has not been such a war since the clash between Peru and Ecuador in the early

1940's. Armies are still substantial, however; in South
America there are over 500,000 men under arms, and those
arms include aircraft carriers and Canberra bombers. Keeping pace with these arms expenses are the increasingly clam-
orous demands, some of them echoes of Castroism, for better
standards of living among the continent's under-privileged
majority. Thus, throughout the developing world there is an
increasingly acute clash of demands for defence and development.

ARMS CUTS?

Not surprisingly, therefore, many governments have been
asking themselves whether they could not reduce their armed
forces. This process, however, is generally hazardous and
can be very dangerous. It seems probable that Mr. Krushchev's
efforts to reduce Russia's army were frustrated by the military and their political allies; this reaction is liable to occur
with varying violence in almost any country where an arms
cut is projected. Even President Eisenhower warned his
successor against the power of the "military-industrial
complex." Among the developing countries, the Shah of Iran
contemplated an arms cut but found the course too dangerous.
Several African leaders, including President Nyerere, have
expressed the heartfelt wish to be able to dispense with armed
forces altogether, but they have never felt strong enough to go
through with it. Probably they were wise; for when President
Sylvanus Olympio of the Togo Republic tried to set a limit to
the size of his army, he was assassinated. The same thing
might happen to any ruler of a developing country who tried a
too abrupt cut in arms. Other West African countries have
provided more recent examples of the danger to a civilian
régime of attempting to reduce the arms budget.

Many governments, realizing this, have been asking themselves the no less fundamental question: "What do we need
armies for?" In parts of Asia, a sufficiently cogent answer
is the traditional one: "To protect ourselves from our neighbours." But this is only part of the answer even in Asia.
Elsewhere it is much less convincing. Often enough, the more
genuine motive is prestige.

MORE REVOLTS THAN WARS

In general, therefore, it can be said that in many parts of the world troops are no longer maintained purely or even predominantly for defensive purposes. Large standing armies, called into being by the continuing unresolved tensions of a bipolar, and even tripolar world, fortunately often remain only standing. Considering the large number of countries which have to live together, small scale international wars are tolerably infrequent in the 1960's. It seems that nations, particularly the smaller ones, have got out of the habit of marauding into other people's territories to see what they can pick up. There must be some especially acute cause of conflict before a nation will launch a war on its neighbours.

Though the reasons for this are not altogether clear, two seem to be relevant. One is the sheer cost of launching a war nowadays, which is likely to ensure the bankruptcy of many potential victors as well as victims. There is also the sheer complexity of the logistic problem, which has been demonstrated most recently in the Punjab, the Yemen, and Borneo. Most emerging countries, in fact, have their hands too full with internal security problems to engage in war.

No doubt there are other explanations, possibly profounder. Certainly it should not be overlooked that Moscow, while promoting "wars of national liberation," has proclaimed that it is not interested in "local wars between states." But whatever the reason, the situation of the world in the 1960's calls for a very different kind of serviceman than the traditional figure who was trained exclusively to defend his frontier and to live and die by the simple doctrine: "They shall not pass." It calls for a serviceman who can deal first and foremost with internal threats to the stability of his country; and this means the ability to attract, by one means or another, the sympathy and support of his fellow-countrymen and to help in eliminating some of the underlying causes of unrest.

Thus, increasing emphasis is being given to finding ways in which the serviceman can (1) reduce the burden that he imposes on society, by pulling his weight economically; and (2) address himself to the task of nation-building and, in some areas, to the threat of subversion. This means that in many countries the modern serviceman finds himself performing a remarkable variety of different functions--as we shall see.

"We still haven't got the benchmarks in," a highly intelligent State Department official declared when asked to assess the record of civic action over the last three years. He meant, of course, that no datum line had been established in any country from which the benefits of civic action could be measured. Perhaps the best that can be done is to record experience to date.

Let us look first at the case where counter-insurgency has been the predominant purpose. This experience breaks down into two categories--what has been termed "curative" and "preventive" civic action, the distinction being whether a counter-insurgency situation actually exists. This is clearly a somewhat loose terminology, since the term "preventive" subsumes the whole range of civic action undertaken when insurgency neither exists nor is expected, but the major distinction between "curative" and "preventive" is worth making. The curative type being the more spectacular, is slightly easier to evaluate. Even here, however, it is hard to say just how much PUMF has contributed to any counter-insurgency operation. It was a conspicuous ingredient of the successful campaigns in Malaya, the Philippines, and Colombia. Yet France's systematic use of it in Algeria proved unable to turn the scales against the FLN. In some countries--Indonesia, for instance--it has sometimes been a liability, since the benefits bestowed there have been annexed by the guerrillas because they were not accompanied by sufficient military force.

Experience has shown that the correct counter-insurgent posture is two-handed--the closed fist of military force and the open hand of friendship. The former by itself cannot be applied with success by any nation which claims to be civilized; the latter by itself is at best wasted effort. Even where this two-handed posture is adopted, however, there remain many mistakes to be avoided. These and other aspects of curative civic action will be considered later. Meanwhile, it is important to understand the consequences--advantages and dangers--of routine civic action in times of comparative calm.

9

EFFECT ON THE ARMED FORCES

It has been well said that one of its most important functions is to "humanize the military" at all levels. For example, in Latin America, which has produced its fair share of "inhuman" servicemen during its history, a palpable change has taken place in recent years. Partly, of course, this has been due to the changing composition of the officer corps, which now contains more middle class representatives than members of the landed oligarchy. But civic action has played its part; at a recent conference of Latin American Chiefs of Staff, this was the subject which aroused far the most sustained interest. The idea had obviously gripped them and provided a much needed outlet for their constructive patriotism.

Likewise, at platoon level, PUMF should humanize the soldier; if it does not, it is being misconducted and can easily be counterproductive. As operated in the Philippines, its whole initial purpose was to improve the image of the ordinary soldier in the field and, therefore, his conduct; to stop him bullying peasants, requisitioning buildings unnecessarily, carrying off food, and generally behaving in a brutal and licentious manner. To check this misbehaviour where it exists must be Stage One in any PUMF operation. For it is the first objective of most subversive movements to establish among the peasantry the conviction that the military are their oppressors and not their friends. This was formerly all too easy in large parts of Latin America. Some would say it has been true in Vietnam.

It is not necessary, admittedly, for an army to perform PUMF to establish a good image with the people at large. In many former British colonies, the army is the most respected force in the country, although these countries are by no means all pioneers in PUMF. This is because it is evidently and manifestly neutral--an apolitical servant of the government.

In the majority of developing countries, however, the armies play a political role. They, therefore, cannot be neutral in the eyes of the peasantry; they are either brothers or oppressors. By adopting PUMF, they automatically opt for the former role. Properly conducted, civic action will have a fundamentally humanizing effect on the troops which operate it. In Colombia today, for instance, a soldier may be severely punished for stealing so much as an orange from a <u>campesino</u>.

PUMF is calculated to bring out the best in a soldier. It calls for qualities of initiative and service as well as of discipline. It is a great educator of the national serviceman. In some countries he is actually, in a sense, conscripted for this purpose; in Colombia, young medical and engineering students are at last being drawn into the conscription net, to reinforce civic action programmes, and they admit deriving benefit from this experience. Also, the very act of instruction is itself educational. The high school students in Iran who are conscripted to work in the Education Corps gain enormously from the experience, and the majority volunteer for a second term.

All in all, few would dispute that one effect of civic action was to humanize the military. But it also brings the army into close contact with the government and with the ordinary villager; what are its effects on them?

Political Effects

It is here that opponents of civic action direct their criticism. It is one thing, they say, to humanize an army; another to de-professionalize it. Civic action, they contend, inevitably brings the armed forces nearer to the seat of power. It may do this directly by giving the army a greater say in the disposition of the country's development effort. It may do it indirectly by acquiring a degree of popularity in the countryside which the civilian authorities have not been able to achieve. When this happens, the popularity attaching to the army can sometimes be invidious, at the expense of the civilian authorities. Some of the beneficiaries may even come to believe that the Minister of Defence actually is the President, as has happened in Latin America, and at least to support any ambitions he has in that direction. (The Fort Gulick Civic Action School in the Canal Zone is known to its critics as a "coup d'état factory.")

These critics, concerned with the principles of liberal democracy, are apprehensive at the spread of military governments in the developing world. This is certainly a major phenomenon of our time. In Latin America alone, the number of military dictatorships, which reached an all-time low a few years ago, has lately returned to around the dozen mark. In Asia--from Suez to Saigon--India, Ceylon, and Malaysia provide practically the only break in the sequence of military governments. In Africa, the same pattern has started to emerge with the take-over in Algeria by Colonel Boumedienne and similar military coups in Dahomey, the Congo, and elsewhere.

This is an extremely important argument. On the other hand, it is a gross exaggeration to claim that an army undertaking civic action will automatically be tempted to stage a coup d'état; a great deal depends on the army. An example of this, perhaps paradoxically, is Pakistan. The most significant thing about the Pakistan military coup d'état was not that it happened, but that it did not happen much earlier. At least three times during the 1950's, the Army was called in to pull the Government's chestnuts out of the fire by undertaking major PUMF projects--and duly returned to its former, apolitical role. This was particularly true of the anti-smuggling operations in East Pakistan; it became abundantly clear that the Army was the only effective and honest force in the country--far too clear for the liking of the politicians. Yet twice it consented to be pulled out. Even as late as 1958, General Ayub Khan told a senior British officer that he would not be a party to any military take-over such as had just occurred in the Sudan. Only when he had conceived it to be absolutely unavoidable did he eventually assume power. By the same token, it is probable that the only thing which would incite the Indian Army to seize power would be culpable negligence and corruption on the part of the civil government.

Secondly, it is at least arguable that all civic action, in the short or long run, tends to promote democracy. By providing education, medical help, agricultural advice, facilities for improved hygiene, and better access to markets, in places where the civilian authorities may have made little, if any, impression, the soldier is not only aiding in development; he is increasing both the political maturity of the ordinary citizen and his economic stake in the country. If generalizations about military dictatorships are to be made, they might with equal validity be extended to show a progression by which the army may, in this way, eventually work itself out of a political job. From totalitarian military rule, this spectrum would ascend through the example of Pakistan, where the military is trying to introduce a responsible government through the creation of basic democracies, and the Sudan, up to Mexico where, after years of PUMF, the Army virtually withdrew from politics-—

having created the necessary framework for responsible government.   Many developing countries find that military rule
may be the only practical alternative to a strongly anti-demo-
cratic social and political régime, which might fairly be char-
acterized as "indigenous colonialism."

In practical terms, the immediate dangers of PUMF are not
so much that it is liable to lead to a suppression of freedom
but that it will create appetites that cannot be assuaged.   The
floating ambulances of the Peruvian Navy on the upper tribu-
taries of the River Amazon are doing magnificent work, but
they are also helping to increase one of the highest birth-rates
in the world. The Peruvian ex-servicemen who receive a prize
for teaching ten of their fellow-villagers to read and write are
likewise conniving at "the revolution of rising expectations."
How can all these babies be fed?   And what sort of literature
will all these new readers imbibe? These are basic problems--
but they are not peculiar to PUMF. They arise out of the whole
policy of aid and development.   PUMF merely brings them
closer at a more challenging rate.

Economic Effects

This raises the second main line of criticism against PUMF,
precipitating the dispute between what are known in economic
circles as "developmentalists" and "impact men." It is perhaps
the most important economic argument of our age. Developmentalists believe broadly that a country cannot progress if
its basic economy is not sound; in concrete terms, this calls
for the development of its infrastructure, its industry and large-
scale agriculture, and its competitive ability in overseas markets.   According to this philosophy, there exists a moment in
an emergent country's development known as "take-off," when
it will no longer stand in need of foreign aid.   To achieve this
requires the creation of an elite--a corps of technical experts,
administrators, and other professional men from whom the im-
pulse for development will automatically emanate in due course.
Some, though not all of them, look askance at "impact" programmes, on the grounds that these make no attempt to go to
the root of the country's economy and merely divert resources
needed for this purpose.

The "impact men" agree with much of this, but with two important qualifications. One is that civic action does in fact embrace a number of programmes which fit into the developmentalists' scheme of things. Road-building programmes, in particular, are designed to increase the scope of the national infrastructure. So, in their way, are land colonization projects; nothing could be more "developmentalist" than the work the Peruvian Army is doing in both these sectors. But secondly--and more important--in areas where there is a serious security threat, the "impact men" would argue that normal economic considerations must be subordinate. There is little value in a stable economy, they say, if a large part of the countryside is in a state of incipient revolt.

Further, they point out that the army has special qualities which make it uniquely suitable for development work. It has comparatively high technical standards, sometimes the most advanced in the country. Often, too, it contains some of the ablest men in the community; many of them widely travelled and patriotic in the most mature way. Thirdly, it is a disciplined force. And, fourthly, it is often economical (see Appendix A).

Thus, "developmentalism" and "impact" are often at one. But where they are at odds, the impact men are by no means always on the defensive. They may legitimately ask the developmentalists to survey the world and say whether they are really satisfied with the results of twenty years of aid in the developing countries. India under Mr. Nehru was a classic example of a developmentalist economy, with its steel mills, dams, and reactors; yet when Mr. Nehru died, the Indian peasant was eating no more than in 1938. Foreign exchange was, and still is, being used to buy food which could well be grown in India. The same is true in many, if not most, developing countries. Somewhere along the line, aid is not fulfilling the hopes once placed in it. There may be practically unavoidable reasons for this; two of them are the population explosion and the terms of trade for primary products. At the same time, the architects of aid may fairly be asked whether they are not thinking in rather too leisurely terms. The ideal target for unrest is the man who believes that he could be making progress but is not doing so. And in these days of transistor radios, he is becoming an increasingly vulnerable target for subversive propaganda all over the world. Allied to the theory of "impact," and likewise stemming from impatience with the notion of "take-off," is the purely civilian theory of "intermediate technology." This is as yet considered somewhat heretical, assailing as it does some of the entrenched doctrines of orthodox economists. Its most eminent proponent, Dr. E.F. Schumacher, an erst-while colleague of Keynes and Beveridge and later economic adviser to the Government of Burma, contends that, with ex-isting policies of industrialization, the bulk of the present pop-ulation of most developing countries can never be absorbed into the economy, and that, meanwhile, their traditional economy is becoming increasingly non-viable. Instead of concentrating on industrialization through modern techniques, he argues, more emphasis should be placed on developing a technology in between the traditional and the modern one, in order to improve the lot of the masses who will otherwise never be employed.

Inasmuch as PUMF is development, and a technique admir-ably suited to the promotion of intermediate technology, it is extremely relevant to pursue this point further. Schumacher notes that, notwithstanding elaborate economic planning--in such countries as India and Turkey--unemployment is steadily rising. Foreign aid as currently practised may be actually in-tensifying the twin disease of unemployment and mushrooming shanty towns; for the heedless rush into modernization extin-guishes old jobs faster than it can create new ones, and all the apparent increases in national income are eaten up, or even more than eaten up, by the crushing economic burdens produced by excessive urban growth. If the current methods and types of foreign aid produce such questionable results, "it is per-haps a bit superficial merely to demand an increase in the vol-ume of aid."

Schumacher attacks the use of a country's gross national product as the decisive criterion. If "the people" are left out of development planning, and if economic growth merely inten-sifies, as it tends to do, the appalling features of the "dual e-conomy"--a small sector of opulence surrounded by an ocean of misery--then the final outcome will be disastrous. He argues that: (1) Work places have to be created in the areas where the people are living now, and not primarily in metropolitan areas into which they tend to migrate. (2) These work places must be, on the average, cheap enough so that they can be erected in large numbers without this calling for an unattainable level of savings and imports. (3) The production methods employed must be relatively simple, so that the demands for high skills are minimized, not only in the production process itself, but also in matters of organization, raw material supply, finance, marketing, and so forth. (4) Production should be largely from local materials for local use.

These four needs, says Schumacher, can only be met "if there is a conscious effort to develop what might be called an 'intermediate technology.'" Putting his finger on perhaps the most crucial economic fact of our time, he says that Western technology has been devised primarily for the purpose of saving labour; it could hardly be appropriate for districts or regions troubled with a large labour surplus. Simply to assume that the "modern" sectors or localities will grow until they account for the remaining 80 per cent of the population is utterly unrealistic, because the 80 per cent cannot simply "hold their breath" and wait; they will migrate in their millions and thereby create chaos even in the "modern sectors." What is wanted is a technology more efficient than the traditional, but less capital-intensive than the modern.

Schumacher points out that design studies undertaken in India have shown that many products are suitable for "intermediate technology" production: practically all basic consumers' goods, building materials, agricultural implements, and many kinds of equipment for the "intermediate technology" industries themselves.

In view of the increasing support he has found for this thesis, he asks himself why more attention has not been given to this subject before. His answers are debatable, indeed provocative, but interesting. Perhaps, he says, there is a kind of technological snobbishness which disdains anything less than the ultra-modern. Perhaps, too, there is a lack of imagination on the part of the planners in resplendent offices who find ratios and coefficients more significant than people.

Schumacher does not at all discount the value of projects on the Western level of technology; and with this important proviso it is difficult to dismiss his argument. Certainly, if the need for increased intermediate technology be accepted in any degree, then PUMF is a natural vehicle for it, whether in the form of Category I or Category II.

It is this training element which is really the purest and often most valuable element in PUMF. Building roads, houses, schools, clinics, or whatever, may have, and should have, a strongly beneficial effect on the economy. But training--the vital principle of self-help--is the greatest economic boon which any defence establishment can confer on the community; and it is one which embodies few of the overtones of the more controversial functions of PUMF.

AN EXAMPLE

In illustration of the foregoing, it is worth noting some of the findings of the Intermediate Technology Development Group, a body set up in the U.K. to study the problems of small-scale industrialization at a level appropriate to developing countries.

According to them, one of the major inhibiting factors in rural development programmes, in the experience of a number of voluntary agencies--Freedom from Hunger, OXFAM, and the African Development Trust--has been lack of accountancy skills.

Few villagers understand the principles of budgeting--what factors are involved; what period a budget covers; what capital expenditure, as opposed to recurrent expenditure, means; etc. Yet the people involved at grass-roots level need to keep and understand accurate, simple accounts, in order to judge their own progress. Professional services of this nature are at a premium in all developing countries, and practically non-existent in rural areas.

One example is probably typical of thousands: the experience of the African Development Trust on one project in Bechuana-land involving an arable 250-acre farm, a 5,000-acre cattle-holding ranch, a trading store with ancillary social services in the form of a school, clinic, and community centre. Three key people--the chairman of the council responsible for local di-rection, the farm manager, and the ranch foreman--were all ex-servicemen; two had been non-commissioned officers. Although these men understood the management of a labour force, were able to handle machinery and direct simple build-ing operations, and supervise the installation of bore-hole equipment and pumps, they were totally unable to grasp the first principles of book-keeping. Because no professional skills were available within the territory, the whole project was threatened by apparent lack of working capital. There were two defects here. One was that the ex-servicemen had not been trained at all in this important subject. The other was that the book-keeping system in operation was quite unnecessarily complicated. It is vitally important that both these defects should be rectified. In this particular case, it was possible to bring a first-class chartered accountant 500 miles to study what was involved. At the end of a week, he returned to his office and devised a system that the men could understand, gave them the information they required to assess the viability of each particular enterprise, and showed them where savings could be made. As a result, within a year the whole enterprise was able to meet its own running costs without further injections of aid funds.

The Intermediate Technology Development Group believes that no enterprise can succeed, however much technical skill is available, unless these accountability factors are taken into consideration; and that there is a strong case for including instruction in this subject in pre-release training arrangements.

FORCED LABOUR

Finally, in this catalogue of PUMF's advantages and dangers, it must be noted that an important line of criticism arises out of the complaints of labour organizations. Sometimes, though less frequently than might be imagined, they raise their voice against the whole principle of armies invading the field of civil development.

The employment of conscripts for development--distinct from their participation in vocational programmes--brings up the question of forced labour. The 1930 Convention of the International Labour Organization on Forced Labour condemns the employment of military conscripts for civil purposes. And as most armies undertaking civic action are conscript armies-- Pakistan is one of the rare exceptions in this respect--a clash of principle is involved.

This is an important objection, since conscription may be perverted to at least four condemnable ends: organized exploitation of labour for compulsory work at low cost; competition for civilian labour with a consequent weakening of labour unions; delay in the development of a purely civilian capacity to do the same jobs; anti-economic action for purposes of indoctrinating and politically neutralizing individuals.

Nevertheless, the question has recently been raised by the ILO as to whether the rigid application of the principles laid down in 1930 is now in keeping with the present realities of developing countries. The provisions of the 1930 Convention were dictated to a large extent by the practices followed in colonial territories at a time when military conscription was applied to constitute workers' brigades at low cost for the execution of public works. At the 1962 ILO Conference, half a dozen West African delegations expressed indignation at what they regarded as a somewhat casual approach by the ILO to the pressing daily problems of their countries for training youth and integrating it in national development.

Following the special research work accomplished by the ILO on this subject--stated in the Director General's report to the 50th session of the Conference (1966)--the ILO General Conference may be called upon, at its forthcoming session, to examine the extent to which the 1930 Convention should be considered as hampering economic and social activities due to its provisions on compulsory national youth service, along the lines of military service. The problem might be examined within the framework of a recommendation dealing more or less broadly with special programmes for the training and employment of youth. Moreover, the ILO has decided to extend forthwith appropriate technical assistance to developing countries by sending experts, offering practical suggestions on the basis of meetings held by experts, and so forth.

As a matter of fact, the ILO criticisms were levelled mainly against organizations which seemed to favour workers' brigades specifically conscripted for civilian labour, although their existence, unlike that of the army, has no justification. The rationale of these latter organizations is outside the scope of this analysis. But experts in this field are coming to the conclusion that conscription is unnecessary for this type of work and, therefore, uneconomical. Sometimes compulsion may be useful when a project is being initiated in a remote area. But once it is under way, the rush of applicants assured of employment frequently far exceeds the number of available jobs; and, of course, volunteers tend to work better than conscripts. This line of approach, opened up by experts of the ILO itself, seems promising.

In point of fact, experience has shown that the organizations of the kind mentioned above for national youth services have essentially been oriented towards the national and vocational training of youth and their integration in development, notably in the rural population; the problem of general conscription for youth, which is not yet possible, is chiefly one for the future.

As to military conscription, several points in mitigation ought to be made. First, major civic action projects are normally undertaken in places where there has been virtually no labour activity before: in the Peruvian Andes, in the jungles of Bolivia, on the Gilgit Road in West Pakistan, in the mountains and back-blocks of Iran. There can hardly be any reasonable complaint, especially from the unions, here. Secondly, where civilian labour is employed on these projects, union rates and conditions of employment are usually taken into consideration. Where they are not, the unions have every right to protest, and deserve international backing. Thirdly, as to the spiriting away of potential trouble-makers, governments strong enough to use this method are generally resourceful enough to think of other ways of silencing individual opponents.

In hard practical terms, the economic question is whether it is better for an army to remain an unqualified burden on the country's economy or whether it should contribute to the country's development. The ideal answer is neither; armies which are big enough to spare time for development should be reduced and, wherever possible, conscription should be ended. But this question of reducing armies is, as already noted, a major stumbling-block. Governments who wish to do it may find themselves in serious trouble in countries where the military carries political weight--as it does in most developing countries. In addition, a great many countries have no wish to do so. Is civic action in these countries to be held up until they change their minds?

The truth is, as already observed, that unnecessarily large armies seem to be an immutable part of the world we live in, however much we may dislike the fact. The desired change is unlikely to come without regional or world-wide disarmament agreements. (It is almost equally difficult to persuade a government to switch to a volunteer army from the conscripted version, which is so much cheaper.) For practical purposes, the most immediate results might be obtained by demanding that trade unions be closely consulted on civic action programmes, and that they should have a say in the location of such programmes and the terms of employment of civilian labour. But to obstruct PUMF in principle would be to cut off a source of expanded employment for the future; for if properly conducted, it can open up the way to new civilian development projects.

3

The techniques of PUMF are still in their infancy. Those governments that have decided that their armed forces can usefully be employed in this type of work have been compelled to make up the rules pretty much as they went along. Inevitably they have encountered obstacles, and these have necessitated rapid decisions. Often they have raised fundamental questions. To what extent does PUMF impair the soldier's capacity to perform his primary function? Can it sometimes, on the contrary, actually help him to perform it? Should the army ever undertake long-term development projects? If not, how are civilian resources to be best deployed so as to ensure that a local breakthrough in development does not disintegrate after the military have moved on, thereby forfeiting the goodwill of the original beneficiaries? How can the maximum benefit be derived from PUMF without incurring the jealousy of civilian agencies and politicians? These are some of the questions that many governments have begun to ask themselves. On the basis of their own experience, some tentative conclusions have begun to emerge.

MILITARY-CIVILIAN RELATIONS

The first requirement for successful civic action is close collaboration between the military and civilian authorities right from the start. The very concept of PUMF is liable to arouse jealousies among the civilian authorities. If it takes place anywhere within the neighbourhood of the capital or larger cities, there is liable to be an element of direct competition about it. On the other hand, if it takes place outside the effective range of the civil authorities, whole regions of the country may conclude that the army is their only friend in the government, coming to their rescue when the civilians have failed. Government departments being what they are all over the world, it may be impossible to eliminate this feeling of rivalry altogether. But if proper precautions are taken at the start, it can be transmuted into a source of healthy competition.

23

The reason why close collaboration is so important is that in most cases the army will sooner or later have to pull out. It cannot be everywhere at the same time, especially if it has heavy military commitments as well. This vital problem of "follow-up" continues to baffle the planners in even the best-run governments. In the words of one high official engaged on this problem: "We still haven't thought this through." But ideally, the basic aim of the follow-up must be the hand-over by the military to the civilian authority. In some countries, such as Thailand, this is a considerable undertaking, and it has so far proved impracticable because the civilian authority lacks the means and capacity to replace the frontier Mobile Development Units. In Colombia, where civic action has otherwise brought tremendous dividends, the cause of the failure appeared to lie to some extent in the relationship between the military and the civilian agencies. Often enough the civilians' attitude, on being asked to relieve the Army in a certain project, is initially that they were not consulted on the project in the first place, and secondly, that they would not have agreed to it if they had been, perhaps because it was physically too remote, or because it would have placed too great a strain on their resources. On the Colombian Army's side, there was considerable extenuation. They were in a hurry, and may well have reckoned that clearing their plans with the civil service and the politicians would cause needless delay and obstruction. They may well have been right. But they laid up for themselves a problem. For how will the villager react if there is no follow-up, and his rising expectations are dashed to the ground? In Indonesia, failure to follow up excellent and elaborate PUMF programmes led to the accolades being reaped by opposing and subversive elements.

The first prerequisite, therefore, is amicable military-civilian relations. These are most likely to be achieved when the head of state has taken a personal interest in the programme and identified himself with its success. (This also applies not only to heads of government but also to political parties.) Obvious examples of such rulers are the Shah of Iran, Houphouët-Boigny of the Ivory Coast, and President Belaunde of Peru. Where this happens and a programme is personally sponsored from the very top, cooperation between the various ministries is enhanced.

RESPONSIBILITY FOR PUMF

What type of organization should be used for coordinating PUMF action at national, regional, and local levels? This question, put to a conference of the Central Treaty Organization powers at Shiraz in Iran in late 1964, received more or less similar answers all around. Project planning, it was a-greed, should be done at ministerial or cabinet level. Planning schedules should indicate a forecast of monetary allocations and also recommend the appropriate implementation agencies. Coordination of military aspects on that level should be done through the Ministry of Defence and should use selec-ted military engineers for this coordinating mission. Staff responsibility should either be delegated to an existing staff agency or, if the project is big enough, that agency may be augmented by a special subsidiary agency.

Some countries have created a coordinating committee on a ministerial level, making it responsible for the planning and direction of these activities. Others maintain special military bodies devoted exclusively to PUMF action. Others again ex-ecute such civic action within the regular military organiza-tion itself. Chile, for example, operates a Military Works Corps, an independent agency under the Army Commander-in-Chief. Honduras has an office of civic action within the armed forces.

But the form of organization seems to matter less than how it is operated. The Colombian system, for instance, would on the surface appear to be enlightened. Presidential Decree No. 1381 created the "National Committee on Military-Civic Action," giving it the function of coordinating such activities; it includes the Ministers of Government, War, Agriculture, Public Health, National Education, and Public Works. It may also include representatives of official and private bodies. Yet even so, civilian ministries constantly complain that they do not know what is going on. Not long ago President Valencia enquired into the reason for these complaints. It was felt that in its eagerness to exploit its success, the Army neglected to keep its civilian counterparts in the picture, though the mach-inery exists for it to do so.

CIVILIAN AUTHORITY

The Pakistani representative at Shiraz was firm about the subordination of these programmes to the over-all civil development plan. "It should be the responsibility of the civil government," he said, to "chalk out the civic development programmes." It should also be their responsibility to assess the resources available for implementing their development schemes. The civil government should decide, in consultation with the military authorities, the areas where military assistance can be provided. Military organizations should assist the civic programmes in spheres which, while supporting the programmes, do not involve military institutions in quasi-governmental activities. Military assistance, he felt, should be limited in scope and should not involve military institutions beyond their normal technical and administrative function.

Finally, though military assistance programmes may be under the over-all direction and control of civil institutions, military institutions should function through their normal command channels.

A good example of military-civilian coordination is to be found in Iran--one of the world's leading three or four countries in this field. The Shah, possessed of an army of over 200,000 men, has gone further than almost any other government to harness military resources to economic purposes. He has used the army, in effect, as an instrument for political and economic reform. When he decided to break the power of the landlords in the early 1960's, following a nationwide plebiscite, he recognized that a new social force was required to take the place of the old one; leadership was required, particularly in the countryside--and it must be greatly superior to that provided by the landlords. Hence, he conceived the idea of drafting the educated young members of the community to perform, as soldiers, largely civilian functions which they would not otherwise have done if they had followed their own instincts and their own pecuniary interests.

The first fruit of this programme was the Education Corps, under which high school graduates, after three months training in both military and civilian subjects, are sent to the villages, where they provide leadership of the most versatile nature. Primarily, their task is education--and since the scheme began, over 15,000 of them have taught around 300,000 Iranians (mostly children) to read and write.   But they also undertake a wide range of civic tasks, from agricultural advice to the construction of schools, bridges, and irrigation projects. Such has been the success of this corps that a second similar organization, the Health Corps, followed hard on its heels in late 1964.   For this, obviously, the qualifications are higher, but the principle is the same: the conscription of the educated, primarily--though not exclusively--for the economic benefit of the community. In addition to these two corps--and a third, the Construction Corps now in process of evolution--the Iranian Army as a whole is seen by the Shah as an instrument which may be called on to promote civil projects;   hence, the need for a sound administrative structure to coordinate such activities.   This penetrates down through three levels. The civic action directive published by the Shah in October, 1962, provided for three types of committees: (1) the permanent committee at ministerial level to supervise the over-all effort; (2) an executive committee of agency representatives to plan and direct implementation; (3) field committees for specific projects. A civic action officer is designated to each major headquarters. Unit civic action officers receive requests from civilian authorities; if they are within unit capabilities, agreement is signed between the unit and the demander, and this is referred to the provincial sub-committees. If they are outside the range of unit capability, the officer seeks support from a higher echelon. Incidentally, in this triple-tier organization there is a close parallel with British counter-insurgency methods.

CRITERIA

By what sort of criteria should such requests be judged? The Shiraz Conference felt that it is important as a general rule that they should, in the first place, be requests.   True, an officer with initiative can, and frequently does, suggest projects which seem to meet a local need.   But it is only human nature that these ideas should appear to have originated among the villagers; clearly, they should appreciate the project sufficiently to maintain it when it is finished. Often enough, this elementary point is overlooked.

Other criteria enunciated at Shiraz were:

A project must not impair military efficiency, except in emergencies and natural disasters.

It should help to build up the fabric of local society.

It should not prejudice initiative, or undermine the authority of the civil administration.

Preference should be given to projects that develop local resourcefulness and capacities, and also those that involve collaboration between troops and civilians.

The ratio of civilian to military participation should be as high as possible. (The army's contribution may be confined to technical advice or the loan of a bulldozer.)

The image of the armed forces should be improved.

The government's ability to anticipate or master any local insurgency should be enhanced.

Projects should be recognizably beneficial to the local population.

As far as possible, the military forces should work with the people, not just for them.

Small, immediate-impact, short-term completion projects should have a high priority.

Finally, if assisted from outside, the project should redound to the credit of the national government and not of the aiding government.

TYPES OF PROJECTS

What type of projects should be undertaken? Experience has shown that the most urgent needs are in the fields of public health, education, farming, and communications. But needs naturally will vary from region to region. For the army, the chief opportunities will be building and improving wells and water supplies; sanitation; roads, afforestation and agricultural help; building schools, hospitals, and other public structures; medical help; fire prevention; education and vocational training; disaster relief and technical aid. The navy is most suited to port and harbour improvements; information on fishing and the training of fishermen; evacuation and medical work in case of disaster; fire prevention and vocational training. Air forces have been most effectively used for airlifts; crop dusting; air communications; airfield building; medical evacuation; locust control; meteorological work; vocational training; and technical aid.

COMMITMENT OF TROOPS

Of the three services, clearly the army will provide the preponderant contribution to civic action. But what proportion of the army may suitably be used and for which projects? In many countries, PUMF is virtually confined to engineering and signals units. In some others, over half the army is engaged at one time or another. The proportion of troops thus designated is to a large extent a political choice. But it will be also conditioned by the attitudes of the military. There will always be generals who frankly bridle at the very mention of "peaceful uses of military forces." Messing about with spades and shovels is bad for a soldier's morale, they will say. In India, this feeling was perhaps reinforced by the set-back on the northeast frontier in 1962.

WHO DOES WHAT?

In countries where the will and the political situation permit it, however, there is a whole range of projects to which not only the specialists but also the technically unskilled mass of the army can be committed. Troop labour is suitable for construction of simple irrigation systems; for the reclamation of land and draining of swamps; for the planting and harvesting of crops, for constructing, repairing, or improving roads, railroads, and airfields; and for evacuating people from disaster areas. In the field of health, non-technical troops can help to improve sanitary standards, to devise acceptable methods of disposing of human waste; to eradicate malaria and other insect-transmitted diseases; and to provide safe water supplies.   In education, those who are literate can help to provide basic training.   In community development, they can prepare plans and engage in the construction of schools, civic centres, churches, orphanages, and medical centres; and they can help initially to operate some of these projects.   Often, they will be working under or alongside engineer units, but their assistance can be of great value.   As an example of such a "mix," a road-building team might consist of a squad of infantry under an Engineer lance corporal.

The range of projects calling specifically for Engineer units includes: grading operations; setting up and operating machinery such as sawmills; devising and constructing flood controls; designing and supervising the construction of buildings; providing larger-scale water supplies and similar types of projects.   Another range of activities calls for signals units: the installation, operation,   and maintenance of telephone,   telegraph, and radio systems;   and the setting up and operation of emergency communications centres, especially in time of disaster.   Among other categories, units with transport facilities can help in the movement of agricultural produce, seeds, and fertilizers; disaster relief; and road building. Lastly, troops with farming experience can be extremely useful in increasing or improving the production of animals, grain, or vegetables. (They can, indeed, be organized and specifically trained with this end in view. In any case, the provision of ex-servicemen trained in the most modern agricultural methods is one of the most important forms of PUMF that any army can perform.)

LIMITATIONS

Such is the range of activities that can in theory be undertaken. In practice, it is constantly limited by several factors. One is the shortage of servicemen who have been trained in PUMF techniques. Another can be the language problem; often enough, the greatest need for PUMF is in areas where racial and linguistic differences have weakened allegiance to the central government.   Again, troops detailed to take part in these operations may have a standard of living as low, or lower than, those whom they are expected to help, which hardly makes for enthusiasm.   In a conscript army, many of them may be of a low intellectual calibre.   An abiding source of trouble is the misuse of equipment by inadequately trained troops; training in the use and maintenance of equipment is an important part of any PUMF programme. Again, as noted above, one rotten apple in a barrel can do untold harm; a stolen chicken or a carelessly driven jeep can create overnight the feeling: "We were better off before they came." The intangible results of PUMF action can be even more important than the concrete ones.

THE MORALE FACTOR

It is vital that this point be understood when the selection of troops for PUMF projects is being made. Experience has shown time and again that, even more important than the feeder road or the new pipeline or school is the feeling among villagers that for the first time, somebody seems to care about them. To see this in action is an unfailingly stimulating experience. If the arrival of a motor-pump to operate the well is a load off the villager's back, the arrival of a senior officer who will listen as well as talk to him has the effect of a shot in the arm. This may or may not be a universal fact of human nature, but it is widespread enough to be taken seriously. Even on the morning after a failure, when post-mortems are being held and high officials are asking, "Why did they turn against us?" the lesson is frequently misunderstood. The true reason is frequently that the army has gravitated to its atavistic, oppressive image--and every army in the world has this to contend with--through a failure to grasp that one of the villager's fundamental needs is to be treated with respect. When a single private rides roughshod over his respect, there will always be other villagers ready to say: "We told you so." Clearly, no army has an unlimited supply of troops and officers imbued with tact and a spirit of service, but where they are not available, PUMF can do more harm than good.

In this context, governments that are really interested in PUMF might well ask themselves whether the quality of their armies is as good as it might be. Conscription--and most armies undertaking wide-scale PUMF have conscription--habitually nets the less fortunate orders of society and misses the better educated. The man who gets caught tends to be the man who cannot run fast enough; the man with influence who evades conscription tends to come from a more educated circle. In particular, students seem to have a habit in many countries of getting their conscription deferred indefinitely.

GETTING THE BEST MEN

This last has always been a major political problem. With the advent of PUMF on the scene, the question arises how long this form of evasion can be allowed to continue. Should the educated be permitted to follow their desires and the labour market exclusively and make their fortunes in the big cities? Or does their very education, largely at the expense of the state, impose on them an obligation to make some temporary sacrifice? It is worthwhile for governments to keep this question under constant review. For nowadays, the sacrifice involved in conscription need not be so great as it might have been in the days when national service represented a total and often apparently futile break in a youngster's career. In Colombia, where attempts are slowly being made to implement the law that requires students to serve in the Army, such medical, teaching, and engineering students as have been called up have found the experience not only interesting but professionally valuable. For an engineering student to lay pipelines or build bridges in the countryside, albeit in uniform, is far from being a time-wasting experience.

Some countries have taken the bull by the horns and adopted a policy which might be described as "Conscript the Educated." Turkey, for example, is able to conduct its massive literacy campaign within the armed forces by conscripting teachers for the task. In Iran, the Education Corps is staffed almost exclusively by conscripted high school graduates, while the Health Corps is staffed by conscripted doctors and medical students. To do this requires a strong government. It also calls for a deliberate decision on the part of that government: a decision which entails opting for an "impact" programme on a nation-wide scale.

THE FOLLOW-UP

If such a programme is to be adopted--and security arguments as well as the principles of democracy would often seem to favour it--the chief difficulty arises in sustaining the momentum. In Iran, for instance, the trouble comes not in the first fourteen months of the teacher-sergeant's mission, but in the follow-up period when he looks in vain for instructors to help him to further the good work. In Morocco, the Army built 1,200 schools in one year, but there is a distressing shortage of teachers to occupy them. In Peru, the shortage of instructors is the main bottleneck in the expansion of pre-release training. "Conscripting the Educated" within the nation can go a long way towards meeting this need.

Still, it is an enormous gap, and the economically advanced nations might perhaps be doing more than they are to fill it. It is time to ask whether these nations themselves could not be conscripting some of their own educated for this purpose.

France and Belgium are, in a sense, already doing just this. A proportion of those who are called up for national service every year are given the option of going abroad, mainly to Africa, as teachers or technical experts. They go on Army pay, though with local allowances. The idea has been a notable success. President de Gaulle has been able to operate it because the decline in France's military manpower needs has coincided with the maturing of a large post-war age group. The latter factor, and sometimes the first as well, applies to the majority of industrialized countries. Almost everywhere, the supply of young men now considerably exceeds the demands of the armed forces. Other nations might well be asking themselves whether they could not be following the General's example.

Some governments are liable to balk at the reaction of their electorate to such a step. Yet, as with the developing countries, so with the industrialized ones, conscription of this sort would be very much more palatable than in its traditional form. The idea is, in fact, spreading. The Peace Corps-- and though it is not a form of conscription, it is for some an alternative to it--has lately been doubled. Other governments are taking tentative steps in the same direction. In Britain, the principle is still voluntary. But here would seem to be scope for a major initiative by Western countries to fill a need that PUMF is accelerating, but that was bound to occur sooner or later. One possible line of approach would be to render every university student liable--in return for the obligation to society he incurs by accepting a State grant--to undertake a year's service in a developing country. Objections to such a radical idea will no doubt spring to many minds. But its cost need not be great; the students would be paid at military rates, while transport--which would represent much the largest budgetary item--could easily be provided by those half-empty aircraft flown by every national airline. As to the popularity or otherwise of the scheme, even military conscripts normally enjoy their service, always provided they feel they are doing something worthwhile, and the urge for service among the young is almost as widespread as the urge to travel. The industrialized countries should be turning their attention to this subject.

CHAPTER **4** VOCATIONAL
TRAINING OF
SERVICEMEN

Advanced and developing countries alike have recently come to see the merits of using the armed forces to train men and women for a constructive role in society on their release. In both groups of countries, shortage of skilled manpower is almost invariably a critical bottleneck. For countries, rich and poor, who have conscription, this provides an opportunity to catch a considerable segment of every age group and offer them the opportunity to improve their qualifications for civil life.

EUROPE

Even in the advanced countries, this development is still at the experimental stage, and the experiments have not always been very successful. In some countries, such as Belgium, the period of national service is too short to provide much time for this type of activity. In most countries, moreover, it seems that the "offer" is not tempting enough to make a very widespread appeal. In Holland, for instance, large numbers of soldiers start on correspondence courses, but few manage to finish them. In the United Kingdom, similar courses are available and there are now three pre-release training centres, but with a small volunteer army--overstretched, at that--the impact on the economy is as yet slight. One abiding trouble in developed areas is the slenderness of the pay "differential" between skilled and unskilled workers. In Europe, the average unskilled worker's pay is over three-quarters of that of a qualified garage mechanic.

The French Army is taking the idea very seriously under its Promotion Sociale programme; and the recent introduction of special officiers conseil into every unit ensures that no soldier need be in ignorance of the vast number of courses open to him. But the proportion of each year's intake that avails itself of these facilities is still very small.

Of all European countries, one would expect France to take the lead in using the armed forces as an instrument for raising the country's supply of skilled manpower.   France has still to complete her evolution of a new defence philosophy following the reduction of her commitments in Algeria. It has even been argued that she no longer needs conscription at all.   But it is deeply engrained in her heritage; and no form of conscription modified by large categories of exemption has lately been established.

Some authorities are reported to have favoured the idea of two or three month's national service primarily to instil discipline into potentially wayward youngsters   "to get their hair cut."   One cannot imagine the regular army relishing such a prospect.   Nor is any army likely to take kindly to the idea of being utilized as a training ground for industry. Nonetheless, the French President is determined to see it so used. At one point it seemed possible,   in view of the insubstantial results achieved, that a measure of compulsion may be introduced into the training scheme.   But this has been ruled out, partly due to improved progress.

In Britain, influential voices have suggested that the Army's extremely effective training system for apprentices might be extended to civilians; that the Army might open technical colleges of its own, which would train both soldiers and civilians. Certainly the training is extremely effective.   Trade unions accept ex-servicemen as qualified after a period of apprenticeship in the Army far shorter than the five years required for civilians.   And now that this "five-year" régime looks likely at last to be broken, training institutes are turning to the Army for guidance in the art of accelerated training.

Obviously, both military and industrial needs and circumstances vary greatly from country to country.   One can only record that most European countries have started to move towards the concept of an army whose members will make a greater contribution to society when they are released.

DEVELOPING COUNTRIES

In some developing countries, this process is even more marked.   Military needs are often fairly slight, while economic needs are pressing.   In a country such as Ceylon, where defence requirements are very small, leading planners are going so far as to contemplate a scheme whereby the Army's intake and training system would be orientated first and foremost to the country's industrial needs. Such a revolutionary programme may be a long way off, though it could be the shape of things to come all over the world. But meanwhile the training of soldiers in civilian skills makes a vital contribution to the economies of many developing countries. The Israelis, indeed, regard it as the most valuable single form of PUMF. They criticize the Americans for placing undue emphasis on the "impact" side of civic action--the direct forms of economic activity. The Americans, for their part, have seen the force of this criticism, and it is now a fundamental principle of the U.S. civic action training teams to do the absolute minimum of direct work themselves, but to concentrate on training and instructing the local troops. In other words, these teams are beginning to concentrate more and more on Category II.

EDUCATION

The U.S. Government is advising on pre-release training programmes in many parts of the world. Such schemes, however, are dependent on an effective educational programme during the soldiers' time in uniform. One reason why there is no pre-release training in India, for instance--apart from a business course for officers--is that few jawans would be able to benefit from it. In developing countries, the average soldier is no more likely to be literate than the average civilian--possibly slightly less. In countries where there is conscription, the more educated members of the community tend to evade it, either by gaining exemption as students or by influence with the authorities. Among volunteer armies, the soldiers are often the pick of the community in terms of character and personality; in India and Ghana, for instance, there may be up to half a dozen applicants for every vacancy. But these are often men who are not educated enough to obtain a job in the civilian sector. Under British rule, indeed, there was a feeling that the uneducated made the best soldiers. Certainly recruiting was largely confined to rural areas, in the belief that the townsman had too much self-seeking sharpness about him. This feeling survives in India and Pakistan today.

This situation is changing as armies adopt increasingly complicated weapons and equipment. Specialists, tradesmen, and clerks all have to be of a higher intellectual calibre than was necessary even ten years ago. By way of illustration, in Nigeria about 70 out of 340 recruits in 1962 were totally illiterate. (All the remainder were semi-literate.) In 1964, the proportion of totally illiterate had dropped to 30 out of 390 (i.e., from 21 per cent to 8 per cent in two years). This in spite of the quota system, which keeps the illiteracy rate up by requiring a minimum percentage of Northerners.

Nevertheless, a high proportion of recruits in all developing countries can barely read or write; and they make an ideal captive audience for adult education. To pursue the Nigerian experience: during their first six months in the depot, recruits are subjected to an intensive literacy course, at the end of which nearly all can read and write. The process is compulsory until the soldier is sufficiently literate to be able to write simple letters and read simple orders in English. Those who cannot do so by the time they reach their unit are given intensive coaching. In 1964, there were only 10 in this category out of the original 30 total illiterates. Further education is voluntary and by selection, educational advancement being required for promotion. This programme has only been introduced in the last few years, and it compares very favourably with many countries.

Israel

Other countries with serious defence problems yet find time to educate their soldiers. Here the CENTO countries have a remarkable record, with massive literacy campaigns in Turkey and Iran. Most outstanding of all is the educational record of the Israeli Ministry of Defence. Its aim is to prepare citizens, over half of whom are immigrants, for their role in the State, as well as soldiers for their role in the Army. Many conscripts have little or no knowledge of Hebrew and not much schooling in other subjects. Those who are not up to standard by the time they are due to leave their basic training camps are kept on for 60 hours of concentrated study. Thereafter, during his national service, the conscript will receive another 450 hours of study under soldiers (most of them women) who are also doing their national service.

There are over 150 of these teachers dealing with elementary education only. This study is dove-tailed into the training programme of each unit; if, for example, the unit has completed a stage of military training and is devoting a few days to cleaning up the camp, the soldiers in the education programme will be excused for studies. They may receive up to 180 hours of Hebrew, 40 hours each on the history and geography of Israel, 50 hours on the Bible, 80 hours on arithmetic, 35 hours on world geography, and 40 hours on world history. This programme is an essential part of Israel's defence effort; experience in the 1949 war showed the difficulties of giving commands in half a dozen languages, while the infusion of a spirit of patriotic pride is considered essential to a country whose survival depends heavily on morale. The Army is in fact a melting-pot for ingredients from 102 countries.

In addition, all conscripts are subject to educational instruction in the form of weekly talks on current affairs by every company commander and question-and-answer periods during route marches designed to stimulate their interest in the countryside through which they are passing. Any group of soldiers interested in a particular subject may apply to its commander to set up a study circle and to provide the necessary instructors. Over 50 of these circles exist at present.

The example of Israel has inspired many developing countries to emulation and, not surprisingly, to requests for advice. The most outstanding recipients of these have been in Latin America and in French-speaking West Africa. In Latin America, the picture is varied, an important factor being length of national service. It is not surprising, for instance, that the amount of education it is possible to impart to a Peruvian conscript, who serves for two years, is greater than that which can be enjoyed by his Brazilian counterpart, who only serves for twelve months.

PRE-RELEASE TRAINING

This is eminently true of pre-release training; some armies can legitimately claim to have less time to spare than others, according to the period of conscription. Some disapprove of the principle. It smacks of welfare rather than warfare. It violates the sacred principle of unit integrity. And it is liable to make a hole in the defence budget. Under the magnificent arrangements for pre-release training in Colombia, for example, the Army contributes pro rata to the maintenance of the impressive civilian apprenticeship school where its soldiers are vocationally trained; in Peru, the training is done entirely within the Army. Such programmes provide a dividend to the Army, sometimes a valuable one, in that they can provide a stimulus to recruiting.

Military opposition to pre-release training, if successful, means that a government must concentrate on post-release training. But wherever one looks, this has proved to be at best a pis-aller. The simple fact seems to be that the average serviceman is not temperamentally inclined to rush to a vocational training centre the moment he takes his uniform off. His first inclination is to go home, to relax, and probably to spend his gratuity, if he has one. He does not particularly want to change the way of life he knew before, especially if this involves any effort. He is certainly not eager to attend a centre at any distance from his home; if this means physical separation from his family, he is deterred not only by natural domestic instincts but also by the fear of having to pay sizable transport bills if he is recalled by sickness in the family. Again, in some countries, the idea of technical or even manual work is alien to the serviceman's martial instincts.

These obstacles can be partially overcome, with proper organization. The impending ex-serviceman must be fully and intensively notified of the courses available to him; these courses must be such as will appeal to him, as well as being appropriate to employment needs; they must be reasonably accessible to him, as far as this is practicable; and travel allowances should be made fairly liberally available. Withal, it is necessary to vet applications for these vacancies with the greatest care, on the basis of interviews and service records. With such precautions, post-release training can yield valuable results. Yet even so, as a stimulus to the economy it cannot be compared with pre-release training, which is beginning to yield some spectacular results.

In Peru, for instance, literally thousands of conscripts spend their last three months being trained in carpentry, plumbing, electricity, masonry, or iron work. There are currently five centres training 750 soldiers each. It is planned that within the next two years the Army will be discharging semi-skilled workers at the rate of 6,000 to 8,000 a year.

The whole programme, which began in the spring of 1962, is financed by the Peruvian Army and subsidized by the U.S. Agency for International Development. Under the direction of civilian instruction, the soldiers built their own centre at Lima, including concrete paving, roof construction, and the installation of work benches, tables, cabinets, etc. This practical work was a valuable complement to the instruction they received, which included instruction in labour laws and community development as well as their specialized trade.

Initially, each of the five centres concentrates on the same half-dozen skills in order to establish its own installations. Thereafter, the choice of trades is determined entirely by local needs. Besides financing the programme, the Army exempts these soldier-students from all military duties during their last three months of service. In each centre, a public relations section carries out instruction on resettlement into civilian life and also provides liaison with industry to help in the employment of the soldiers on their discharge.

An important departure in 1965 was the establishment of an agricultural training centre in the Cuzco area. This was designed to train up to 900 students a year in cycles of six months each. Courses, which include tuition in cooperative farming as well as small farm methods, are open to civilians as well as soldiers.

Another new centre will be the Heavy Equipment Training Centre, which will train operators of engineer road construction equipment in support of the Army's road programme. Here, too, it is planned to accept civilians. These two centres are potentially the most important of all. As to machine maintenance, neglect of valuable equipment is one of the most heart-breaking of all development problems, and the foundation of this particular centre is the fruit of bitter experience. As to agriculture, pre-release training in this subject could have a profound effect on the economics of developing countries.

AGRICULTURE

The more progressive countries are beginning to switch their training programmes towards agriculture--Pakistan, for instance. Here there is a vigorous vocational training programme for soldiers and ex-servicemen, based on the Post War Services Reconstruction Fund, which was established during World War II for demobilized rankers and divided between Pakistan and India at the time of Partition. It has been noticeable that neither here nor in India have the vacancies allocated for ex-servicemen in industrial training institutes been fully taken up. Various explanations of this have been offered; for example, that the facilities are not always very up-to-date. This might help to explain the fact that allegedly trained ex-servicemen are sometimes found by employers to lack the skill they claim to possess. But a truer explanation is probably that in the Indian sub-continent, as in many other parts of the world, the serviceman comes from a farm and often wishes nothing more than the chance to return to it. In Pakistan, the most popular course for ex-servicemen--belying the notion that they will not be bothered to travel far for vocational training--has been the agricultural course near Hyderabad.

This point is crucial to the problem of resettlement over large parts of the world. To ignore it is both to waste money and miss a valuable opportunity. The example of Peru is as relevant as that of Pakistan. There has been distressing wastage of skill among Peruvian Indians trained at the centres mentioned above; too many have simply drifted back to their plots in the Andes, equipped with a skill that they do not intend to use and sorely in need of the agricultural training that they might have been given.

The fact that many ex-servicemen in developing countries hang around street corners in the bigger towns pathetically hoping to pick up jobs as commissionaires or night-watchmen can lead to false conclusions. Some, no doubt, do prefer battening on their relations to doing a day's work on a farm. But often enough they have no choice. In India, for example, there is a real shortage of cultivable land. Where the soldier has an option, in the form of a well-organized land settlement scheme, preceded by land clearance, he is glad to avail himself of it.

Herein lies the most important contribution that the ex-serviceman can make in the economic advance of the developing countries. Yet in most countries it is being neglected. This may be due partly to basic government policies towards farming vis-à-vis industry. There is a tendency among economists and planners, accepted by many governments, to make agriculture the Cinderella of society. At a recent lengthy conference on vocational training in South Asia, the word "agriculture" was barely even mentioned; too many speakers seemed to be animated by a form of snobbery about industry, a desperate desire to catch up with the industrialized Joneses.

Ex-servicemen are, as a group, one sector of the community not automatically inclined to float with the drift to the towns, which is the bane of so many young countries' economies. Naturally, there are large numbers of exceptions. But, in general, the ex-serviceman has shown in many countries that, given the right circumstances, he can make an outstandingly efficient farmer.

What are the right circumstances? First, to be efficient he should have pre-release training in agriculture. The Pakistan Army, whose pre-release training programme dates from 1957, did not take long to include such training among their facilities. Initially, the chief training programmes were in textile mills, sugar mills, and rubber, cement, and shoe-making factories; these now absorb well over 1,500 soldiers a year on courses of up to six months. Recently there has been an important emphasis on farming. Since then, well over 1,000 servicemen have been trained in dairy farming and bee-keeping, and several hundred in tractor driving. Also of benefit to farming is the emphasis on the training of tube-well operators--well over 100 in all.

It should go without saying, but unfortunately does not, that applicants must be carefully selected. Pakistan is very far from being alone in finding that these facilities are being made available to men who have not the necessary qualities to make use of them. The problem seems almost universal in one form or another; facilities seem to have been introduced faster than the machinery for vetting candidates through interviews and aptitude tests. The result is not just a waste of money, but also may lead to a loss of faith in the system among the civilian sector.

An example of wasted agricultural training was the original Service Civique experiment at Bouaké in the Ivory Coast-- since successfully amended in the light of experience. There, under the guidance of Israeli experts, an Army school was set up that would help soldiers to become farmers. The idea had been working with spectacular success in Israel; members of the Nahal (Pioneer Fighting Group) receive training in agriculture and soldiering alternately, and sometimes practise them more or less simultaneously. In the Ivory Coast, the scheme foundered on the quality of conscripts. It was found that the first twelve months of their service was not long enough to teach them to be soldiers, nor the second twelve months long enough to teach them to be farmers. The objective of the scheme--that the servicemen should go back to their villages and propagate the new farming methods that they had learnt--was not achieved. In the phraseology of the official report, the servicemen simply "éparpillaient"--dispersed without making any such impact on the economy.

On the advice of the Israeli experts, a number of radical reforms are being made; and since they represent the latest thinking of highly intelligent people about a widespread and fundamental problem, they are worth recounting.

First, all new recruits, though drawn from the ranks of national servicemen, are volunteers for this type of work. They wear uniform, like their predecessors, and come fully under military discipline; but they are not trained as soldiers.

Second, progressive villages are being set up around existing Service Civique farms. They are being run on cooperative lines in respect of farm machinery and distribution methods; otherwise the property--farm buildings and cattle--is strictly private. Every farmer is able to apply to the Service Civique centre for machinery and financial credit. The village's initial capacity is 60 families spread over 800 acres. Land clearance is being done mechanically with Army help, but cultivation is done by cattle-drawn plough. The villages will pass through several organizational stages, starting as a paramilitary organization and ending at the moment, after some eighteen months, when the farmers achieve economic independence. At this stage, the village will pass out of the hands of the Army into the authority of the Ministry of Agriculture. The recruit has by now completed his legal service. He may leave if he wishes to; but if he does, he will be relinquishing a steady livelihood.

Third, the development of selected villages is to be accelerated. The method is an adaptation of the Israeli garin, or group of young people who learn, live, and work together. Recruits are being drawn in groups of about twenty from the same village. They are given six months' training at a farm school; this is considered to be the maximum desirable period beyond which the recruit may be mentally uprooted altogether and will lose interest in his own village. The following six months he spends back at his village, still in his original group and under the same instructor who trained him at the farm school. As with the Progressive Villages, he will have the backing of regional Service Civique centres in the clearance of land and the supply of implements, seed, etc.

It is too early yet to know how this determined effort to grapple with an intractable world-wide problem will work out. The Israelis believe that, in the long run, the only sure way to "keep him down on the farm," as the ditty has it, is to provide the same facilities, amenities, and opportunities for recreation as he can get in the towns. But this seems an eminently practical start.

The Israelis, of course, aim even higher in other countries; where there is a need for it, they are ready to advise on the creation of farm settlements on the frontier for defence against invasion or infiltration. Their experts have advised the South Koreans on the use of this technique on the 38th Parallel; they have also been in touch with the Indians with regard to similar schemes in the Himalayan valleys. Other countries have spontaneously evolved schemes of their own--most conspicuously Thailand on the frontiers with Laos and Malaya.

Finally, the value of pre-release training can best be computed against the economic background of developing countries. There is a major shortage of skilled labour in these countries; what is the limiting factor in the filling of these vacancies? The pay "differential" is nothing like such a serious deterrent as it is in the developed countries; whereas in Europe a garage mechanic only earns one-third again as much as an unskilled labourer, in Africa he earns over twice as much. As to training facilities, these are now growing impressively. There are perhaps two major reasons why a man who could benefit from vocational training does not see fit to undertake it. One is the sheer inconvenience--the inaccessibility of the nearest training establishment. The other is the obligation to postpone a full and regular wage during the training period.

Both these obstacles are surmounted by pre-release training.

CHAPTER **5** PUMF AND
PEACE-KEEPING

The current concept of United Nations peace-keeping operations is one which was not foreseen in the Charter--the latter
dealing as it does with the more classical use of the military
in enforcement actions. In a very real sense, these current
peace-keeping operations may essentially be viewed as falling within our subject--the peaceful uses of military forces.
Much has been written about the order-keeping side of these
operations; very little has been written about the role they have
played or could increasingly play in helping to avoid a breakdown of the civilian infrastructure of a country in which the
United Nations has been called upon to intervene. Sometimes
chaos, confusion, and the disruption of vital services with
resulting loss of life are not involved. Where they are
involved, a U.N. peace-keeping force possessing civilian
skills has much to recommend it in an emergency situation.
But in any case, the experience of PUMF on a national basis
has much of relevance to both order-keeping and disaster
relief and reconstruction by the U.N., which is our Category III
of PUMF action.

PUMF AND CATEGORY III

As noted above, the three categories are all to some extent
interlocking. A serving soldier who has engaged in Category I
will be a much more useful civilian (Category II) than one who
has not; he will also be a much more useful member of a U.N.
peace-keeping force (Category III). There are, however, few
skills called for in Category III which are not required in
Category I; for most countries, Category III will essentially
be an extension of Category I, taking in a small number of
additional skills.

Experience has shown that far and away the most necessary
skills of a soldier engaging in a peace-keeping operation are
those that he should normally possess if he is to be an

47

effective soldier in his own country; and overriding all others is the capacity to establish and maintain law and order. This is not, it is true, the traditional function of soldiery; in days gone by, the soldier was trained first and foremost to fight--to shoot to kill, to overwhelm enemy forces without too much concern for loss of life. The maintenance of law and order is a much more sophisticated art. To kill a man under these circumstances is a confession of failure, rather than a mark of success.

In the Congo, many contingents took quickly to the role of peace-keeping. These tended to be those already accustomed to the task of internal security; the Indians, Ghanaians, and Nigerians proved extraordinarily adept. They had had experience of aid to the civil power at home, and been trained in it. They knew that the first essential is to keep tempers down; never to use more force than is necessary. Indeed, the Ghanaians developed a doctrine of never appearing in more force than was necessary, for fear of inflaming a situation. Sometimes they would go even further, and their officers, in particular, would deliberately discard their arms before undertaking a specially delicate piece of public diplomacy; they knew from experience that to carry them may be to invite the other side to disarm one violently.

Such tactics and such objectives--the cooling of tempers-- call for one quality above all others: discipline. A contingent that uses more force than is necessary in dispersing a mob, so that the mob turns and rends its persecutors, is no use in a peace-keeping operation. It is a difficult quality to inculcate; and it is harder still to sustain in the circumstances of a peace- keeping operation, where the normal hazards of soldiering-- homesickness, fluctuating morale, etc.--are compounded by almost constant provocation. In the Congo, there was hardly a U.N. contingent that did not have trouble with its troops, either in that country or after they had returned home. For this reason, it is desirable that normally no unit should be asked to serve in such an operation for more than six months.

Clearly, some of the U.N. contingents in the Congo were barely fitted to stay for that long; and some individual soldiers should not have been allowed in at all. The determining factor must be this capacity for cool conduct in exceptionally dif- ficult circumstances. If there is one need more than another for military training in countries contemplating possible future participation in peace-keeping operations, it is in this art of aid to the civil power--an art whose rules are known to all, but which only practice can perfect.

The reason this art is of such paramount importance and of relevance to PUMF as a whole is that if it is present, the civilian life of the local population will tend to function fairly normally, and to that extent the need for PUMF action will be reduced; whereas its absence precipitates all those ills that can only be cured by PUMF action. To take one example, the town of Tshiakiapa in the Congo was brought to a standstill by terror. The famine, the closure of the two main mines and the cotton mill, and the breakdown of the medical services were caused not by the absence of food in the vicinity or the non-existence of factory operatives and medical workers so much as by the breakdown of law and order, which prevented anybody coming into the open to provide these services.

The blame for this particular situation did not lie with the U.N. troops on the spot, but higher up. Yet the situation was a classic U.N. peace-keeping problem, and the moral is clearly that the capacity to restore law and order must rank as the overriding prerequisite of a U.N. contingent. Nor, it should be added, is this simply a matter of self-control and good will, though these are important ingredients. The Ghana contingent suffered two grievous tragedies through the practice of going unarmed--normally a highly effective practice, but not, unfortunately, always.

Nowhere is the need for this type of training more urgent than in the developing countries for, of course, with the industrialized countries being frequently disqualified from making purely combatant contributions to peace-keeping operations on political grounds, the burden of peace-keeping is most likely to fall on these shoulders. Nevertheless, the pioneer work being done by the industrialized nations, notably Canada, the Netherlands, and the four countries of Scandinavia, is of obvious relevance to any government concerned with this subject. The methods of recruitment and training of the Scandinavian U.N. Stand-By Force are cited here as being the most recent developments in this field.

Recruits for this force are required to meet the highest standard of conduct and morals. A knowledge of languages is also considered desirable. It is felt that, though the training of these units should not necessarily follow the service pattern established for military units, a complete military education is a necessary basis for such service.

Training includes an orientation on the U.N. organization, tasks, and procedures; the preconditions and principles for the organization and commitment of U.N. forces; a thorough examination of the Geneva conventions; police conduct; instruction on potential areas of U.N. commitment, as far as practicable; the personal duties and rights of the individual participating in the U.N. force; and the significance of correct, authoritative, and decisive conduct for the purpose of maintaining the U.N.'s authority, and the possibilities for peaceful resolution of international conflicts.

The Norwegians are undertaking a two-step training programme for their component battalion. The first part consists of a course for battalion officers, lasting one week, which is intended to give the officers general information about the U.N. as well as an introduction to some disciplines characteristic of U.N. operations, to which not much attention is paid in normal military training. The second part is in two phases: a one-week course for officers and NCO's, and a three-week course for the whole battalion. This aims at welding the whole battalion into an effective instrument and qualifying the squads, platoons, and companies to carry out tasks such as riot control, patrol duty, observation service, and cooperation with U.N. observers and local civilian authorities.

The officers' course, some forty strong, deserves close attention. It provides (a) knowledge about the U.N.'s structure and activities; (b) knowledge as to which conflict-types the U.N. might be confronted with, and which tactics and techniques should be applied; (c) knowledge of planning and carrying out air transportation of a military detachment; (d) knowledge about rights and duties of the U.N. forces as a whole; (e) information about the religious, social, and political problems with which they might be confronted; (f) information about problems of a medical, ethnical, and climatic nature; (g) information about previous peace-keeping operations and evaluation of experiences gained.

Under these heads are included:

The U.N.'s history, tasks, and working methods.

Instruction in riot control--principles of command of intelligence planning, of logistics planning, and operational planning; in patrol duties, especially in jungle and desert areas; in principles of cooperation with the local police.

A mock transport exercise.

Under "Rights and Duties": instruction on the Basic Agreement, the Status of Forces Agreement, and Transit and Base Agreements. Instruction on the Status of Forces Agreement included a study of the status, privileges, and immunity of U.N. forces, decisions on disputes and claims for damages, the use of the uniform and carrying of weapons, use of the U.N. flag, currency regulations, communication services, water, power, and other public utilities.

For a developing country to institute such a course would be aiming high indeed--although not too high for some. But the basic moral of U.N. peace-keeping is that its units should be prepared for just about everything--including urgent demands for PUMF, whether in the form of a breakdown in communications, of public hygiene, or of supplies of one form or another.

These problems arise every week in a U.N. peace-keeping operation; to cite only one example out of thousands, a British medical officer parachuted into Cyprus, supposedly to minister to members of the U.N. Force, was amicably hi-jacked by some Turkish Cypriots who wanted him to save the life of a baby with a "blue face" (heart condition). He saved its life and had it despatched to London for an operation. This, in fact, had nothing whatever to do with the political crisis, but--quite aside from its humanitarian aspects--it must have improved the "image" of the U.N. Force and made one village, at least, more amenable to its presence.

The ideal U.N. soldier is, without doubt, an impossibly perfect creature--one with the instincts of a policeman, the knowledge of a "doctor-cum-engineer," and superhuman energy. But is he not, rather than the old-style cannon-fodder, the ideal at which armies in developing countries should be aiming simply in their own interest? For surely he, rather than the traditional type of soldier, is the sort of man who can be most use to his government and his fellow-citizens in his own country. Unlike the latter, he is equipped to meet trouble when it breaks out within his own borders--not only by the use of minimum force, but also by his contribution to measures to alleviate the cause of the trouble.

From this analysis, one very important point arises. Is the U.N. to stand passively by, merely hoping that developing countries will recognize that it is in their own interest to turn out soldiers on this pattern, and thereby be able to supply appropriate contingents of them when asked? It has so far proved impossible to provide the U.N. with many of its military needs--for instance, a Military Staff in New York. But here is a task which could be undertaken with comparatively little difficulty, and with possibly far-reaching beneficial consequences. Just as its new Research and Training Institute is designed to help both the U.N. and the countries who send representatives to attend it, by turning out administrators which can be of use both nationally and internationally, so it could provide an analogous service for the military arm of these countries. There exist fairly large numbers of officers who have taken part in operations under the U.N. flag. These men could be seconded on invitation, to instruct units of national armies in the art of peace-keeping--including, as this does, the art of PUMF. This would be a form of advisory mission to which few governments should take exception, and which would bring them much the same dividends on the military plane as the Research and Training Institute is designed to do on the civilian plane.

The idea of a U.N. Staff College has often been mooted, and is still a good one. But the approach suggested here would provide a more direct and compelling form of instruction, based on experience at first hand. In its potential contribution both to future peace-keeping operations and to the security and stability of developing countries, this could be the most accurately aimed blow for peace which the U.N. could strike at its present stage of development.

CHAPTER **6** BELGIUM

In Belgium, as in most developed countries, the trade unions watch zealously for any sign of the armed forces performing civilian work in competition with the civilian labour force. On occasion--as in harvesting--the unions seem to go even beyond this principle. In spite of this, however, the Belgian armed forces manage to undertake a remarkable amount of "peaceful uses," particularly in the field of engineering and recently-- most dramatically--that of medicine (see Appendix B for the decree that authorizes and describes the system under which the Belgian Army engages in emergency non-military work).

ARMY

The Engineers are constantly at it. Their record for the first nine months of 1964 included the construction of two Bailey bridges for the Belgian Federation of Boy Scouts; levelling work at an aerodrome; building a swimming pool and parking place for the Arc-en-Ciel, an organization similar to the Boy Scouts; demolishing three chimneys for a private firm; building 5,000 metres of road for the Ministry of the Interior; building a dance hall, a platform, and a small bridge for the Federation of Ex-Prisoners of War; building a Bailey bridge for a private firm; more levelling work--this time for a clerical brotherhood which looks after the mentally hand- icapped; making a football ground and a road for the YMCA; mending a road for the Father Pire University of Peace; levelling 100 square metres of ground for the Burgomaster of Eghezee; removing a Bailey bridge at Tournai; and building a Bailey bridge for the Ministry of Works at Godsheide.

Such work goes on year in, year out; it is naturally inten- sified during a hard winter--for instance, when snow and ice clearance are needed. It is carried out entirely on an ad hoc basis. Bridging projects for the civil authorities come under a convention between the Ministry of National Defence and the Ministry of Public Works signed in 1956. In the event of a disaster, the use of the armed forces is determined by Royal Decree No. 13 of March 3, 1934, and by an agreement made between the Department of National Defence and other ministerial departments concerned. The part of the Army consists in lending assistance as normal labour and/or in specialized equipment to the civilian authorities responsible for rescue work. The intervention of the armed forces must wait on a preliminary request by the relevant civilian authorities or the police to the local military commanders. Military resources are placed under the orders of a "Military Commander of the Catastrophe" who orders them into action according to the directions of the official representing the authority which called for them. In each case, the work follows an approach by the authority concerned to the Ministry of National Defence.

In all emergency operations, improvisation is the paramount factor. During the heavy snow of January, 1963, for instance, the Army formed an organization colloquially known as the "Oil Company" to come to the aid of industrial concerns who were finding it impossible to distribute their oil. The drivers were drafted from every corner of the country--some from a transport battalion in Brussels, others from artillery schools, others again from various engineering schools and depots. The officers came from Transport Command. The vehicles consisted of Army tractors and of Air Force half-trucks. This company was placed under the orders of the big oil organizations. The operation was supervised by the Commandant of the 7th Transport Group. In the space of three weeks, the lorries had covered nearly 80,000 kilometres and transported 6,000,000 litres of oil. The team of thirty-four tractors and thirty lorries was kept operating by four mechanics under a Transport Command lieutenant.

The same winter, the Engineers were called in to blow up ice which was sealing off the inland coaling port of Genk.

Other occasional tasks that have done much to improve the Army's image include: a major rescue operation from a building which collapsed in the middle of Brussels in 1962; the restoration of the Boyau de la Mort, the celebrated trench from World War I, which is to Dixmude what the Tranchée des Baïonnettes is to Verdun; and the attempted rescue of workers in the collapsed mushroom caves at Zichen-Zussen-Bolder.

AIR FORCE

The Belgian Air Force is frequently used for disaster work. During the catastrophe of Marcinelle, when miners were trapped underground, the Air Force provided masks, oxygen cylinders, and ambulances on request from the Mines Department. At the time of the floods around Antwerp, the Air Force was invaluable in providing photographic information about the impact of the disaster. During the 1953 floods, military aircraft transported materials for repairing dikes and emergency food supplies.

It has been equally active overseas. After the Agadir earthquake in 1960, the Air Force provided transport for some 50 tons of equipment and about 300 civilian refugees. It evacuated large numbers of refugees from the Congo; in particular, it ferried some 1,700 people out of Elisabethville to Usumbura and Salisbury in 1961. The following year, it transported nine tons of medical supplies from the Red Cross to help the Algerian people. Members of the Air Force performing missions of this type remain dependent on the Army authorities, with which they are in close liaison, for changes of orders or additional directives. The Air Force has no units maintained specially for these operations except for the Search and Rescue Service at Coxyde, which is equipped with Air Force helicopters. They get no special training for these tasks.

The Air Force carries out topographical surveys in the form of aerial photography. These include:

1. Photometric surveys carried out in Belgium on behalf of the Military Geographical Institute in order to bring the map of the country up to date;

2. Aerial photographs on behalf of the Royal Institute of Artistic Heirlooms;

3. Aerial photometric surveys of the whole of the territory of Katanga on behalf of the Special Committee on Katanga--a long-term project carried out over many

years through close collaboration between the MGI, the Special Committee, and the Air Force. These surveys made it possible to map the whole of that fertile province in a very short time.

NAVY

The Navy undertakes emergency engineering works, such as dike repairs, when its units come under the Army's Engineer-in-Chief in response to an appeal from the ground forces. In case of catastrophe, such as a tidal wave, the request for help will originate from the Belgian minister concerned. If it is an overseas disaster, this, of course, will be the Minister of Foreign Affairs. The Belgian Navy also operates fast escort vessels on behalf of boats fishing on the high seas.

CIVIC EDUCATION

For all these non-military operations, there is no special training. However, it is official policy to ensure the widest possible education for Belgian officers. The Military Academy, through which 85 per cent of all officers go, provides such education for technical and non-technical officers alike. Courses are as follows:

Non-Technical Officers:

1st year	Social Philosophy	88	hours
	Law	53	hours
2nd year	Psychology	102	hours
	Sociology	176	hours
	Public Law and		
	Military Law	106	hours
	Political Economy	136	hours
	Economic History	90	hours

3rd year	Social Psychology	30	hours
	Social Philosophy	88	hours
	Political Economy	132	hours
	International Law	50	hours
4th year	Military Leadership	88	hours
	Military Sociology	44	hours
	Social Economy	59	hours
	Political Economy	44	hours

At the Polytechnic, where ballistics, telecommunications, and engineer officers study, these courses are shorter, but great store is set by them. In addition, a wide range of courses is open to officers and warrant officers on such subjects as public relations, journalism, television, the army as a social phenomenon, professional guidance, knowledge of Russia, knowledge of NATO, knowledge of the developing countries, psychological warfare, etc.

HEALTH

The Military Health Service collaborates with the Ministry of Public Health in matters which concern the notification of contagious diseases, medical and hygiene measures in case of catastrophe, and first aid measures for road accident victims including the provision of rescue service ambulances and hospital beds. The Service works in collaboration with the transfusion service of the Belgian Red Cross, providing blood from the military blood transfusion service and addresses of ex-service blood donors. It lends tents and blankets to youth organizations and provides accommodation for large youth rallies, and also first aid facilities. At certain sports meetings, it makes helicopters available for evacuating the injured.

The Army regularly supplies civilian hospitals with blood; the average per year is nearly 300 x 400 c.c. bottles. (This was more than doubled at the time of the Congo flare-up in 1960.) All soldiers are checked for blood group, and personnel of the Health Service are checked for Rh factors, a point of particular pride. (The Health Service of the U.S. forces does not undertake this systematic investigation into the Rh factor, while the French only make the examination for their naval forces.)

During the doctors' strike in 1964, the Minister of Defence, M. Segers, moved into action with vigour.* On April 2, he ordered General Geuens, Inspector-General of the Health Service, to coordinate action with a view to keeping the civilian medical services going. Immediately 200 beds in the Brussels Military Hospital were turned over to civilians. Four days later a military hospital opened at Anderlecht where 550 beds were in due course installed. Staff reinforcements came from the CRS (Centre de Recrutement et de Sélection) and from the CSS (Centre du Service de Santé); twelve doctors and a number of staff were recalled from Germany. Extra ambulances were moved into Brussels, some from Germany. By April 7, the Military Hospital at Brussels--thanks to the removal of a certain number of transportable military cases-- contained 450 civilian patients. The Medical Military Centre at Namur was reopened, as were later those at Ghent and Tournai. An infirmary of 80 beds was set up at Bogelsang.

As the situation became more pressing, the civil authorities asked the Army to prepare for the recall of 3,685 medical officers on reserve. This was decided on April 12 at 5 o'clock in the morning. A medical headquarters was set up in each military command and 135 liaison officers of all arms were appointed to every civilian hospital with more than 100 beds. Their job was to tell the commanders the requirements in each hospital. Two days later a new wing of 100 beds was set up in the hospital of La Louvière, and a helicopter was sent to Arlon and placed at the disposal of the Luxembourg Province headquarters for the urgent transport of medical specialists. The Pharmacie Militaire Centrale organized 400 medical supply kits and distributed 360 of them. Extra beds were supplied in the military hospitals at Antwerp and Ostend. A dispensary was opened at Mons and further reinforcements of ambulances were set up. By April 17, 336 liaison officers were operating. By the 18th, 1,351 civilians were in hospital in military establishments, but on this day the emergency ended, and with it a remarkable operation.

---

*The World Veterans Federation passes no judgement on the principle of the use of military forces in this context. It is concerned here simply to describe the technique.

VOCATIONAL TRAINING

Considerable trouble is taken to ensure that the serviceman is satisfactorily settled into civilian life on his release and, therefore, makes the best possible member of society. A wide range of courses is provided for him during his service; these are optional and free but, unless he has good reason, a beneficiary of the scheme may not abandon his course unless he refunds the expenses he has incurred. He is at liberty to take which course he likes entirely on his own decision, though he is always informed in advance of the economic and employment situation. He will also be guided by the estimate of his capabilities given by the Centre of Psychological Advice and Vocational Guidance, which examines all applicants and administers a vocational guidance test.* At present, some 2,000 soldiers are enjoying one of the following forms of training:

1. Correspondence courses for the examination of the Board of Secondary Education. This takes one or two years according to the serviceman's level of education.

2. A course for the examination of the Board of Lower Secondary Studies. Technical studies in mechanical or electrical engineering (available only to certain categories of career soldiers) take two years, of which six months are practical work.

3. A three-year course for the examination of the Confirmation Board (this Board relates military with civilian attainments).

4. A course preparing candidates for the competitive examinations for posts as Second, Third, or Fourth Grade civil servants. The length of the course is two years, one year, and four months respectively.

---

*The institution of an Officier-Conseil (see France) does exist in Belgium, but his services are available only to regulars, not conscripts. The latter, however, are interested in availing themselves of the services of the Orientation Centre.

5. Specialization without official qualifications. Subjects
    include motor mechanic, mechanical fitter, welder,
    precision mechanic, machine-tool worker, and operator
    of bulldozers and cranes.

6. Training by apprenticeship contracts for the occupation
    of motor mechanic. This is reserved for volunteers
    performing one of the following military functions:
    mechanic or repairer of wheeled vehicles, mechanic or
    repairer of track vehicles, and Diesel mechanic.

7. Private institutes for cases not covered by the provisions
    above, on the advice of the Centre of Psychological
    Advice and Vocational Guidance for the Army.

The first four types of courses come under the Ministry of
National Education and Culture. Specialization without official qualifications comes under the Military School. Apprenticeship contracts come under the Ministry of Middle
Classes.

Diplomas are given for those who complete their courses
successfully. For Central Boards: a legal diploma. For correspondence course institutes: a certificate, not of legal force.
For training in workshops: a record of specialization without
legal qualifications. For apprenticeship contract: a diploma.
Thus, only the first and fourth have legal force of the same
value as any diploma acquired in a State school or institution.

Following his release, the Government does not assist the
serviceman to continue his general or occupational studies
further. However, the Ministry of Employment and Labour
has created, under the auspices of the National Office of
Employment, Centres of Accelerated Vocational Training
available to all demobilized soldiers.

RESETTLEMENT

The National Office of Placement and Unemployment helps to resettle ex-servicemen by informing them of vacant situations. This department edits information bulletins giving all useful information on jobs offered both in Government and private employment.

Regular competitive examinations for the civil service are organized by the Permanent Secretariat of Recruitment, which comes under the Prime Minister's office. The department undertakes the transmission of offers of jobs and the centralization and transmission of requests concerning career servicemen. The costs of entering for these examinations are refunded to the examinees.

In practice, such general and vocational education as is provided in the Belgian armed forces is mainly received by the career soldiers. For, at twelve months, Belgium's period of conscription is one of the shortest in the world. (An attempt to make good the gaps by instituting the short-service career man, or NATO technician, was instituted in 1959--see below.)

As far as general education is concerned, the armed forces are legally obliged to give literacy courses to those who cannot read and write fluently. This education occupies a considerable part of the soldier's initial four months' training period. The instructors are often conscripts with teaching diplomas. Thereafter, soldiers who still need it are given an hour's basic education a day. There has been some introspection about the indifferent results of this whole system. However, the situation is to a large extent solving itself, thanks to the improvement in civilian educational standards.

In addition to mastering their own language, servicemen are strongly encouraged to learn their country's second language, Belgium being divided into French and Flemish speakers. Before the war, this division was acute in the Army. Nearly all the officers spoke French, and some refused even to give orders in Flemish, regardless of whether those orders were fully comprehended. Today, the mastery of a foreign language is compulsory only for officers. To become a major, an officer must pass examinations in both languages. But the Government has undertaken a strong propaganda campaign to persuade other ranks to learn the second language. This has to be done in their spare time. However, if in any battalion there are fifteen applicants for any one course, the Government will pay for a professor to teach them. The majority of such courses now being operated are in languages.

As for vocational training, Belgium suffers like most Western countries from the fact that young men can earn large sums without being skilled, and consequently, many do not trouble to take the courses. In addition, there is little time for a conscript to settle down to this sort of work. Certainly it is impossible to acquire a skill from scratch in that time--with the single exception of vehicle driving.

For the conscript, the post-release system of accelerated training, which is open to all civilians, has greater attraction. This system, which is paid for by the Ministry of Labour on condition the applicant has done the job for two years or one year plus Army service, has been going since 1961, when seventy-three centres were made available; by 1964 the number was considerably higher. However, only a few hundred ex-servicemen, including career men, take the courses in welding, plumbing, building, carpentry, and mechanics every year, and some consider the system is not working as efficiently as it might for lack of applicants. There would no doubt be more if the Ministry of Labour waived or modified their two-year rule. But they are under no pressure to do so from the armed forces, which thereby benefit from an increased number of servicemen signing on for another year. In 1965 alone, some 450 NATO technicians did this.

NATO TECHNICIANS

In an effort to increase the regular number of tradesmen in the armed forces, and equally the number of skilled workers in industry, the Belgian Government in 1959 invented the

concept of the NATO technician.[*] He is a third category between the long-service volunteer and the conscript who serves
for twelve months only. He will sign on customarily for five
years, sometimes for three years and sometimes for even
less, taking his decision either before being enlisted or at the
end of his twelve months' national service. The attractions
are the prospect of being trained in a civilian trade and also
a terminal grant, which ascends according to the length of
service to the remarkable peak of $2,000 at the end of five
years. The NATO technician also has the opportunity on
release of taking a post on special terms either in the gen-
darmerie or the customs service. The scheme has run into
some difficultues in execution; promises have been made--
such as in the provision of housing--that have proved quite
impossible to fulfil. Recruitment has been unsatisfactory
both in quantity and in quality. Too many of those who joined
have had little idea of what they wanted to do, or ambition to
do it, and have been attracted largely by the money. Worse,
the regular NCO's morale suffered heavily from the sight of
inferior soldiers earning much more than they themselves.

Today, the public appeals for NATO technicians have
stopped. Indeed, in their efforts to find a new solution to this
recruiting problem, the Belgian armed forces have turned to
study of the British approach. Nevertheless, the scheme was
a commendable attempt to solve this widespread and intractable problem.

---

[*]So-called because most members of the Belgian armed
forces come under the North Atlantic Treaty Organization.

In the field of "peaceful uses," Brazil has a long tradition stretching back several generations in the exploration of the jungle and the opening up of communications by Army units. Today, the picture may be summed up by saying that these vital communication works continue vigorously--over half the country's major roads are being built by the Army--and that the Army provides primary, secondary, and higher education for a considerable number of civilians, but that as far as pre- or post-release training goes, this is negligible or non-existent. The latter fact is due to the remarkably short period of conscription--between eight and twelve months. Thus, the striking experiments in Colombia and Peru have no counter-part in Brazil.

ROAD BUILDING

The biggest civic action programme is road building--obviously vital to a country which until recently was described by the Brazilians themselves as virtually a series of islands. Military-civic action is mainly confined to the Engineers, working jointly with civilians. An Engineer battalion on a road-building project is likely to consist of about 700 troops and anything from about 300 to 20,000 civilians under contract. One of the merits of this system is that a conscript working with the Engineers may receive special technical training and, on completion of his term of service, he may then stay on with the battalion as a civilian. He is thus launched smoothly on a career in which there will be no shortage of work. These operations are not paid for by the Army, but by the Ministry of Works. There is little clash with private industry, inasmuch as private firms have little desire to operate in these outlying areas. However, once a section of the road has been built, civilian firms often move in and obtain the contract to maintain it. Also, the Army sometimes sub-contracts stretches of roads to civilian firms in the less remote areas.

In the Northeast (the most pressingly under-developed area) public works--including railroads, dams, irrigation works, and water supply systems--are currently being undertaken by four construction battalions, a service battalion, and a group headquarters. In addition to their construction work, these units have wide social responsibilities covering health, literacy, food supplies, and transport. In Southern Brazil, there are four Engineer Construction Battalions whose functions are confined to construction. At present, they are concentrating on the building of the main southern railway line to accelerate communications between São Paulo, Pôrto Alegre, and the South. The Army is building over 350 miles of track plus a great many maintenance installations.

These public works are carried out under the direction of civilian agencies. Under agreements stemming from Decree No. 37148 - A, of April 5, 1955 (see Appendix C), the civilian agencies supply the over-all direction, the programme specifications, and the money; the Army does the work under contract with its own men, equipment, and vehicles. By the middle of 1964, it had received more than 1 billion cruzeiros for roads, nearly 2.5 billion for railways, and 187 million for irrigation work. In the Northeast, the agencies involved are the Ministry of Communications and Public Works, the Directorate of Transport, and the Superintendency for the Development of the Northeast (SUDENE). It is estimated that the Army has built or has in hand the construction of 1,300 miles of roads, 430 miles of railways, and irrigation systems with a water volume capacity of 52 million cubic metres.

The trade unions tend to be suspicious of the whole concept of military-civilian battalions. But according to the Army, these civilians are employed under a simple contract, with no question of military discipline attaching to it, and they enjoy at least the same benefits as their purely civilian counterparts, including sickness care and fifteen days' dismissal notice. In addition, of course, the civilian may qualify for specialized technical training by the Army.

FRONTIER UNITS

Another phenomenon of some international interest is the Frontier Unit. Six years ago, the Army set up military establishments along the north and northwestern borders with a headquarters in Manaos. This headquarters, known as the Frontier Elements Group, comes under the 8th Military Region and the Amazon Military Command in Belém. There are at present seven Frontier Units varying in size from platoon to company strength. (These troops are all regular soldiers, including former draftees who have signed on.) Besides normal frontier and anti-contraband operations, these units have engaged in a vigorous civic action programme. They have set up sawmill and brick workshops, flour mills, rice-husking machinery, and small hydroelectric plants; they have helped local farmers by seed distribution, cattle improvement programmes, and the building of stables; they have built at least five rural schools and established the same number of dental and medical mobile units; and they have set up sewage systems and water storage facilities.

Even allowing for the size of the country, these projects are small-scale affairs. But they are extremely successful and popular, and may be considered to show what could be done if more of the Brazilian Army were engaged in them.

EDUCATION

The Brazilian Army makes an important contribution to education through its military colleges and its engineering institute. It operates seven military colleges, in the first instance for sons and orphans of military personnel, but with a considerable number of sons of civilians. More important, over half of those thus educated make a career outside the armed forces. These colleges are situated at Pôrto Alegre, Curitiba, Rio de Janeiro, Belo Horizonte, Salvador, Recife, and Fortaleza. There is great competition for places in these colleges. The six outside Rio nominally have an establishment of 700 students, while that at Rio numbers over 2,584.   Of these, 1,355 are sons of civilians;   428 are being educated free.   The term of instruction ranges from between three and seven years at the different colleges.   The intention is that all colleges should be expanded to seven-year institutions--four years of primary and three years of secondary education.   These establishments are entirely financed by the Brazilian Army and staffed mainly with Army personnel, and combine their educational programme with basic military instruction.

ENGINEERING INSTITUTE

The Military Engineering Institute at Rio provides a five-year course for about 300 students between the ages of eighteen and twenty-three.   Of these, currently some 60 are civilians. These students start at eighteen; most of the soldiers are given general basic training elsewhere and join at the age of twenty for three years.   The Institute provides places for students from other parts of Latin America; at present, Paraguay and Venezuela are represented, and there is a girl student from Guatemala.   As to the subjects for specialization, current practice is that the Army will specify which kind of technician it requires, so that civilians tend to fill up the remaining quotas. During their course, the civilians get training as reserve officers.   The course, being completely free, is enormously popular. Principal subjects are electronics, communications, chemistry, metallurgy, geodesics, and civil engineering. There is also a post-graduate course in nuclear engineering.

The ultimate aim is to expand the college to some 500 places, out of which 200 will be open to civilians.   As usual, the main limiting factor is shortage of teachers (although with the falling rate of exchange of the cruzeiro, it has in the past been difficult to get adequate equipment).

The Institute is under the primary jurisdiction of the Ministry of War, also supported by the Ministry of Education and Culture, the National Commission for Nuclear Energy, and the Superior Council for Institute Planning.   It collaborates in technical activities with the other Brazilian armed forces and civilian organizations, mainly with the object of stimulating industrial development important to national security. It collaborates with all agencies concerned with industrial, technical, and scientific mobilization of the nation. Academic degrees are not granted, but students completing the course are recognized to have reached a standard equivalent to a good B.A. degree. Those who complete the graduate course of twelve months' duration have the equivalent of a good M.A. degree. From time to time, technical courses are arranged for sergeants and other ranks. Naturally, most of the staff are Army officers.

These, then, are the Army's main projects in the field of technical education. It will be seen that while no effort is made in the way of pre-release training of soldiers, a good deal is achieved in the on-the-spot training of conscripts working with Engineer batallions. Conspicuous by its absence, however, is any provision for agricultural training. At any rate, an attempt to provide such instruction in São Paulo failed. It is reported that some 200 teachers were available and only 18 pupils enrolled. The establishment was closed and turned into a medical school.

THE NAVY

The Brazilian Navy, perhaps because it is something of a political and social force in its own right, has a more vigorous civic action programme than is to be found in most countries. Under Law 1658 (1952) it has the responsibility of providing technical assistance and professional training to maritime and fishing personnel. It provides, in the Merchant Marine School, training for merchant marine officers and prepares pilots for the fishing industry.

It is also carrying out hydrographic and oceanographic surveys off the Brazilian coast. One survey ship is now working under contract with UNESCO, helping to train men in under-sea survey work. In this connection, naturally, the migration of fish is studied--their habits and the likely depths at which they are to be found. Since this particular ship operates well out into the Atlantic, its findings have as yet been of limited value to fishermen, but they may be more so as the project develops. Already, extensive measurements have been taken of the changing temperature and salinity of the water at different depths and at different times of the year, the movement of horizontal and vertical currents, luminosity at different depths, and the presence of various types of plankton.

The Navy has carried out surveys for port construction, e.g., selecting a site on the coast of Espíritu Santo for shipping minerals; it has surveyed the north channel of the Amazon, in the territory of Amapá, to promote the export of manganese ore, and in these and similar projects it has had the close cooperation of the Agency for the Economic Development of the Northeast (SUDENE).

All told, the hydrographic and oceanographic service maintains six to eight ships on survey work. In addition to those required to man them, another 1,000 are employed ashore. The service also carries out coastguard work covering the coastline and river waterways.

The Brazilian Navy provides very considerable ship repair facilities. In the past three years, the Rio shipyard dry dock has accommodated an average of over 15 million ton-days per year of which almost exactly one-half were merchant vessels. Of the remainder, some ships were from the Uruguayan Navy. Out of 849,331 man-hours expended on all categories of ship repairs, the shipyard expended rather over a quarter on repair of merchant vessels in 1963. During the same period, the industrial shops, out of 1,439,386 man-hours, utilized 408,046 in work on private industry. The bases at Belém, Matao, and Recife are smaller, and an even larger proportion of their activities are devoted to private shipping and industry.

The Navy is frequently called on as a source of technical know-how by other Government agencies. Agencies which have called on naval personnel for advice or direction include the Merchant Marine Commission, SUDENE (Northeast Development), SUDEPE (Fishing Industry Development), PETROBRAS (Federal Petroleum Industry), SRONAPE (Federal Petroleum Fleet), LLOYD BRADILEIRO (Federal Shipping Lines), COSTEIRA (Federal Shipping Lines), Tribunal Maritimo (Maritime Admiralty Court), National Telecommunications Council, and SNAP (Amazon and other major river direction traffic management).

AIR FORCE

As in many South American countries, the Brazilian Air Force plays an important role in the country's economy. It provides transport to all remote areas where civilian airlines do not operate and supplements existing airlines. The Brazilian Air Force has been conducting these civil transport operations for more than thirty years. The Air Force estimates that it files 1,000 hours a month on purely civic action flights. The bigger airfields are used jointly by the military and civilian aircraft. The Air Force maintains some 300 landing strips of greater or lesser size throughout Brazil, and a study has recently been undertaken of the practicability of concrete runways in many remote areas.

Brazilian Air Force planes make many deliveries of food, medical supplies, and mail to distant areas as weather permits. They fly in medical teams on a monthly basis; they are also subject to calls for any type of disaster in the country. Likewise, the Air Force is liable to be called on to evacuate stricken people from flooded areas or those hit by disease or drought. It has been particularly active in bringing social, educational, and medical help to the northern and western frontiers of the country. This is done through the National Air Mail, the agencies of the First Air Zone, and the Aviation Health Directory, which supervises emergency cases. A steady service is supplied by the medical officers in the Air Mail crews, with striking results. The work of the Air Medical Units is reported to be outstanding; since their foundation in 1956, they have taken more than a million X-rays and provided more than 4 million treatments in these outlying areas. This work is said to have made a valuable contribution to the development of tropical medicine.

Another vital function of the Brazilian Air Force is the surveying of the vast sub-continent which constitutes Brazil. At present only one tenth of the country has been mapped. The most urgent target for this work is the Northeast of the country, the fastest growing area in terms of population. This important work is supervised by the Directoria do Servicio Geografico. Among its more spectacular successes has been the discovery of iron and oil by aerial photography. Though it is not the only organization working in this field, it is in effect the parent body; other companies will obtain the major survey from the DSG and work from it to more detailed surveying. The organization, which numbers 600 employees, civilian and military, is doing work whose value can scarcely be computed. I was told, though without being able to confirm it, that it carried out a survey of 40 square kilometres for the town of Aracajú, capital of Sergipe State, at a vast saving for that city; a civil organization, it is said, asked 2 million cruzeiros per square kilometre surveyed, while the price charged for the whole area by the DSG was a total of 8 million.

It remains to record that proposals were made through bills in Congress in 1948 and 1959 to establish a compulsory civic service for young men, not required by the armed forces, who would be trained while promoting the country's development. But nothing has come of these proposals.

Colombia is a classical example of a country that has successfully used PUMF as an integral part of a counter-insurgency campaign.

It was General Ruiz Novoa, a veteran of the Korean War, who, in the two years of his appointment as War Minister (1962-64) broke the back of the sixteen-year-old guerrilla war, which up to that point is estimated to have cost no fewer than 200,000 lives. This he did by a judicious combination of the mailed fist and Acción Cívica-Militar. Clearly the security aspect was the more important factor. The villagers were left in no doubt as to what might happen to them if they failed to provide the necessary information about guerrilla activities in their vicinity. A degree of toughness was necessary to out-bid the extraordinarily unpleasant methods of some of these guerrillas. The Army had to assert its authority with vigour and keep on attacking. Today, in the violence areas, it has an extensive network of observation posts that will provide minute details about the smallest activities in the villages. These observers know when any newcomer arrives in a village and where he is staying. They even know when a child fails to go to school and are liable to send a party to check on the reason. If their methods are sometimes rough, there would seem to be little alternative. For those of the guerrillas are frequently horrifying.

It is against this background that civic action is proving so timely. It would be wrong to exaggerate its importance as a factor in the country's economic development. But it is absolutely vital in enlisting the confidence of the campesino and in bringing order to areas cleared of the guerrillas. It is also, in the view of the Colombian Army, a new combat weapon in the campaign against the guerrillas, aimed at denying them their previous support in the countryside. Part of it is straightforward propaganda--the dissemination of information through leaflets, public address systems, radios, and films. But in addition, a considerable segment of the Colombian Army is geared to civic action in the form of health, education, and road-building programmes. The Navy and Air Force are equally active.

ORGANIZATION

The effort of all three forces is coordinated under a unique body in the Ministry of Defence: Department No. 6. This, in collaboration with other joint services departments, plans civic action for the year ahead. On the basis of this plan, the commanding general gives orders to each of the three armed forces as to what has to be done. The head of this department is supposed to coordinate with other ministries and agencies-- Foreign Affairs, Public Works, Health, etc. and also the U.S. Agency for International Development--to determine what funds are available. There is no special budget for civic action; funds are taken from the normal appropriation budget.

The programme covers the entire Army; every unit receives basic training in civic action and is supposed to carry out a mission. All five Engineer battalions are doing road-building or well-drilling work. Other arms of the service have responsibility for geographical divisions of the country-- cavalry, artillery, infantry, etc.--an arrangement that originally led to excessive competition, but that is now subject to fairly effective coordination and financial control from headquarters in Bogotá.

Today this competition is healthy, and ensures vigorous initiative even in areas unaffected by guerrillas. The infantry school, for instance, has an area of responsibility around Bogotá without any violence problems at the moment. But owing to the drift of the bandits out of the countryside into the towns, thanks to the Army's success in the countryside, this area is potentially explosive. The Army has therefore conducted a survey of educational and road problems and has estimated the needs of the region. One survey reached the conclusion that the land was too infertile for widespread arable agriculture. The Army therefore undertook a campaign to persuade farmers to switch to developing a pork industry, and also fruit growing; to this end they induced the Ministry of Agriculture to supply the necessary help in the form of a good strain of pigs, and also seeds. For such surveys, the Army can borrow technicians, doctors, etc., from the University.

ESCAPING THE NET

This borrowing is necessitated, among other things, by the calibre of the raw material recruited into the Colombian Army. As in so many countries, though military service is theoretically universal, those of advanced education systematically manage to elude it. In practice, only about 20 per cent of those of a given age-group get called up; and foremost among those who succeed in obtaining exemption are students of all faculties, who generally manage to postpone conscription indefinitely. This is recognized by the Army as one of the major deficiencies in its civic action programme, and steps are being taken to put it right. As an initial measure, some 150 students--medical, legal, dental, etc.--are being recruited on a short-term basis. They are called up for three months, receiving one month of military training and operating for two months in their own professional field in the villages. The Army hoped to extend this system both in time and in numbers. Certainly it seems successful, inasmuch as the students find it provides valuable practical training. Their hope was to enlist some 1,000 of these students by the end of 1965; influential opposition, however, was anticipated. This opposition has already successfully diluted the existing law, which requires all medical students to serve with the Army.

This problem is, of course, a world-wide one--including the element that doctors are normally disinclined to work in the villages when they can earn so much more in the big towns. Colombia's attempt to solve it may well be of interest to other countries.

For those who are conscripted, there is a basic military training period of twenty weeks, followed by anti-guerrilla instruction lasting nine weeks. The second period includes education on relationships with the civilian population, how to befriend the campesino and how to undertake simple tasks of hygiene and rural development. Officers and NCO's receive more elaborate training. The promotion course for lieutenants to captains is strongly orientated towards civic action.

CONFLICT WITH CIVILIAN AGENCIES

A crucial aspect of this civic action programme is, inevitably, relationship with the various agencies. In theory, the combination of these agencies, which possess the necessary funds, with the Army, which possesses the executive means, should be complementary and fruitful. However, at least in its early stages, it seems that the relationship has not always been too happy, for reasons inherent in any civic action programme. In particular, the Army must tend to be guided primarily, sometimes exclusively, by security considerations in its selection of tasks to be undertaken This has meant frequently by-passing the civilian agencies, who may not merely be affronted by this procedure, but sometimes genuinely question the choice of tasks. It has been found that special allocations of funds for civic action programmes are necessary within the budget of the Ministry of Defence. Total dependence of the military projects upon appropriation of funds by each civilian agency concerned has been found to hamper--if not positively frustrate--the object of a programme. This is because the needs for development projects, as seen by the military, usually cover tasks that have not been contemplated within the scope of the national or sectional budgets.

At any rate, for good reasons or bad, when the time comes for the Army to move out of a civic action area and hand over to the civilian agencies, these agencies can always, and frequently do, object that they would never have undertaken the task in the first place and have no desire to carry it on. The experience of Colombia in the last two years has shown that though "developmentalism" and "impact" need not necessarily be incompatible, very careful forethought is required if the two concepts are not to become at loggerheads with each other.

EX-SERVICEMEN

The impetus behind Colombia's terrorism is a matter for debate. It long antedates Castroism, and even lately it does not seem to have been particularly "Castro-ite." Some of these terrorists have been ex-servicemen. Most of them former campesinos, they returned to their old areas--unarmed, it is true; but the lessons learnt during their service helped them to capture arms and settle down to a life of terrorism. The whole experience provides a warning that an ex-serviceman can not only be of benefit to society if he is properly trained for it, but can be a serious menace if he is not. Today a major pre-release training programme is under way (see below). But there is still no registration for ex-servicemen. Such registration, and a requirement to report regularly to the local commanding officer, might simplify the task of identifying the subversives; it could also help to enlist in antiterrorist operations and in the provision of intelligence, ex-servicemen who are by nature inclined to help. The same advantages would be equally true in the towns.

Meanwhile, steps are being taken to ensure that the largest possible number of ex-servicemen are trained for civilian work before they leave. This is done through SENA (Servicio Nacional de Aprendizaje). It was hoped that by 1966 all service-men would be put through this technical training organization, which is undoubtedly one of the finest in Latin America. It is financed by a tax on private business. Every firm that employs more than ten people must pay 2 per cent of its total wage bill to SENA. The Army will eventually pay 5 per cent of its total wage bill. There are twenty-seven SENA instructional schools in the country specializing in various forms of manual skills.

Since it is industry which directs the organization, it is industry which calls the tune in respect of number and type of training given. As far as servicemen are concerned, a principal limiting factor is not the availability of places so much as the number of servicemen sufficiently educated to benefit by this form of training.

The Colombian Government claims that this is the oldest such training centre in South America except for the one in Brazil; the others, they say, followed Colombia's example. Be this as it may, the buildings and equipment in Bogotá are dazzlingly up-to-date. In addition to training students, SENA has an international training centre for student instructors from the rest of South America.

As in Peru, the initial emphasis on industrial skills is being shifted to embrace major agricultural training facilities.

Supporting this programme is a literacy training programme designed to teach about 9,000 illiterate recruits annually to read, write, and do simple arithmetic. This was launched in October, 1963. Teaching laboratories have been installed in the seven Army recruit training centres. Recruits receive 100 hours of instruction based on pre-recorded tapes and text-books. The programme appears to be working very well. Training is continued, where necessary, after arrival at the unit by military or civilian instructors.

CIVIC ACTION IN A VIOLENCE AREA

Civic action in Colombia covers a wide spectrum of activities from road-building projects to one-shot operations known as Civic Action Field Days. The most important road-building project has been the Tolima Highway, which was initiated several years ago as a joint effort of the Colombian Army and the Ministry of Public Works. The project involves construction of 96 miles of a trunk-line highway between Ataco, Tolima, and Palmira, Calle, together with about 30 miles of connecting road at the eastern end. The network will bisect an area of over 2,000 square miles that has been one of the most active violence areas in Colombia. It is essential both to effective military movement and to the development of the region.

Although a vital project, it was moving very slowly before 1963 because of a shortage of funds and equipment. These were to a large extent remedied by U.S. aid. Five Army companies are currently working on the project. It was due for completion by September, 1965. The road will incidentally shorten the distance from Bogotá to the port of Buenaventura by about sixty miles.

In addition, two civic action road projects were completed in 1965 by an Engineer battalion. One company built a gravel-surface forty-mile road in the Department of Santander. These road works, though not on quite the massive scale of those in Peru, are clearly of development and strategic importance.

HEALTH

The construction of health clinics has been an important feature of Colombia's civic action programme. The planning for this project was directed by the Army Command with the assistance of U.S. officers. Its objectives were to supply free medical care in areas where it is not available, to develop a health plan, and to develop a first-aid education programme. It is also designed to improve the sanitation conditions of the towns, to provide information about the nutritional values of food, and to instruct those engaged in house building to meet minimum hygiene standards. The aim of the project, which began in February, 1964, is to provide these services for about 100,000 people living in nineteen separate areas. Over half of these live in the violence areas. Up to that time, these areas had no medical facilities whatever. As of autumn 1964, eighteen fixed health centres had been established.

Those engaged in the work are convinced that their operation is a vital force in the development of civic pride in the towns and villages concerned. They provide a spur to the formation of local community development committees for the accomplishment of other civic projects. The project engages seven Colombian officers and twenty NCO's, thirty-two Colombian civilians (doctors, dentists, and nurses), and one U.S. military adviser. The main problem here, inevitably, is shortage of medical personnel.

Another important undertaking is the provision of increased supplies of drinking water. The work consists of drilling wells, installing chlorination equipment, building storage tanks, and treating water. Its direction is under the Armed Forces General Command; its administration is under the commanding officer of a battalion of support engineers. The project envisages the drilling of nineteen water wells in areas where water is insufficient and often contaminated. Up to 3,000 people are estimated to benefit from each well. The time calculated for drilling the wells is twelve months. The armed forces also train personnel to operate this system, giving theoretical and practical instruction on procedures. By autumn 1964, two wells and one potable water supply system had been completed. There appears to be a bottleneck in the operation of the equipment available; in autumn 1964, the Ministry of Health had received five rigs from U.S. sources but lacks the personnel to operate them. Those engaged in this work are two Colombian officers, twenty-two Colombian other ranks, one Colombian civilian geologist, and two U.S. officers.

FIELD DAYS

At the extreme "impact" end of the spectrum is a phenomenon apparently peculiar to Colombia, at least in the consistency and regularity with which it is employed: the monthly Civic Action Field Day. This is a dramatic occasion--a cross between an outsize village fête and an army manoeuvre--to which campesinos will come from up to ten miles around for the various services it provides. They may have their ailments attended to, their teeth drawn, their hair cut, their shoes soled, and many other facilities free of charge. These occasions are taken extremely seriously by the Army and frequently attended by top level generals and politicians. In the course of them, these VIP's will listen attentively to the needs and complaints of the local headman, judge, or leader of the communal junta, the local organization which the Government is anxious to build up in all areas as a supplement to civic action. Between December, 1963, and August, 1964, these operations provided 53,000 medical consultations, 40,000 dental operations, 42,000 first aid and immunization treatments, and 51,000 haircuts and shoe repairs.

There can be no question as to the popularity of these occasions. They take place in areas where the services provided by the Army are unique and unprecedented; there are likely to be no medical and dental facilities whatever. Undoubtedly the proceedings do a great deal for the Army's image. But here, of course, par excellence, arises the problem of follow-up. It may be months before a man given medical treatment in one of these field days will see a doctor again; he will be lucky if he sees a nurse with the most rudimentary ideas of medicine. Probably the campesino's reaction to this failure to follow up is more compounded of bewilderment than resentment. But certainly the Government is conscious of the problem. Peace Corps volunteers and their Colombian counterparts have been urged to assist in follow-up health education and to stimulate community interest.

THE NAVY

Remarkable medical work is carried on by the Navy in areas where the rivers are the only form of transport. In the Amazon area, four river gunboats, five transports and tugs, and one patrol boat have been assigned to provide medical services, supplies,passenger transportation, and other services. Along the Magdalena River, gunboats and a river transport provide similar services along some 600 miles of navigable waters upstream from Barranquilla. On the Meta River, besides performing these functions, the Navy provides medical supplies, services,and evacuation to the hospital in Orocué. The Navy also treats patients from Colombia, Peru, and Ecuador at Leguizamo Naval Hospital. This hospital is the only medical facility available to inhabitants of these three countries in a jungle area of thousands of square miles. The only access is by boat or air. Likewise, Leticia Naval Hospital provides services to the inhabitants of Colombia, Peru, and Brazil in the area (Leticia is on the extreme southern salient of Colombia, immediately adjacent to both the other countries). The hospital is administered and operated by a committee consisting of Colombian Navy, City, and State officials, and civic leaders. It is being steadily expanded.

AIR FORCE

As in other Latin American countries, the Air Force is in the forefront of civic action. It operates its own civic action airline (SATENA) which now runs six aircraft on daily service. This provides freight and passenger transport at extremely low rates. One understands that travelling by these aircraft can be a convivial experience, rather like travelling in a village bus, with livestock well in evidence. The aircraft are supplied from U.S. Government surplus at no cost to either U.S. AID or MAP.

A flying dispensary was formally inaugurated in July, 1964. Its personnel were to include:

Ministry of Health: One doctor, one dentist, one medical technician (immunization), and one nurse.

Ministry of Government: One dietician and one adviser on animal husbandry.

Colombian Air Force: One pilot, one co-pilot, one crew chief, one sergeant (administration), and one general labourer.

The plane was to operate in the Llanos-Amazonas area, providing vitally needed medical services to the indigenous population and to colonists. The plane was to off-load medical equipment and supplies and be available for air evacuation purposes.

As with the Army and Navy, the Air Force operates an intensive literacy programme among the 300 conscripts recruited every six months, of whom it is estimated that half cannot read or write. Electronic teaching material is provided by the U.S. AID at the Air Force basic training centre, Madrid Air Depot; the literacy rate is reported to have reached 95 per cent as a result.*

---

*Similar success has been achieved by the other two services: the Army induction centres, AIC, claim to have raised literacy from 40 per cent to 85 per cent on completion of basic training. Likewise, the Navy claims to have reduced illiteracy to approximately 10 per cent of the basic trainees.

YOUTH CAMP PROGRAMME

It remains to note the work of the Youth Camp Programme. Critics of civic action fasten on this programme as a questionable form of indoctrination. Its supporters would argue that with so many more sinister influences at work, some effort to direct the thoughts of young people to positive ends is justified. At any rate, four pilot camps were held in 1964 in violence-affected areas: Neiva, Tunja, Palmira, and Calarcá. Over 200 boys between the ages of nine and fifteen took part for two weeks. The programmes included a conference on Colombian history, government, patriotic songs, personal hygiene, and group athletics. The programme was actively supported by local industry, agriculturalists, schools, and churches. For 1965, an additional sixteen camps were on the schedule. These youth centres, which are in effect Army schools, are looked upon as a vital aspect of civic action in violence areas.

The French armed forces are in the middle of a period of reconstruction. The ending of the colonial era, coupled with the investment in nuclear weaponry, has pointed towards a drastic reduction in forces coupled with a bid to raise the quality and education of those who remain. Among the most interesting aspects of French defence policy have been the two chief consequences of these factors. The reduction in forces has made possible the creation of, in effect, a conscript overseas peace corps, albeit of relatively small scale at the moment; while the need to increase education has led to a new step to bring the Army in as an instrument in promoting the national policy known as <u>Promotion Sociale</u>.

The need for smaller forces of around 550,000* as against over a million, coupled with the dramatic post-war birth bulge, faced the French Government with a number of alternatives. Though some official voices pressed for the ending of universal conscription, this tradition has been ingrained in the French way of life for generations; what is more, public opinion polls have shown that the majority of young people favour conscription. These findings, echoed elsewhere, may be of interest to other countries that regard it as axiomatic that conscription is a political liability. Questions were asked of a cross-section of young men of whom a third had done their military service and 56 per cent had still to do it. To one question, "Do you think that military service provides something useful in the education of a man?" 64 per cent said "Yes," 21 per cent said "No," and 15 per cent were undecided. (The majority of the "No's" came from the larger towns and from the higher educational groups.) The percentage of girls in favour of conscription was even higher than that of young men. Among

---

*Total French armed forces in 1966: 583,956, This includes Navy: 69,723, and Air Force: 108,584 (official figures).

other findings was the fact that a substantial majority of students considered that the Army is a "necessary element for the prestige of the country"; this group also provided the smallest percentage of people who regarded the Army as an object of useless expenses.

Nevertheless, conscription in its traditional form could not realistically be continued. The size of the call-up group has been increasing at a prodigious rate. That of 1961 was 265,000, the really sharp increase occurred in 1965, and recent estimates expect the figure 416,000 for 1966 and a steady plateau of just over 400,000 for the next few years. This same steep curve is, of course, to be found in many parts of the world.

Even a reduction in length of service could not reduce the figure to the appropriate dimensions. Thus, the French Government hit on the idea of differentiated service. This enabled a small part of the call-up group to spend only a short time--if any--with the colours and to be employed during the rest of the time within the very extensive framework of the defence services on mutual aid tasks overseas.

A form of precedent for differentiated service already existed in the case of below-surface miners who, since 1945, and particularly since their military status was defined in 1960 by legislation, do only a reduced period of service so long as they continue to work underground. These contracts are accepted by about 2,000 miners every year. Nobody thinks of considering them privileged persons.

Some of the arguments used against differentiated service are germane to this study. Those who opposed it pointed out that, while international technical cooperation may be desirable, the countries concerned require fully trained technicians with experience of handling men: Not many, they said, would be found among boys aged from nineteen to twenty and a half. In any case, the Army had no desire to deprive itself of its best technical or commanding cadres.

The armed forces in general were opposed to the idea of differentiated service. They contended firstly, that Frenchmen would never agree to inequality of military duties, and secondly, that the Army's task is first and last military and that it is both unwise and unprofitable to entrust it with duties which are not strictly its own business.

OVERSEAS TECHNICAL ASSISTANCE

The machinery for channelling recruits into technical overseas aid was based on four conventions--between the Minister
of the Army and, respectively, the Minister of Cooperation,
the Minister of Foreign Affairs, the Minister of State in charge
of Departments and Territories Overseas, and the Secretary
of State in charge of Algerian Affairs--concluded between
December, 1962, and November, 1963. These conventions
permit the recruitment of personnel which the Minister of the
Army puts at the disposal of the interested ministerial departments. But conscripts come under military jurisdiction
throughout the whole of their detachment. Once arrived at
their posts, they are integrated in one of the administrative
organizations of the country where they are serving; they are
then under the authority of that country.

In this service, there are three main forms of cooperation: teaching, which is considered to be much the most
important (70 per cent of all those involved); technical services; and civic and agricultural services. In the last category, the young Frenchmen are expected to play the role of
instructor in a variety of specialized techniques.

This operation is confined almost entirely at present to
territories presently or formerly ruled by the French. In the
past, the largest proportion have been sent to the African ex-
French countries, but the group coming under the Minister for
Foreign Affairs--Tunisia, Cambodia, Laos, Vietnam, and
Morocco--is catching up. At the end of 1965, 1,600 conscripts
were working in ex-French Africa, 91 in the West Indies
Departments and Pacific territories, and 1,682 in the "Foreign
Affairs" group. These, together with 1,696 in Algeria, could
be expected to bring the total to over 5,600.

Candidates for these posts must be volunteers and must
possess professional qualifications. Originally, every
successful volunteer had to do four months' training either
before or after going overseas (but that obligation was withdrawn on January 1, 1965). While overseas, he comes under

the discipline and administration of the nearest cultural attaché to the place in which he is employed, after July, 1966. If married, he is not normally allowed to have his wife or family with him.   He receives a subsistence allowance varying between 800 and 1,200 francs a month, according to the place where he is working.   He receives free lodging and furnishings and is obliged to wear civilian clothing.

A candidate has to apply at least three months before call-up, listing the four ministries in order of preference. If he fails in his first choice, he may be referred to the ministry of his second choice.   In any case, he will know his fate at least a month and a half in advance of call-up.

A precedent for this concept already existed in the Service Militaire Adapté (SMA) instituted in the Antilles and French Guiana.   There, conscripts have for several years been directed to combating economic backwardness.   The Army is the only organization capable of handling these problems; it is employed to initiate projects and is a decisive economic factor only in their early stages.   In 1962, for the first time, some 3,000 young conscripts from the Antilles, under the supervision of cadres selected for their specialist ability, were constituted into working groups for enterprises in their own territory.   In Guiana, the effort was concentrated on heavy engineering to open up the undeveloped hinterland. Projects undertaken in Martinique and Guadeloupe have included: improving the road network, particularly tourist routes to attract the hotel industries; bringing land into cultivation; and building houses. In Guiana, work has been done in this way on the coastal route, which is part of the great American road system from Fairbanks to Cape Horn, and thence, the opening up of land for the building of villages in the interior.

As a military formation with a civil objective, the SMA has a mixed structure.   The Organisme Central du SMA is located in Paris under the Minister of State in charge of Departments and Territories Overseas. It prepares the budget and ensures coordination with the Ministry of the Army. In the Antilles and French Guiana, the commanding officer of SMA directs the activities in liaison with the local préfets, who propose the work to be undertaken and define the training specialities according to the economic needs of their department. The préfet draws up a list of work projects in consultation with the elected conseils généraux. This is then submitted to a mixed commission that brings together, under the préfet's chairmanship, the heads of the departmental technical services plus the SMA commander. The SMA work programme must be finally approved each year by the Minister of State.

The SMA absorbs around half the conscript intake in the Antilles. They are given special professional training which, of course, is of great value to them and the community when they leave the service. SMA is as much as anything, therefore, a means of preparing young people for the vital tasks of civil development.

PROMOTION SOCIALE[*]

At home the French armed forces are contributing to the civilian economy through their participation in the nation-wide plan for improving the supply of skilled manpower known as Promotion Sociale. Until recently, the French Army, with its strong fighting tradition, was not conspicuous for its help to the civilian sector. Nor had it laid much emphasis on seeing that the soldier, when released, can make a maximum contribution to society. There are no pre-release training programmes as such, though there are certain schemes for officers, and not only those who wish to enter the teaching profession. Only lately has there been much concentration on improving the general educational level of the serviceman.

The Law of 1910, it is true, requires every serviceman to be taught to read, but this is not in force. There is a three-day test for every recruit to see where he can be most usefully placed in the Army, and this gives the French Government a complete survey of the educational achievements of French

---

[*]See Appendix D, "Extracts from Ministry of Defence Note for Company Commanders Regarding the Establishment of General and Technical Training Courses."

boys of twenty years. The survey is handed on to the Ministry of Education, the Ministry of Labour, and other interested authorities. It would appear that at least 10 per cent of the population is semi-illiterate, i.e., they cannot either read, write, or count fluently. One surprising result of this nation-wide review is that the percentage of the population incapable of passing the Certificat d'Etudes Primaires is higher for twenty-year-olds than it is for fourteen-year-olds. Clearly some 10 per cent of the population has relapsed in the interval, presumably through having read very little for the previous six years.

There has been very little post-release training specifically scheduled up to the present time for ex-servicemen. They could, however, avail themselves of the accelerated training courses open to all civilians.

A law was passed following the Algerian War to organize post-release training but almost nothing came of it.

The problem is now for the French Government to find sufficient men who will enlist on a voluntary basis in order to pass from the present conscription system to differentiated and shorter conscript service. The Law of July, 1965, provides that all men having served for more than thirty-two months (double the legally required service time) can receive professional training if they ask for it so as to prepare themselves for return to civilian life. The French Government hopes to find thus the enlisted men that are needed.*

Accordingly, four different approaches are being made:

1. Men are professionally trained in the Army (when the training has something to do with Army needs). They are

---

*The French Government would like to arrive at an enlistment period of from three to five years but not more. The men find enlistment financially advantageous for a period of from three to five or even seven years, but after this the advantages decline.

encouraged to obtain civilian diplomas as soon as possible after they enlist. The Army uses their skill and knowledge during the enlistment period. (Air Force schools always ask the men to present civilian diplomas.   These men find ready re-employment after they leave the Army.)

2. Men are professionally trained in the Army at the end of their enlistment (during the six months before they leave the Army) but the Army gets no benefits of their knowledge.

3. Men go to civilian training centres during the last six months before they leave the Army.

4. Men go to civilian training centres during the six months that follow their departure from the Army.

Of course, the Army favours systems (1) and (4), but all the systems are now being tried out.

French armies need about 30,000 volunteers every year. The problem is to train all these men professionally accord-ing to the 1965 law. This is supposed to be done through dif-ferent channels (civilian or military). It is generally thought that the best way to find enlisted men is not money, but is to give them a good professional training and valuable experience that will enable them to find a good job at the end of their enlistment time.*

The Promotion Sociale, when it began in 1962, was at first limited strictly to professional education, but it was very quickly extended to general and technical education carried out in conjunction with the civilian ministries concerned. While 1963 was somewhat of an experimental year, it was hoped that by 1965 practically all recruits would have the possibility of following courses organized by the Army in conjunction with the Ministries of National Education, Labour, and

---

*This is quite true for electronics--the volunteers for the Signal Corps are very good, and quite numerous. Will there be volunteers for infantry ...??

Agriculture. The Government is quite deliberately putting great weight on this operation, inasmuch as most of the country's youth passes successively through the military channel. A good many military leaders originally opposed the whole system, but the results of the last two years have proved that Promotion Sociale can be reconciled with the requirements of purely military instruction. The programme has demonstrated an amicable cooperation between the Army and the ministries and public organizations involved.

The operation has two main facets. One is information, by which the young man is invited to consider his future and is informed of the ways in which, during his service, he can improve his professional competence or even prepare to change his profession. Instruction comprises the courses he may take to achieve this end. The object is to ensure that military service is not a break in the man's professional career, but a spur to advance himself in it.

Information

It had previously been discovered that, far more than laziness or feebleness, ignorance was the greatest barrier to what the French call ascension sociale. Young Frenchmen simply did not know what opportunities were open to them. In rectifying this ignorance, the key figure is the officier-conseil, a new important figure in the French Army.   The creation of this post owes much to the Armed Forces Youth Commission. This was set up in 1953 by the Minister of Defence. The object was to establish a permanent dialogue between representatives of the Army and those of youth.

Military men often say that youth is not interested in the Army. Youth sometimes replies that it is misused by the Army. The Army needs to know more about the problems and aspirations of young people. They, on the other hand, should be prepared for the responsibilities they must carry in the Army. The Commission is thus primarily an organisme de dialogue.

On the national level, the Commission has ten to fifteen officers with a specialized knowledge of training and organizing young people, plus ten to fifteen representatives of youth movements, institutions, and associations. At the regional level, its committees have the job of encouraging contacts between the military and young people.

Among its most important achievements has been the establishment of the principle, in 1957, of equivalence between military and civilian certificates. In 1962, the Commission was able to establish that holders of first degree military certificates can enter for examinations for civil certificates, counting their practical experience in the Army as equivalent to that in a civilian profession. The Commission can also take much credit for the introduction of the officiers-conseil.

Every unit in the French Army now has its own officier-conseil, and every conscript has access to one. He generally has other responsibilities as well, but in compensation for this, he will often accumulate a team of conscripts who are particularly interested in teaching. In this way he can ensure a full range of contacts with the conscripts in his unit. The officier-conseil works in direct and constant liaison with the departmental or regional services of the different ministries, the local labour exchanges, educational inspectorates, etc. These bodies give him all necessary help and the documentation he will need to answer the questions he is likely to receive from the conscripts. Besides the specialist reviews to which he can subscribe, he is provided with a guide, kept constantly up to date in the form of a "Three Monthly Bulletin of Liaison" put out by the Secrétariat Général pour l'Administration.

Almost as soon as he arrives at his unit, the recruit receives a lecture from the officier-conseil. Later, instructors come from industrial and agricultural establishments and from teaching organizations. Unit journals also help in this work.

If the conscript already has a profession and desires only to obtain employment, the officier-conseil and his team will tell him of the openings available in his profession and the employment situation in various regions; they will give him the address of the information offices of the ministries concerned; and they will show him how to draw up an application for employment, how to fill out an official record sheet, etc.

If the man wants to change his profession, the officier-conseil, helped by the teachers among his conscripts, explains the level of studies and diplomas required for the profession he has in mind, the duration of the courses, the method of preparing for the examinations, and the openings he can pursue during his service. The officer will arrange for him, if appropriate, a direct contact with the Bureau Universitaire des Statistiques, or with the departmental offices of the Ministry of Labour or other appropriate ministry. It is hoped that before long this work of the officier-conseil will be greatly strengthened by the existence, in local departments of the Ministry of Labour, of an official specializing in liaison with the Army.

The task of the officier-conseil is a delicate one; he must win the confidence of young conscripts, some of whom may be suspicious or frightened. Thus, an older man is often selected for the job--a captain or major--because of his greater experience and diplomacy. But he may be assisted by a second lieutenant, and the concept of a team of young conscripts working with him is clearly a vital part of the programme.

Instruction

In October, 1962, seven units began experimenting with various types of instruction; today, the greater part of the Army has organized these courses of general and technical instruction. The period of instruction does not begin until the recruits have finished their initial military training. Courses take place only in spare time from military activities. In spite of this, some progress has already been made. More than 600 young soldiers passed their CEP in 1963 out of the original seven units of 2,550 men plus a small number of other units.

The figures for successful candidates are as follows:

	1962-63	1963-64	1964-65
CEP	620	1,100	1,126
Technical Instruction	194	650	1,304
Admissions to the FPA courses	234	623	1,310
Baccalauréat	59	142	190
Other examinations	23	120	383
	1,130	2,635	4,313

As far as possible, the courses are given by civilian teachers; it is up to the officiers-conseil to make the necessary contacts. Wherever possible, the crucial task of determining the precise educational level and capability of the candidate is entrusted to civilian specialists, though where it is not possible, it will be done by the officier-conseil and his team. This work is very necessary to offset a tendency of young conscripts to over-estimate their capabilities.

Investigations have revealed that astonishing gaps are to be found in the knowledge of adult students who might have been expected to be better educated, and the value of the psycho-technical tests is that they help lay them bare before the student enters into a course for which he is not qualified. One enquiry some years ago, for instance, showed that out of eighty-nine candidates for training to first grade in important industrial skills, only 60 per cent could multiply decimal numbers accurately and 34 per cent could add simple fractions reliably. Nearly all of these had their CEP, and their results were compared with those of school children fifteen days before they themselves took their CEP. In each category, the children came out well on top. (It would appear that mastery of decimals and fractions is one of the most easily forgotten arts.)

The principal courses are as follows:

Correspondence courses

These courses are conducted mainly by the Centre National de Télé-Enseignement. In January, 1964, 1,400 conscripts were taking courses from the CNTE. Today the figure is over 4,000.

General educational courses preparatory to entering a centre
for adult vocational training

Previously, these were limited geographically to the North
and East of France, but they have since been extended.   The
military instructors are trained in Paris in courses organized
by the Institut National de Formation Professionnelle. Two hundred of these instructors were taking this course in 1965 for
bringing students up to the level of the CEP.

Evening courses, either in the Army or in an outside educational establishment

Refresher courses preparing for the Certificat d'Aptitude
Professionnelle. By the summer of 1965, more than 9,000
conscripts were participating in these courses--most of them,
around 6,400, doing courses organized within the Army with
the aid of teachers in uniform.

Courses by radio

These are still experimental--at Lille and Toulouse. Some
450 recruits followed the one in 1963, while around 700 followed
the course beginning in March, 1964. The results of the CEP
examinations were being awaited before any conclusions were
drawn on the efficacy of this method of instruction.

Agricultural education

Finally, but by no means least, agricultural education is
imparted through the interesting medium of agricultural clubs.
These clubs, to be found in over 300 units, number more than
7,500 members. The accent is on discussion and cooperation
rather than lectures. The leaders--there is no precise word
to convey the nuance of animateur--are instructed in courses
organized in liaison with the Ministry of Agriculture, of which
there were twelve last year. Though the clubs function under the
guidance of the Ministries of War and Agriculture, they are
run entirely by the conscripts themselves, who fix their own
programme activities. They are considered very successful
by the French Government.

Correspondence courses in agriculture have lately been
introduced. Other plans in gestation include the participation
of career soldiers in these activities, and the admission of

conscripts after their demobilization to the centres of vocational training of the Office National des Anciens Combattants et Victimes de Guerre. These latter centres have, in fact, just started to operate.

The number of beneficiaries from Promotion Sociale, 35,831 in all, may appear slender in relation to the 300,000 total of conscripts, but the project was bound to pass through an ice-breaking stage.

In the summer of 1965, a cross-section of French ex-servicemen was asked in the course of a questionnaire prepared by the Armed Forces Youth Commission:

1. Have you profited by your leisure to work for your own social betterment? The answers were: 25.8 per cent Yes, 74.2 per cent No. Of the former, 6.6 per cent have benefited by courses of the Ministry of Education, 1.1 per cent by those of the Ministry of Labour, 1.4 per cent by those of the Ministry of Agriculture, and 14.7 per cent--over half--by those organized in the private sector.

2. Is there an officier-conseil in your unit? 52 per cent Yes, 44 per cent No.

3. Are you a member of a leisure club? 25 per cent Yes, 68 per cent No.

Some French officials believe that it would be a good idea to start drawing young people's attention to these possibilities before call-up. This, they feel, would be the best way to get at those 33 per cent of young men, at a scholastic level below that of CEP, whose education is considered to be most urgent. Meanwhile, there is a growing feeling that the key to stimulating interest in Promotion Sociale may lie with the educational leisure clubs.

CHAPTER **10** INDIA

For any discussion of the Indian Army today, the starting point must be the Chinese war of 1962, after which the Army doubled in size from 450,000 to over 800,000. Many Indians saw for the first time in their lives that they really did need an army, and that as a matter of self-interest, they must treat their soldiers better than they had done in the past. By the very act of doubling its size, the Army was claiming a larger share of the attention of the civilian economy.

The convergence of all these factors has led to a hard look at the question of educating the ex-serviceman and resettling him in civilian life. (See Appendix F, Part I, "Extracts from a Circular by the Director General Resettlement to All Resettlement Officers, 24th May 1965.") In such matters as prerelease training, the Indians still have some way to go. In fact, India has today virtually no pre-release training of servicemen, although this was done on a large scale at the end of the war. However, a scheme is under consideration and is likely to be implemented soon as a pilot measure. Even among officers, there were practically no pre-release courses of any sort until 1964, when an orientation course on industrial management was established and has become a regular feature. It is also proposed to run specialist courses of longer duration on various techniques of industrial management. As to post-release training, most vocational training schemes have lapsed since the early days of independence. It is true that courses are available at industrial training institutes, and that 200 stipends are available for ex-servicemen and more than 100 for disabled ex-servicemen. Some states reserve 5 per cent of their places for ex-servicemen in these institutes. Although a number of concessions are available for admission, these places, however, are not being taken up-- partly, it is true, owing to the disinterest among country-born ex-servicemen, but fundamentally for two other reasons beyond their control.

First, the standard of education of the average jawan (soldier) is simply not high enough to enable him to take advantage of these facilities; and second, publicity and guidance are not available to the extent desirable; besides, the number of jobs available to him is extremely limited due to keen competition. There is some Government pressure to allocate places for ex-servicemen in Central Services. The states, the public sector, and private industries need to be persuaded to follow suit. There is no statutory reservation, but ex-servicemen have been given the highest priority among a dozen other categories, for names being sponsored against vacancies notified to employment exchanges. However, to make this more effective, administrative instructions are being issued for reservations in Class III and Class IV appointments under the Central Government. This would appear to be a substantial advance from the position obtaining so far.

The Post War Services Reconstruction Fund established at the end of World War II to help ex-servicemen has been useful. Invested largely in securities, it has been handled with considerable energy. Some states, notably the Punjab, have a very good record in providing education for children of servicemen, in helping hardship cases, supplying widows with the wherewithal to work--such as sewing machines--lending money to ex-servicemen to set up in business, and operating veterans' homes.

In 1964, however, an important new chapter was opened with the setting up of a Special Services Fund for reconstruction and rehabilitation, mainly for the benefit of ex-servicemen not covered by the earlier "Fund." The Fund consists of Rs. 50 million, and an annual allocation of about Rs. 10 million is also to be made from the defence budget, provided that state governments agree to make matching grants. Eighty per cent will be kept as reserve at the Centre. (See Appendix F, Part II, "Special Fund for the Reconstruction and Rehabilitation of Ex-Servicemen.")

Following this important development, new arrangements have been made for the expansion of training in industrial training institutes. Any soldier under the age of thirty-six holding the middle school certificate is eligible for these courses. They are free, and the student receives 35 rupees a month in addition to hostel accommodation, medical facilities, and workshop clothing. Additional facilities for the disabled, including their employment, are also receiving new attention. The courses, which will take nine to twelve months, will include such subjects as dyeing, knitting, manufacture of sports goods,

printing, and bookbinding. Longer courses in technical trades
will be available for those who have matriculated. These will
include plumbing, tool-making, blacksmithy, and mechanical
trades. They will entail eighteen months' institutional training. With the growing industrialization of the country, efforts
are being made to expand cooperative activities among ex-
servicemen and to encourage them to undertake small-scale
industrial ventures. At the same time, increased utilization
of technical manpower released from the armed forces is being made both in the public and private sector.

A large number of soldiers on release are employed with the
civil defence, home guards, and other security forces.

Service technical skills and experience have now been equated to civilian standards, significantly assisting in the proper
placement of released service personnel.

Action is in hand to provide increased opportunities for
technical and operative training of personnel due to be released, as well as those who have already left the service.
A number of "training-cum-production" centres have been
established, which are producing hosiery and other textile
goods as well as blankets. These have been registered as
Suppliers to the Directorate General Supplies and Disposals.
On tenders as small-scale units, they are entitled to price pre-
ferences over larger units.

A number of correspondence courses are also available for
serving personnel, and the Ministry of Defence has organized
a series of technical training courses to improve the skills of
the participants.

But as in Pakistan, the vast majority of servicemen come
from the country, and it is to the country that their first wish
is to return. Granted, there is a shortage of skilled and semi-
skilled industrial workers in India. But in a world where the
drift from the land seems almost universal, good working men
who wish to move in the opposite direction are a valuable com-
modity. One of the greatest benefits that India could derive
from its ex-servicemen would be to help by all means possible
those who wish to return to agricultural life.

India has a fairly good record in this respect. The most
successful ventures have been the land colonies, fourteen in
all, jointly sponsored by the Centre and states, which ex-

servicemen operate under special facilities, including loans, granted by the Central Government. Some of those in Central India have fallen on hard times owing to lack of water, but in general, they have more than proved their worth. Even more encouraging have been the recent experiments in provincial land colonies. Still better results would have been achieved if a certain element of leadership could have been injected into these colonies in the initial stages. (The rules for these colonies were laid down during World War II, when officers were not allowed to participate.) This has been rectified for future plans. But, in general, there is little wrong with these colonies that cannot be cured by more vigorous official support.

Some would argue that it is a wiser policy to integrate the ex-servicemen with civilian projects; otherwise, there is a danger of perpetuating the notion of "a race apart." Unfortunately, as far as the community development schemes go, it is alleged that there is a hostility to the ex-serviceman that entails positive discrimination against him in many cases. Possibly, this may be one of several reasons why the community development schemes, which were to have rescued the Indian economy, have proved disappointing. But at all events, it seems more sensible at this moment to concentrate on the development of all-ex-servicemen farming projects, through which an example may be set to the rest of the country.

This concept of example-setting is not a fanciful one, as some might imagine. One of the most notable features of Indian farming at the peasant level has been the failure to experiment owing to sheer lack of knowledge. To take a couple of examples at random, some Israeli experts recently suggested that large parts of Northern India were suitable for growing vines. This surprised many quite well-informed Indians who had always thought of vines as a temperate-climate crop. Again, the introduction of Napier grass might assist in the solution of the biggest of India's farm problems, that of cattle-feeding, if more farmers knew about it--and has in fact done so where it has been undertaken.

Though there is resistance to new ideas, example has undoubtedly proved a good way to break it down. Most observers agree that, with a little additional know-how, the average Indian farmer could greatly improve his crop without any greater effort or expenditure. Recent experiments near Delhi, which have shown that both soil and climate are amenable to a remarkable range of fruit-growing, have made an impressive impact on the neighbourhood. The improvement of Indian agriculture may well lie to a large extent in physical demonstration to the Indian farmer of what he can do if he has a mind to.

It is here that ex-service colonies might be playing an even more important part. They should be able to show the neighbourhood what can be done with no outside assistance except expert advice. These projects deserve all the help the Indian authorities and outside agencies can give them. And they could well be reinforced by pre-release training courses in farming for servicemen who are capable of benefiting by it.

To promote this work, it would be no bad thing to strengthen the office of Director General Resettlement. This office is strong in terms of quality, but its establishment is slender; it is run by a brigadier and only six other officers. There is a strong case for a larger organization with higher status and powers.

However, all in all, a new and happier relationship is now being built up between the Indian Army and the Indian people. A much more positive attitude towards ex-servicemen is being taken by the Government. Mr. Shastri had urged industrialists to employ more of them. The old barriers of mutual suspicion are being broken down. It remains to be seen how far this process will go, but the logic of the situation suggests that it might go a great deal further.

The Indian economy, of which the most conspicuous feature is the fast-rising birth rate, is having to sustain an army over four times as numerous as the British Army. Such a burden could soon become intolerable. It is surely necessary that those in authority should ask themselves how far the Army-- an otherwise unproductive burden--could be going towards contributing to the economy of the country.

At all events, such intervention would be nothing new to the Indian Army. Their record in relieving distress and hardship in the face of national disasters has been magnificent. Nor is it confined to the less well-organized areas of the country, as the recent history of Delhi bears witness. Two years ago, large parts of the city would have been under water had it not been for the timely intervention of the Army in stemming the flood of the Jumna River. Perhaps even more dramatic was the Army's action at the time when the Jumna altered its course in 1958 and threatened the city with a total breakdown of its water supplies. As an example of what the Indian Army can and frequently does perform, it is worth recounting.

On August 17 of that year at 4:15 P.M. the Delhi Municipal Corporation requested immediate military assistance at the Wazirabad pumping station. By that night, 200 soldiers and four bulldozers were already at work. At 2 P.M. the next day, the Army received instructions to take over the whole responsibility for ensuring the flow of water to the station. Within 48 hours, the Army had dug a temporary channel and restored the water supply. The main channel was completed ten days later, and thereafter, the Army continued to maintain the channel until the end of October, when they handed the operation back to the Delhi Municipal Corporation.

In February of the same year, the Army helped to pump water from the Ghawra Colliery near Dhanbad following a disaster. They also undertook flood relief work in Uttar Pradesh and East Punjab and, following a breakdown in electric and water supply in Simla the same summer, they lent the city generating sets and soldiers to operate them for about two weeks.

The Indian Air Force carried out aerial reconnaissance of the flood-affected areas in Andhra Pradesh during September and in Assam and West Bengal during October. Bridging equipment was loaned to the Government of Bombay for restoring a breach on the Bombay-Konkan-Goa road. Engineering equipment was provided to the Oil and Natural Gas Commission for use in the Hoshiarpur and Cambay region and in the drilling operations at Jwalamukhi.

In July of the following year, unprecedented floods took place in Jammu and Kashmir, badly affecting a large number of roads and washing away many bridges. Considerable damage was caused to property throughout the Srinagar Valley. A combined civil-military headquarters was set up at Srinagar to coordinate the relief work. The electric supply in Jammu was restored by the Army, and breaches in the River Tawi were repaired. In addition, a great deal of bridging equipment

was released for the restoration of communications. Twelve
large bridges were built, and at one stage, all Engineer troops
in the state had to be deployed on this task.

The same October, large-scale flood relief operations were
carried out in West Bengal. Four hundred troops were engaged in an amphibious operation to rescue and supply marooned people. In nearby Calcutta, sixteen pumping sets were
provided for draining waterlogged areas. Fifteen boats were
also provided for ferrying foodstuffs supplied by civil authorities to marooned villages in the district of Burdwan. Similar
operations were carried out in the summer in Bombay, Punjab,
and Assam. In most of these, the Navy and the Indian Air
Force were also active. The Navy sent a medical team to help
flood victims in Surat, and the Air Force carried out reconnaissance of the flooded areas and dropped food supplies where
necessary.

After an accident to the hoist chamber of a tunnel of the
Bhakra Dam, the civil authorities asked the Army for troops
and stores to close the mouth of the tunnel as rapidly as possible. Two hundred troops were sent to Nangal on September 16. Engineer stores such as Sommerfield track, steel-
wire ropes, etc., were released for this work. More than
700 troops helped the authorities to block the mouth of the tunnel. The task involved dumping thousands of tons of boulders
in crates of about ten tons each. In addition, a vast border
roads organization exists to make roads in difficult and inhos-
pitable terrain; this is primarily service-based and employs
a large number of ex-soldiers.

Nor have these operations been confined to India. The Army
played an invaluable role during the floods in Ceylon at the end
of 1957. Together with the Air Force, it ferried more than
100,000 lbs. of stores and about 50,000 people from the disaster areas. It built timber bridges, repaired roads, and established a ferry across the Galoya River near Amparai to
bring urgently needed supplies to the southeast sector of Ceylon.
Nine Indian aircraft and two helicopters played an important
part in relief operations from Colombo. The aircraft carried
a medical team and supplies and two Army rescue teams, along
with assault and collapsible boats. Some 600,000 lbs. of food
and medical supplies were airlifted or airdropped. Over 300
stranded people were airlifted to safety. Recently, the Army

provided substantial and prompt relief for a large number of displaced persons from the border and set up their own liaison organization to supplement the civilian staff.

From the largest disasters down to the smallest, the Army has time and again proved itself indispensable.   It rendered assistance following a rail crash near Igatpuri. It rescued six men trapped in a sewage disaster in Delhi.   It played a decisive part in the strike of Central Government employees in July, 1960, helping to operate telephone exchanges, wireless communications, railway yards and railway workshops, navigational and communication services of civil aviation and essential meteorological, wireless, and teleprinter channels.

The Navy regularly loans divers and diving equipment for help in the construction of hydroelectric projects.   Naval divers went down to a depth of 180 feet while working on the Bhakra Dam.   They used an underwater television camera for detailed survey and inspection of the two spillway aprons that had become damaged. Recently, they were called in to assess and chart the coral formations near the Malacca jetty at Car Nicobar, which were dangerous to navigation.   As a result, it was decided to blast a channel through the coral.   But perhaps the Navy's most valuable contribution in recent times has been the complete survey of all the ports of India, carried out by the Naval Hydrographic Office--a survey covering the best part of 140,000 square miles (the NHO is virtually the only authority in India that could prepare such navigational charts).

The Indian Air Force, besides being heavily involved in flood disasters and in individual air-sea rescue operations, has undertaken aerial surveys for flood control projects, dam sites, and desert control. In the latter category, during 1953, the Air Force was engaged in the survey of the Rajasthan Desert with a view to finding ways of controlling its advance; later, it helped to check this advance by the aerial broadcast of special types of seeds.   In addition, the successful location of oilfields has been in no small measure due to the surveys carried out by the IAF.

Finally, one of the most dramatic steps taken by India in this field was announced in December, 1965, by Defence Minister Chavan.   He revealed a plan to call up schoolboys and university graduates for national service--the first example of Indian conscription on a national scale.

The Government proposes to select 10,000 graduates a year, 2,000 of them being for training as officers; they will serve for two years.   Boys entering the university will do a year's national service, including three months' military training, and then work on defence tasks such as road building in forward (border) areas.

Contemplating its record, of which only a cross-section has been given above, one may wonder whether any army in history has made a greater or more direct contribution to the cause of humanity.   Some of those concerned would say it was excessive and damaging to military morale. This danger must certainly be watched. There was considerable grumbling over the Amar project, for instance, under which an Infantry division in Ambala built a township of about 1,450 tenements for themselves and their families.   It is not to squat on his haunches with trowel and mortar that the jawan joins a world-famous regiment.

Still, there are few more generous spirits than the Indian soldier, and he is glad to help, provided that he is not treated as a pariah when the trouble is past. Were the full story told to the Indian people, the gulf between soldier and civilian could not long survive. Happily, the story is being told. It is now Government policy to publicize the peaceful uses of the armed forces not only by the printed word but in the cinema through short but effective documentaries.   This augurs well for a further improvement in Indian civil-military relations. It is certainly due, and nothing but good can come of it.

EDUCATION CORPS

The Government of Iran claims to be "probably the first country to use part of the budget and manpower destined for its national defence for the purposes of educating its population."

If the claim is slightly overpitched, there is no doubt that the experiment of the last two years has been both impressive and highly original. The Education Corps, which sends several thousand soldiers into the most primitive parts of the country every year, has lately been followed up by a Health Corps, and a third body, the Extension and Development Corps, is now well beyond the blue-print stage. The Shah was recently confident enough to have invited representatives from all over the world to watch the Education Corps in operation, and every country invited accepted with enthusiasm.

The Corps originated in the Shah's six-point assault on ignorance, poverty, corruption, and landlordism launched at the end of 1962. Up till that time, his struggle against corruption had been unrewarding. He decided that the obstructive power of big land interests could only be safely broken if a simultaneous campaign was launched to promote democracy; otherwise, he feared, a vacuum of power, both political and economic, would be created. He himself--to some extent like President Ayub in Pakistan--was the source and generator of democracy.

Thus, the six-point programme provided simultaneously for an assault on entrenched interests and the promotion of democracy through education. His programme comprised:

1. Land reform setting a limit to the big estates--some of them almost the size of Belgium--and providing land for the peasants.

2. Nationalization of forests.

3. The sale of State-owned industries to finance land reform and agricultural projects.

4.   Implementation of profit-sharing plans for the industrial workers.

5.   Amendment of electoral laws to include, for the first time, women voters.

6.   Establishment of a Literacy Corps--more commonly referred to now as the Education Corps because of the breadth of its undertakings.

The task before the Corps was prodigious. A recent survey showed that less than 20 per cent of the population could read and write.   Although 75 per cent of Iranians live in villages, the Government's educational efforts had been almost entirely concentrated in the towns.   Only about a quarter of the education budget was allocated to three-quarters of the population. While 84 per cent of school-age children in towns attended school, less than 25 per cent in the villages had any education at all.

This is a picture distressingly familiar among developing countries.   Too often the educational structure seems to resemble a mushroom, with towering educational facilities in the capital and large towns, while the mass of the population is completely neglected. This deliberate cultivation of the mushroom must tend to exacerbate many countries' economic problems, for it has two undesirable consequences: the perpetuation of a large backward and potentially disgruntled class in the countryside and the creation of an unemployable group of graduates educated beyond their prospects.

It is greatly to the Shah's credit that, after five years of attempting to solve this problem by largely persuasive methods, he eventually decided that nature could not be safely allowed to take its course, but that an all-out crusade would have to be launched to rectify the imbalance between town and country.   He thus became one of the first leaders of the developing countries to turn his back on the "mushroom" formula and adopt what might be called the "pyramid" structure. His intention was to kill two birds with one stone.   He planned to raise the standard of living of the primitive three-quarters of the country while at the same time syphoning off the potential trouble-makers among the young educated townsmen. Since his problem was common to many countries, his remarkable success in handling it deserves their attention.

Certainly the scheme has run into snags. Notable among these is the failure to plan for a second stage after the corpsman has completed his fourteen months in a village and is due to return to civilian life. Even if he is prepared to stay on as a civilian in the village--and an astonishing number of them are--there remains the problem of equipping him to satisfy the appetite for further education that he himself has created. Again, in spite of elaborate screening in selection, black sheep find their way into the Corps; young sergeants from the towns do not relish spending a winter in icy mountainous conditions, and some have deserted to the towns. But by and large, the progress has been remarkable.

I was fortunate to attend an assembly in the offices of Dr. Birjandi, Director of Education, at which eighteen prize-winning corpsmen were hoping to win the supreme nomination of national hero. Each was accompanied by his village headman. They looked a sturdy, enterprising lot in their smart khaki uniforms with black velvet collars, brass buttons, and red epaulets.

The bases on which prizes are allotted are:

1. The number of students in the school in proportion to the village population.

2. The percentage of girls in these classes (in a Moslem country, an obvious sign of the villagers' confidence in the corpsmen).

3. Popularity with the villagers.

4. Achievements in health and sanitation.

5. Creativity in carrying on educational, hygiene, and development work.

Listening to the stories of some of these young corpsmen, all to be authenticated later by a travelling jury, there was no doubt of their creative energy; one, in fact, got into trouble for showing excess of zeal. He reported that he was trying to build a bridge across the River Zoyanderood near Isfahan to give a village access to its graveyard. He asserted that the bridge had been badly needed for the past seventy years and that it would also be useful as a feeder communication. He had been undeterred by a warning from the Isfahan public authorities that the bridge would take ten years to build. With obvious sincerity, he pleaded the need for such a bridge. Dr. Birjandi commended his initiative in amassing money for the project and also having had elected a board of five directors to run the project. But here was a case where initiative had outrun hard-headedness; the scale of the project was too ambitious.

Other corpsmen spoke of more projects: the building of schools; the introduction of vegetable gardens into villages that had never known vegetables, but that eagerly followed the corpsman's example; the separation of human and animal drinking facilities by means of a simple two-inch pipeline.

There seemed no doubt that these young men had enjoyed playing the role of king of their small castle--a role reinforced by the authority of the Army and directly backed by the Shah himself. It is worth examining how they were prepared for it.

The Corps was set up immediately after the referendum in January, 1963, which overwhelmingly endorsed the Shah's six-point programme. Iran, like many other developing countries, has a birth-rate in excess of what can usefully be absorbed into the Army by universal conscription. Thus, it was decided to recruit for the Education Corps by earmarking a certain number of conscripts who had achieved high school graduation. The youngster's fate is decided by drawing lots. Those who draw a blank can obtain exemption certificates at a cost of 5,000 rials ($66); if they choose not to pay, they must take part in a later draft. If they draw a blank on the second occasion, they are not further liable for military service.

Of those high school graduates who took part in the first lottery at Teheran in 1963, nearly two-fifths were allocated to the Education Corps. Out of 2,758 taking part, 721 were conscripted into the Army, 991 were exempted for five years, and 1,040 were enrolled in the Education Corps. In Isfahan, the figure was rather over 50 per cent--208 corpsmen out of 406 taking part in the lottery.

The basic syllabus for a corpsman is four months' training and fourteen months in the field. During the first period he
receives, at one of 21 centres situated throughout the country,
372 hours of purely military training and 336 hours designed
to instruct him in the civilian arts that he will be practising
during his fourteen months in the field. He receives 32 hours
training in agriculture, 56 in psychology and educational science, 32 in rural health and first aid, 32 in rural development,
18 in the establishment of "peace houses," and 14 in religious
instruction. Within this syllabus, emphasis is laid on the
teaching of Farsi and mathematics. There is also a week's
course in organizing scout camps.

At the end of his four months' period he takes five tests: in
the Persian language; in general intelligence, speaking, and
understanding;   in general knowledge (geography, history,
physics, mathematics, etc.); in teacher competence; and in
"teacher attitude inventory," under which he is required to
express an opinion on a number out of 145 topics--such as, for
instance, How do you cope with a bashful student?

On completion of his training, the conscript receives the
rank of sergeant. The pay is 2,400 rials a month for a sergeant third class, 3,000 for a sergeant second class, and 3,600
for a sergeant first class. He is then sent, where practicable,
to a village with whose customs and dialect he is familiar.

Here his paramount duty, which he must never allow to be
subordinated to more ambitious activities, is the education of
children between the ages of six and twelve who have never
previously been to school. The aim is to bring them up at
least to the second grade of primary education and, if possible, as far as the fourth. In addition, he will hold evening
classes for adults and encourage them to read on their own by
starting small village libraries and circulating reading material supplied by the Ministry.

Second only to the spread of literacy are three other major
activities: hygiene, farming, and community development.
Under hygiene come the basic problems of changing open la-
trines to sanitary ones, building hygiene mortuaries, sep-
arating livestock from living quarters, and conducting special
classes for midwives.

Agriculture is particularly important inasmuch as the elimination of all large estates under the Land Reform Programme--under the second stage, no one may own more than about 300 acres--has removed from the scene a landlord who may have been rapacious but did at least ensure subsistence. Into this vacuum the Shah has recognized that he must rush an organization of his own; and his emissary is the corpsman. It is for him to acquaint the farmer with the help available from the Ministry of Agriculture and to inform him of procedures for obtaining new information on insecticides, fertilizers, farm implements, and livestock breeding. Also, as we have seen, the example of intelligent farming may quickly spread throughout the village. Community developments will most commonly take the form of feeder roads but they may also, as noted above, embrace more ambitious projects.

Though the Shah is anxious to avoid the notion of inspectors, some form of supervision is obviously necessary. Theoretically, one supervisor is appointed for every ten corpsmen; the actual figure is nearer one in fifteen. The supervisor is a graduate of the College of Education with at least five years of experience in elementary school supervision. He is supposed to visit every corpsman for half a day each week; unfortunately, this does not happen in practice. Other regular visitors to the villages include the local Agricultural Extension Agent, the Health Agent, and the Cooperative Expert, who well provide technical assistance. Overseeing the operation are the Education Corps Committee composed of the Governor (Chairman), and the Directors of Education, Agriculture, Health, Justice, Police, Community Development, and the Agricultural Bank. At every level there is close coordination with Army commanders. On the national level the National High Council is presided over by the Prime Minister himself. The Council members are the Ministers of Education, Agriculture, Health, Interior, and Justice; the Director of the Iranian Plan Organization; the Chief of Staff of the Iranian Army; and the Commander of the Police.

There is a strong competitive element in the programme. "Service to people" contests are held on the basis of criteria listed above, in which the judges are a committee composed of the Director of Education, the Agricultural Extension Agent, and the Health Agent. The winners receive prizes, such as transistor radios donated by UNESCO. These contests are carried on to a higher level and final winners receive prizes from the Shah himself.

Perhaps the most striking feature of the programme is the way in which corpsmen volunteer to stay on after their term of service is finished. Over 80 per cent of the first consignment applied for teaching positions under the Ministry of Education--90 per cent of them in the villages where they had served. Without a doubt, one reason behind this surge of idealism is their knowledge that jobs or university places will be hard to come by if they return to the towns. None the less, the figures reflect a remarkably high degree of harmony between corpsmen and villages. Corpsmen have been far more successful than expected in persuading women to come forward as pupils. Many have been made headmen of their villages, while others have married into the village. At least one instance is on record of a Zoroastrian marrying into a Moslem family-- than which there can be few higher tests of confidence.

The fact is--and it has been noted in many other countries, advanced as well as developing--that Army instructors as a race are at least the equal of civilian teachers, and often superior. When Dr. Birjandi was first told of the Shah's scheme, he was appalled by the prospect of roughnecks from the Cossack Brigade trying to teach others what they barely knew themselves. In point of fact, the combination of a high school education with military discipline turned out to be remarkably strong; in fact, most impartial observers will agree that these instructors are considerably superior to the average run of Iranian teachers, not only in zeal but also in technique.

The chief difficulty and stumbling block of the scheme, in fact, is the problem of further education for a corpsman after he has completed his fourteen months and before he returns to his village as a civilian teacher. It has turned out that he has little or nothing to learn from the civilian authorities on the subjects which could be of practical value to the villages. The four months' refresher course provided for the corpsmen has definitely proved a failure. Owing to lack of instructors, it has been cut to a two months' course held in agricultural colleges, since these are the only boarding schools available. The corpsmen complain that they are learning nothing that they have not already found out for themselves the hard way, or that they have not been taught in their initial training period.

Partly because of this sense of futility, discipline tends to deteriorate. Here is a very real problem--how to sustain the momentum of this remarkably successful exercise--and the Iranian Government is keenly conscious of it.

The other problem to which it is giving priority is the short-age of supervisors and the poor quality of too many of them. It was on this rock that a similar enterprise by Turkey found-ered some years ago, as the Turks themselves admit. Should the supervision fail, undoubtedly morale will become slack and the whole enterprise may degenerate. For Iran is rugged ter-ritory where a corpsman can easily be lost without report of it coming through to headquarters--particularly so if the su-pervisor is unwilling to face the slogging journeys, often through thick snow, that his job requires.

Against these major drawbacks must be set very real achievements. Military discipline may break down, but it is infinitely more efficacious than the haphazard system of sup-ply and demand that is proving so inadequate in many parts of the world. Also, though costly, this method of instruction is much cheaper than purely civilian education. It is esti-mated that the school expense per child is only a quarter of the cost in the regular Ministry of Education schools. Final-ly, the results themselves are impressive. Over 10,000 corpsmen have already been in action (1965). They have taught around a quarter of a million children, though only one-tenth that number of adults; built some 4,000 two-room schools; helped to construct over 1,000 miles of feeder roads; and repaired or built 56 mosques, 185 bath-houses, and 143 bridges.

HEALTH CORPS

On January 21, 1964, the Shah ordered the creation of a Health Corps to be run on similar lines to the Education Corps. It would be composed of mobile teams operating throughout the rural areas and consisting of fully trained physicians, univer-sity graduates, and secondary school graduates. The first batch set out in October, 1965. Each group consists of one physician and three assistants, together with a car or jeep,

pharmaceutical drugs, and surgical equipment. Each group
has about thirty villages with between 10,000 and 15,000 people
under its supervision.

The Health Corpsmen are recruited in much the same way
as the Education Corpsmen, though the doctors are naturally
enlisted at a later age; having been exempted as medical students, they are liable for conscription around the age of twenty-
five. There are two quite distinct categories: graduated doctors start with the rank and pay of second lieutenant, while
the medical assistants are enrolled as sergeants. Like the
Education Corpsmen, they receive an initial training course.
Doctors are given 210 hours refresher instruction in general
health education, with the emphasis on epidemics and hygiene.
Assistants are given 345 hours in a much wider range of subjects including nutrition, child health, accident prevention,
school health, nursing, and general occupational hazards.

The need for this Corps is if possible even greater than that
of the Education Corps, for the top-heaviness of the urban population is even more marked healthwise than it is in education. Of the 7,000 doctors in Iran, some 3,000 work in
Teheran--a proportion of more than one per 1,000 of population. Worse, having been attracted by city salaries, all too
many of them go overseas. Under the Health Corps scheme,
this leak has been firmly stopped. No doctor, veterinarian, or
pharmacist is allowed to leave the country until he has done
his eighteen months' service; the necessary exit permit is
denied by the police department.

Obviously, until clean water can be brought to all these villages and nutritional standards can be raised, medical work
cannot be more than palliative. Yet the stoppage of this leak
abroad and the diversion of medical effort from town to country means that literally millions of Iranians will be seeing a
doctor for the first time. And though the root causes and conditions of disease may not be eradicable for some years, these
mobile teams will be well equipped to cope with the deadlier
epidemics, such as cholera and typhoid fever and the grim
mountain killer, pneumonia. They will be backed by twelve
stations, one to every twelve groups at most, providing heav-
ier equipment, drugs, a dental clinic, and a public health educational service.

As with the Education Corps, the term of service is four-teen months. It was hoped that there would be three intakes of about 100 doctors and 300 assistants every year. Whether it will prove so easy to persuade doctors to stay on in these back-ward areas remains to be seen. But the monetary inducement held out by the Government is very much higher. The doctor who stays on will receive very nearly twice as much as a Gov-ernment civilian doctor in Teheran. In addition, he may be able to accumulate a private practice of his own in the country.

EXTENSION AND DEVELOPMENT CORPS

The latest project in this remarkable series is the Exten-sion and Development Corps, for which legislation was brought in by the Prime Minister in October, 1965. Its task would appear to be to build on the foundations of the Education Corps. Agronomists, architects, and other skilled men will introduce new farming methods and bring in new techniques for road building and rural development. Recruitment will be on sim-ilar lines to the other two Corps and confined to holders of a high school diploma. The initial training will be determined jointly by the Ministries of War, Agriculture, and Housing and Development at their own new training centres. The High Council for the Corps will consist of the Ministers of these three departments plus those of Health, Interior, Economy, and Labour.

Introducing the Bill, the Prime Minister declared, "The foundations of our Government must be at village level. We must realize that Iran is not Teheran or a few towns and cities, but consists of 50-odd thousand villages where most of the population live. We must consider the village as the first unit of the nation's economy and society and begin all social and economic programmes at this level." There is a philosophy here which will find an echo in other progressive societies.

The extraordinary development of "peaceful uses" that has come to fruition in Israel today has roots long antedating the creation of the modern Zionist state. The people of Israel could almost be said to have invented the concept. The Jew has traditionally been on the defensive, but this has not stopped him from working. In the time of the prophet Nehemiah, he rebuilt Jerusalem with a sword in one hand. Today he finds himself in his new home for the first time in centuries no longer in a minority; yet he is still on the defensive inasmuch as his Arab neighbours consider themselves at war with him. At the same time, an enormous amount of work is required to make the State of Israel viable. The need for military readiness is matched by a comparable need to mobilize the nation against a harsh and unrewarding physical environment. To this need they have responded by building on tradition and modernizing the concept of the soldier-farmer.

The idea of the kibbutz, or collective farm, which was used for settling the country, goes back long before the creation of Israel in 1948. Since the creation of the state, the Nahal-- the Fighting Pioneer Youth--which has impressed several developing countries to the point of emulation, has served the same purpose.

Nahal is a branch of the Israeli defence forces that combines military training with preparation for a life of cooperative agriculture in one of Israel's frontier settlements. These settlements are, of course, fundamental to Israeli defence thinking. With a long frontier and a population of barely 2.5 million to hold it, the Israeli Government decided from the start that the surest way to maintain an outpost or to secure a strategic route was to settle it. The first problem, therefore, was how to provide enough farmers out of a population of predominantly urban origin. Part of the answer lay in military conscription, and the Nahal was the embodiment of the drive to settle Israel's frontiers with soldier-farmers.

The basis of the Nahal is the garin, or group of young people who all join the Army as a unit. The great majority of Israeli youth takes part in group activities. Most political parties-- and there are over a dozen of them in Israel--maintain some

119

sort of youth group, which serves to channel the energies of the young towards the national goals. They have clubs everywhere and run cultural and social activities for children and teenagers under the guidance of youth leaders.

Each garin is part of a youth movement or other organization (Boy Scouts, National Youth Organization, Gadna,* etc.). There are also garinim from the Cooperative Movement and of the young generation of the collective farms (kibbutz). The working principle is that every group of recruits that has been organized prior to enlistment with the aim of fulfilling the pioneering demands of the country is formally recognized and approved by the Ministry of Defence as a garin.

By the time a youngster reaches the age of military conscription, he is generally both physically fit and extremely well-informed about the problems and purposes of the State of Israel. The garins are highly organized societies each with their own elected functionaries and internal administration in matters of social nature. The hope is to keep them together as one unit as far as possible throughout the twenty-six months of military service and a good number of them afterwards on a collective farm.

The Nahal member joins up at eighteen and plunges straight into the basic training of an infantryman for three months. From this course are excluded the girls and the less robust boys, who form two separate categories throughout the conscription period. However, every effort is made to keep the garin members in contact even during their periods of official separation.

The next stage is a year at a kibbutz or moshav--the latter being a farm in which, unlike the kibbutz, each member is allowed to own private property, but in which marketing and

---

*The Gadna (35,000 members) is a Government-sponsored youth organization run jointly by the Israeli defence forces, the Ministry of Defence, and the Ministry of Education and Culture. It specializes in military and technical trades to be used by the future recruits. Founded long before the War of Independence, it trained youth for service in the Hagana, the military underground movement under the British.

education of children is done communally. Within this farm
the garin lives separately in a military camp, its members
wearing uniforms and still being subject to military discipline.
Their basic task is farming, and they are sent for specialized
courses at Nahal agricultural institutes to study one of a wide
range of technical farming subjects. But they are also soldiers,
and during this year they are sent on military courses and
given training in scouting and patrolling and the use of special
types of armaments. Already in this period they are considered to be members of the regional defence organization.
They will also continue their military training in the evenings.

As a result of this farming work, Nahal is almost unique
among the world's military organizations in paying for itself
and even bringing the Army a small income. Agricultural settlements (kibbutz or moshav), which benefit from the work of
Nahal, pay the Ministry of Defence for work done according to
the average farm-worker's salary rate. From this sum, deduction is made for food and services rendered by the settlement. The balance pays for part of the upkeep of Nahal, especially its education system and special social programme,
which is unique to this corps and stems from the fact that it
deals with groups rather than with the individual. The Nahal
serviceman receives the same salary as any other recruit doing his national service.

The next phase, for those who are physically fit enough, is
five months' intensive military training including parachuting
and assault courses. Those not fit enough, together with the
girls, are moved to a frontier settlement--possibly a new one,
or more likely one that has previously been established by
earlier Nahal groups and requires reinforcements. These two
groups need no longer wear uniforms, and they do not receive
Army pay, but they have to remain at this settlement until they
are demobilized and are still considered soldiers on reserve.

On completion of their military course, the combat-fit
members of the garin rejoin them. The garin is now gradually
integrated within the settlement. The Nahal member wears no
uniform. The settlement becomes completely responsible for
his support. If he should wish to leave the garin at this stage,
he is re-drafted into one of the regular units of the Army.

Apart from forming a ginger group that serves to assist in developing existing settlements, the Nahal has developed a special type of settlement of its own: the he'achsuth, or foothold. These are established at critical strategic points in which military requirements take priority over agricultural. The he'achsuth is in fact not a civilian settlement like the kibbutz, but a Nahal Army settlement. It is set up in places previously uninhabited for security reasons. It is settled usually by the better-qualified members of the Nahal who are sent in a garin to occupy the area immediately after their recruit training period.

As regards the direction of garinim to kibbutzim or he'achsuth, the decision is made in two stages:

1. On completion of military service, the garin, in coordination with the movement of which it is a part, decides on its ultimate settlement destination with no intervention on the part of the defence authorities.

2. During service, the choice of kibbutz, he'achsuth, or other form of pioneering activity is made by the garin members themselves (in some cases even prior to enlistment).

The garin and its movement suggest a desirable place for settlement to the Ministry of Defence. Approval is given according to considerations of security, settlement requirements, and spread of population. The he'achsuth is a military frontier settlement, and garinim serve their turn of duty according to decisions of the Nahal authorities after consultation with the movement.

Though an Army settlement, the he'achsuth is a joint enterprise of the Nahal and the Settlement Department of the Jewish Agency, the body that normally looks after Israel's agricultural settlement. The eventual objective is to farm these areas productively, but the initial emphasis must be on defence. The Nahal groups occupy the he'achsuth for a year, corresponding to the agricultural training period of the Nahal group. In due course, the settlement is developed to the point where it can be taken over as a civilian undertaking. The hope is that the garin will stay on permanently as a civilian group.

Nahal does more than train the young man or girl in purely military and agricultural arts. It is a comprehensive social force. Its educational activities include a steady programme of instruction in the problems that Israel faces; tuition in the Hebrew language--particularly for new immigrants; and special courses such as singing, acting, and folk dancing. Nahal also has its own monthly magazine, its own extremely able dramatic corps, and a cultural division that provides its garin groups with libraries, radios, and newspapers. The Israeli Government makes no bones about declaring that the inculcation of team spirit and group morale is among its foremost objectives.

A glimpse of these settlements at work may be of interest. At Nahal Oz (Valley of Courage) near the Gaza Strip, the settlement consists of 75 basic members plus 40 children and 35 members of Nahal. This settlement, which grew out of a Nahal "foothold," provides a training ground for Nahal members, and it is hoped that ultimately some of them will settle there for good. The Secretary, Eleazar Shavit, went there with his garin over 11 years ago. It was then 60 strong; today 25 members of it still remain. For his specialized farming course, Shavit studied agricultural mechanics as a result of a collective decision by his garin. Although the United Nations Force stands guard across the border, the state of vigilance is constant.

Further along the border at the junction of the Gaza Strip and the Egyptian frontier stands Kerem Shalom (Vineyard of Peace). This kibbutz is run by Mapam, one of the major left-wing parties. Obviously of vital strategic importance, it is commanded by a lieutenant from another kibbutz whom the Army had transferred there for twelve months. (In less exposed kibbutzim, decisions that are not of a military nature are normally taken by vote; in this one the lieutenant in charge has the final authority.) The average age is around nineteen.

Kerem Shalom was settled just over eight years ago, but owing to the shortage of water, it is still in an early stage of agricultural development. The main product is winter vegetables, though a large acreage of soil is being brought in by planting elephant grass. If there is little farming, however, there is no shortage of creative activity. Here, as in most

settlements, is conducted the vital work of teaching immi-
grants--particularly Orientals, who now outnumber the European stock.   Here one can see the melting pot at work--con-
scripted girls teaching Moroccans, South Americans, etc.,
to speak and write Hebrew.

While about half this settlement came from a garin, and
consequently have a full education, the other half are new immigrants with lower educational standards. Some such immigrants who did not have the benefit of completing their elementary education in their countries of origin after their period of
military training may spend up to five months at one of the educational centres of the Army, which brings them up to the
standard of eight years at primary school. Others, whose hand-
icap is due to the language, go through an intensive course in
Hebrew.   But if they are still deficient, they will get three
hours a day further instruction, mainly in Hebrew, at their
unit. Undoubtedly, the melting pot seems to work well here--
even better than it does in the towns.   The mutual dependence
of educated and uneducated, of European and of Oriental origin, is undoubtedly a powerful unifying factor.

The Nahal experiment has aroused a great deal of interest
in developing countries as a possible way of tackling their own
defence and economic problems--one of its great attractions
being that it is a form of defence that is not inflationary.
Israeli advisers have been sent on request to introduce a form
of Nahal suited to the particular requirements of overseas
countries. Indeed, the most striking aspect of Israel's "peaceful uses" is their suitability for export.   Israel is not, of
course, a "have-not" country--she has a standard of living as
high as Austria or Italy, but neither can she reasonably be
called a "have" country; most of her standard of living she
owes to sheer hard work and organization. And the point from
which she started seventeen years ago was close enough to that
of many developing countries to make them ask how she has
achieved a rate of growth faster than that of any country in the
world, except possibly Japan.

In addition, of course, Israel is free from the stigma of
colonialism attaching to other countries that might otherwise
provide good advice.

Israeli advisers--frequently appointed as they emerge from the armed forces--are therefore widely welcomed, most especially in the former French colonies of Africa, but also in former British colonies of that continent and as far afield as Latin America. Apart from know-how they bring with them the gift of sympathy. Informally dressed, unpretentious in manner, they are just as anxious to get on with the job of development as their hosts--sometimes more so. Part of their success is due to the regard in which they are held by their hosts at government level. Their most obvious differences from, say the U.S. Peace Corps--and it is no disparagement to that very effective body to say so--is that they are capable of reorienting the economic and even social philosophy of host governments. A case in point is Liberia, where three Israeli experts have had a marked effect in central government policies.

The diversity of languages now present in Israel gives her an enormous advantage over competitors in the field of cooperation and human aid, particularly vis-à-vis the Arab world. Between 1958 and 1962, Israel had aid missions in no fewer than 85 countries. In the medical field she had 131 experts in 15 countries; in agriculture, 184 in 35 countries; in youth leadership, 58 in 10 countries; in education, 84 in another 10 countries; in industry, engineering and building, 75 in 19 countries; in economics and administration, 56 in 12 countries; and in other fields, 228 in 39 countries.

Many recipient countries have placed emphasis on agriculture and irrigation. In Burma, Israeli experts have created an oasis of fertile farming in the depth of the arid zone of Namsang in the Shan States. More than 100 Burmese ex-servicemen spent over a year in agricultural settlements in Israel, while Israeli soil conservation and irrigation specialists were surveying Namsang and making their plans. When the Burmese ex-servicemen returned, equipped with new experience, they worked alongside Israelis in their own homeland.

Another party from Burma came to study Israel's irrigation methods in Negev, and an Israeli mission later drew up a project for the Burmese to develop similar areas in Burma-- Nyaung-Oo, Chauk, and Yenang-Yaung. This scheme involves the introduction of sisal into Burma in areas where rice cannot be grown because of water shortage. While the sisal is in process of introduction and maturing, which may take some years, experiments are being conducted with new types of millet and groundnuts.

In Liberia, President Tubman invited Israelis to help establish an eye clinic. Israeli surgeons and physicians in due course helped to open the clinic in Monrovia. At the same time, a Liberian doctor and ten nurses from Liberia were given specialized instruction in the Hadassah-Hebrew University Hospital in Jerusalem. Within eighteen months, 13,000 patients had been treated in the clinic in Monrovia, and subclinics had been established in outlying places. Today, Africans with eye complaints come from all over West Africa to Monrovia. Soon the Liberians themselves will be able to take over the central clinic, and will then replace the Israeli personnel and be qualified to undertake training on their own. A similar plan is being carried out in Tanzania. In Sierra Leone, an Israeli mission helped to build the Parliament in Freetown, one of the most impressive buildings in Africa.

Another form of cooperation is the joint company, in which an Israeli enterprise usually holds 40 per cent of the share capital and the foreign government holds the rest. It is understood that the Israeli partner will withdraw as soon as the company achieves solvency. The classic example of this was the agreement under which Zim, Israel's national shipping line, ran the Black Star line together with the Government of Ghana. Zim set up a nautical school at Accra to provide marine officers and crews. As the Ghanaians were trained in seamanship, the Israeli crews returned to the Israeli merchant navy and Israeli capital was withdrawn. Likewise, in Nigeria an Israeli company in partnership with the host government has built roads and public buildings and trained Nigerians to build.

Likewise, Israel plays host to a large number of trainees from overseas. In 1957, the number was 137 from 26 countries. The number jumped dramatically to 1,547 from 77 countries in 1962. The largest number of requests are for agricultural training, though there is a wide variety of courses. In agriculture, there are eleven main courses (e.g., poultry husbandry, agriculture in arid zones, the use of fertilizers, etc.) most of which are in more than one language (English and French) and at least one of which is in English, French, and

Spanish. The courses last for not longer than four months. In educational and vocational training, similarly available in two or three languages, the subjects include courses for physical education teachers, youth leadership, agro-mechanics, and telecommunications. Some of these courses (e.g., agro-mechanics) take two years, though most are much shorter.

There are six different nursing courses of duration up to six months. Shorter courses are held in cooperation and labour; subjects here include development problems, trade unionism, and labour economics. There is a three-months' accelerated course in public administration. There is also a wide range of courses in community development, including handicrafts for home industries and cooperative marketing; a study-tour and symposium on rural integration and rehabilitation projects; food and health techniques and institutional management; adult education, including the teaching of illiterates and the preparation of visual aids; a seminar and symposium on the role of voluntary agencies in the advancement of the community; and an accelerated course for kindergarten and nursery teachers. Also, in response to many requests, the Israeli Government instituted six-year courses leading to a degree in medicine for English-speaking students.

EDUCATION

The task of integrating at high speed immigrants from half the countries in the world, many of them illiterate, devolves to a large extent on the armed forces. Compulsory courses in Hebrew, the Bible, Israeli and general history, geography, mathematics, biology, and civics are designed to bring every recruit up to the standard of eight years of elementary education, and it is hoped that this can soon be extended to ten years. The courses are taught from Army textbooks.

About one-fifth of the Army is involved in these compulsory courses, which start with three weeks' reading and writing, followed by mathematics. In his last three months of service, the soldier goes to the Central School in Haifa, where he takes an intensive course in the subjects listed above. If successful, he is given a certificate stating that he is up to the standard of eight years of elementary education. If unsuccessful, he is aided, after his release, in further study by a special section in the Ministry of Defence.

Education is not confined to the classroom, but is a continuous inculcated process throughout service. For instance, officers will hold meetings with their men to discuss current events. When a unit moves to a new area, it first learns about the geography and history of that area. (The Army issues a whole range of pamphlets for this purpose.) The interweaving of history and geography in Israel--and of "peaceful" and "military" uses--was brilliantly illustrated at the time of the War of Independence when General Yadin, who was in charge of military operations around Jerusalem, put to striking effect his knowledge of the terrain gained as one of the country's foremost Biblical scholars and archaeologists.

A route march undertaken by a battalion through 200 miles of desert country was used to provide instruction in history and geography. The battalion was divided into nineteen classes according to educational attainment. For ten days, with the aid of lectures and films, it studied the places it would pass. During the march itself, each section commander had a fact sheet from which he explained the historical associations and current uses of the places his unit passed. During halts, company commanders addressed their units and questioned them on their knowledge.

Thousands of officers and men voluntarily receive free secondary school education during their service. Free textbooks and special examination leave provide an added incentive. Regular soldiers obtain a 50 per cent cut in tuition fees in institutes of higher learning. At any one moment about 150 may be studying at the Technion in Haifa and the University in Jerusalem. Some are sent abroad to universities and technical colleges.

The Army also provides courses for senior officers on Jewish thought and ideals and the role of Hebrew culture, given by University staff. Courses in comparative government are provided, and officers are encouraged to study foreign languages.

Any group of soldiers interested in a particular subject may apply to its commander to set up a study circle and to provide the required instructors. Over fifty of these circles exist at present. The Army has also undertaken to help in training teachers for the elementary schools and, together with the Ministry of Education, maintains several teachers' colleges where soldiers with over twelve years of schooling study for two years during the evenings after work in their units. After completing their course of study, they pass Government examinations and receive teachers' certificates. Over 100 soldiers each year are certified and as the whole course of study is tuition-free, the graduates repay the Government by serving as teachers in new settlements. Nearly 1,300 girls have been trained and have since joined the State educational system. Only in this way can education reach the more remote districts.

Graduates of the teachers' colleges of the country are con-scripted and serve, after basic training, as teachers in uniform. Some serve, after a special course of adult teach-ing, as teachers in the education centres of the Army. The rest are sent to border settlements and to settlements of new immigrants to teach school children. Most of Israel's im-migrant children are taught by teachers in uniform.

The Army also trains first-class journalists and actors. The former get their training on the weekly magazine Bamahane (In the Camp); the latter are trained in an extremely expert theatrical company.

Every non-commissioned officer goes for a leadership course, which includes the study of the Israeli regime, group dynamics, and allied subjects. Officers go to a special school in Jerusalem where courses in leadership include the study of the cultural heritage of Judaism, democracy, and "Man in the Modern World." Israelis believe that an educated army is strong in morale, particularly in its relationship between of-ficers and other ranks.

Another form of education undertaken by the Army is the publication of good, cheap books. The Israelis feel that now-adays, most cheap books are extremely second-rate, and they have set about rectifying this. They sell versions of classics at the equivalent of only 30 cents (US) to the public and to the soldier at half that price. This practise has aroused complaints from civilian publishers on the grounds of interference with private business, but it continues to flourish.

The growing strength of private enterprise has indeed not unnaturally had its effect on the purely peaceful uses of the Israeli armed forces. In the early days of almost frantic improvisation, the forces took an active part in the economy, growing vegetables to help out the serious shortage, building the road to Eilath, doing relief work during the floods that in 1951-52 inundated the immigrant camps, and building the communications in the Negev. Nowadays, this work is virtually not needed and is seldom done.

RESETTLEMENT AND VOCATIONAL TRAINING

Resettlement is no problem in Israel; it is often said that the most gruesome place in the country is the labour exchange -- for it is always deserted. Nonetheless, Israel is, like many countries, desperately short of skilled technicians--for a special reason. In the first flush of independence, the Government decided that the only quick route to viability was the settlement of lands that had been vacated by the Arabs. There was thus a heavy emphasis on agriculture, involving the contortion of converting into farmers men and women who mostly came from an urban background. The emphasis has now swung the other way. If Israel is to continue her success as a trading centre, she must clearly sell her brains in the form of industrial products. More and more, kibbutzim incorporate industrial projects; the Nahal is switching towards industry. All this requires a greater output of technicians, in which the armed forces play an important part.

At the Air Force Technical Centre in Haifa, for example, the training is not specifically in military subjects, but is suitable for a wide range of civilian technical jobs and is rewarded with Ministry of Labour certificates. Where military needs would have dictated a reduction in training, the Government insisted that the numbers should be kept up. More than 12,000 technicians now in Israeli civilian life graduated at this centre, and civilian instructors are trained here. Students are given at least one week of general education as well as technical and, thereafter, at least two hours every week. This and similar centres set the pace for technical training in the country, and civilian schools study according to its syllabus. From them come manuals and primers used by civil schools.

The accelerated training courses here are enormously popular; thousands of boys wait often for three or four months for a course. The most advanced training aids, though expensive, can often cut tuition time, as compared with civilian training, by a half or even two-thirds. In one technical instrument course it is claimed that the student will cover as much ground in five weeks as he would in six months in a civilian technical school--though there, of course, he would be studying a much wider range of subjects.

A close liaison is maintained between the military technical training centres and civilian official organizations. If the Ministry of Labour, for instance, is told of a sudden demand for instrument mechanics as the result of the construction of a new factory, it will refer this demand to the Army, which may release the necessary technicians. Of those who pass through the Air Force Technical Centre, about a quarter are allowed to obtain exemption from military service by going into Israel Aircraft Industries for at least four years. It is intended that these men should be foremen (a scheme originally resisted by the Army). At this factory, which comes under the Ministry of Defence, there is intensive emphasis on training, including training of foreigners. In 1958, 21 courses were available and being studied by 242 employees; by 1963, nearly 1,000 employees were studying a range of 70 courses, all of them free. Technical courses take place during working hours and general educational courses in spare time. The chief limitation on the number of courses is inevitably the shortage of instructors.

All in all, the armed forces of Israel play a fundamental role in the country's civilian life.

CHAPTER **13** IVORY COAST

The philosophy of the Ivory Coast in the context of this report was recently summed up by an Ivoirian official: "In the very near future, the Army will cease to be a liability and will become a financial asset to the nation. Its methods will serve as examples, and once the young men have completed their military service, they will be able to go back to civilian life fully equipped with modern technical training that they will be able to pass on to the men of their villages."

The most spectacular feature of this programme is the Civic Service Centre at Bouaké. Here the Israelis, who are supervising the operation, are carrying to great lengths the campaign to halt that world-wide problem, the drift from the land. They have met with setbacks in their effort to train soldiers as farmers and make the training "stick," but the new measures they are putting in hand to overcome these setbacks must be of interest to many other countries with similar problems.

The school was founded in May, 1962. Its purpose was to give Ivory Coast conscripts, in addition to military training, a civic and general education, and intensive instruction in agricultural methods. For this purpose an Israeli mission was imported. Cadres of command and instruction were formed from both Ivory Coast and Israeli officers and NCO's. The Israelis were at pains not to overassert themselves; as far as possible they established themselves as "shadows" to their Ivoirian counterparts, although the inspiration and expertise naturally came from them.

The scheme had from the first the vigorous support, indeed the paternity, of President Houphouët-Boigny, who had earlier become extremely impressed by Israeli methods. He was enthusiastic about the concept symbolized by the centre's crest: the crossed gun and farming implement. The objective was the improvement of Ivory Coast agriculture through the encadrement de la paysannerie. Soldiers on release would inculcate the practices they had learned in the villages whence they came.

QUALITY OF RECRUITS

After two years, however, the scheme in its original guise has been written off as a failure. Why was this? The official answer is that the national service syllabus, designed to produce in two years citizens trained as both fighters and farmers, was in fact producing neither. Such are the complications of both professions in these days, it is said, that the first twelve months were not long enough to train a soldier, nor the second to train a farmer.

The difficulty of finding in the ranks of young conscripts men capable of not only assimilating new farming methods, but also propagating them on their release from the service, is obvious. Such a role calls for definite qualities of initiative and, if possible, leadership. The Abidjan Government admits that it made a mistake in drafting conscripts compulsorily into the Civic Service. The intake--some 600 at a time--is now voluntary and is understood to be working very much more satisfactorily. There is no longer any specifically military training. But the Civic Service is still basically a military organization, coming under the Ministry of the Armed Forces, budgeted for within the Army budget, and run with military discipline.

FOLLOW-UP

Along with the new method of recruitment, a bold plan of action has been drawn up by the Ivory Coast Government with the object of ensuring that the methods inculcated in the Civic Service are transplanted to and take root in the villages. Foremost among the measures being put in hand at this moment are: (1) intensification of the instruction at the Civic Service Centre; (2) the use of the farms established in the regional centres for instruction in agriculture, animal husbandry, and poultry keeping; (3) the creation of "progressive villages," i.e., new hamlets; (4) the earmarking of existing villages, under supervision, to spearhead the drive for improved farm methods; (5) the creation of a company of pioneers capable of carrying out national tasks.

Instruction at the Civic Service School

This is now to be accelerated--principally to reduce the period of separation from the recruit's village. The course is now six months and includes carpentry and metal work, as well as agricultural mechanics and driving, poultry keeping and animal husbandry. The number of recruits in each course is rather over 160.

Regional Centres

The object of these is to serve as a base of agricultural instruction and demonstration and to provide the Progressive Villages and the Villages Under Supervision (see below) with materials, seed, and agricultural machinery. It is also to serve as the base for processing farm products. Two of the existing Civic Service farms are being transformed into Regional Centres and in due course this will happen to all of them. In addition, there are to be two specialist centres-- one for poultry keeping and one for animal husbandry. These will be in close touch with the Progressive Villages. The introduction of cattle is particularly important in the North, where valuable land is being under-used. An important function of the animal husbandry farm in Nangré is to breed an animal of more value to the Ivory Coast than the local Baoulé. In pursuit of this, ten milk cows were imported from Israel and acclimatized in the Ivory Coast.

Progressive Villages

Here the object is to create a new type of village in which the farmer will enjoy a better standard of living by employing more intensive methods of production. There are two villages, both of them established around existing farms of the Civic Service, one at Béoumi and the other at Fergessedougou. The villages are run on cooperative lines in respect of farm machinery and of distribution; otherwise, the property--farm buildings and cattle--are strictly private. Every farmer will be able to apply to the centre for farm machinery and for

financial credit. Initially, the village will provide for 60 families and will cover just over 800 acres. The two villages have
been deliberately sited so as to provide the greatest possible
contrast in climate conditions and agricultural requirements.

While land clearance is being done mechanically, the cultivation of the land is being done by cattle-drawn plough. For this
purpose each farmer receives three Indama cows--more suitable for this work than the local breed, the Baoulé (the Indama
has a greater resistance to disease and produces more meat).
The farmer is also supplied with twenty-five hens from the
Civic Service poultry centre. It is estimated that each farmer
should be able to make around $250 a year, which should be
greatly increased as, in the course to time, he is able to sell
cattle for veal.   He is not required to start repaying capital
until his fifth year, by which time he is expected to have reached
a maximum level of production. In addition, of course, he will
receive an advance of running expenses during the season,
such as the employment of tractor operators and the purchase
of fertilizers and insecticides; these he will not be required
to repay until the end of the season.

The village will pass through several organizational stages,
starting as a paramilitary organization and ending at the moment when the farmers achieve economic independence. At
this stage the village will pass out of the hands of the Army
into the authority of the Ministry of Agriculture.   Right from
the start, the students have been obtaining intensive agricultural training; they are also, incidentally, being transformed
from a highly heterogeneous group into a civic unit with common aims and methods of work.

Four stages of operation were scheduled as follows:

1. August, 1964--Recruited to the Civic Service Centre.
    Tasks: Clearing of land, civic and agricultural instruc-
    tion and partitioning out of the land.

2. March, 1965--The recruit starts operating on his own,
    sowing his plot, collecting tools and beginning work on
    buildings with the aid of the centre.

3. August, 1965--The recruit is now living in his own
    house and his family takes up residence with him.   In

this stage he acquires his cows, starts ploughing, and sells his first harvest to the centre. Community buildings are being put up.

4. March, 1966--The recruit has now completed his legal service and is on unpaid leave up till the time of his discharge. He is continuing his individual work and helping in the administration of the village, which is now directly under the authority of the Ministry of Agriculture.

Villages Under Supervision

The object is to accelerate the development of selected villages and thus slow down the rural exodus. Here we see the concept of the garin. Recruits are to be drawn in groups of about twenty from the same village. They will be given civic and agricultural education at the nearest farm school for six months. This period is considered, in the light of experience, to be quite sufficient; anything much longer is liable to uproot the recruit altogether, so that he will merely gravitate to the towns and fail to make use of his education. Thus, his instruction will be of a highly intensive nature for six months, and he will then spend the next six months in his group back at their original village. As with the Progressive Villages, these recruits will have the backing of the centre in clearing land and in the provision of financial credit. Altogether, seven villages have been taken in charge in this way and 140 young farmers own 575 acres of cultivated land. An important feature of the Villages Under Supervision is the introduction of unusual crops such as cotton, tobacco, and rice.

For the initial detachment, the farmer's schedule was as follows:

1. August, 1964--The recruit spends six months at the farm school. In this period he receives civic education and instruction in reading and writing; he works on the farm in company with other members of his group under the supervision of a group instructor. In this period the land is parcelled out and prepared.

2. March, 1965--Returns to his village with his group under the control of the instructor. The necessary tools are acquired, and cultivation of land and poultry-keeping begins.

3. August, 1965--He is now discharged and continues to farm his plot of land with the backing of the centre.

The estimated annual budget for these operations may be of interest:

		African Francs*
Progressive Villages		39,000,000
Villages Under Supervision	(nearly)	11,000,000
Upkeep of the Farms		9,000,000
Poultry-Keeping Centre	(nearly)	9,000,000
Regional Centres		7,000,000
Civic Service School		11,000,000
Farm at Nangré		3,000,000

A Company of Pioneers

One of the reasons for forming this company, which will undertake a wide range of construction and other civic work, was the fact that the Civic Service has an excess of machinery which, in spite of the levelling and bringing in of land, remained under-utilized. The company is headed by an Ivoirian officer, aided by an Israeli technical adviser and the local representative of the Ministry of Public Works. The officers and NCO's of the company are seconded from the Army. There is one captain, four other officers, and about one hundred other ranks. These include a number of specialists, such as nurses, telephone operators, surveyors, builders, carpenters, and motor mechanics.

On balance, the Civic Service represents a determined attempt to grapple with a major problem that besets nearly all developing countries and that some have scarcely been willing to recognize, let alone solve. It signifies an unusual, and no doubt admirable, sense of priorities--the determination to secure a firm agricultural base on which to build the country's

---

*245 African Francs = US $1

economy.   Ultimately, the Ivory Coast Government believes
that the only sure way to counteract the attractions of the city--
pleasant living quarters, electricity, cinemas,etc.--is to provide these very same facilities in the country. But in the meanwhile, this enterprising scheme has provided experience from
which other countries besides the Ivory Coast may benefit.

WOMEN'S CORPS

Finally, mention must be made of the highly successful
Women's Corps. Its object is officially defined as "helping the
Ivory Coast woman to progress"; for if she does not, it is believed, all achievements of the menfolk will be frustrated because of her influence on her husband and in the future on her
children. The first course was inaugurated at Bouaké in July,
1964.   It consisted of 330 young women of between fifteen and
eighteen from every part of the country. The Israeli advisory
mission is headed by a woman colonel, Dina Werth, aided by
other Israeli women officers.   The course lasts one year for
ordinary recruits and two years for instructors.

There is a definite educational requirement for entry. The
official aim is to try to help those who have left school at this
level but have no opportunity of becoming typists or nurses.
"We are giving them," it is said, "a chance to lead just as interesting a life in their villages as these typists." Subjects
include domestic economy and child care as well as animal
husbandry and poultry-keeping. After their service, the girls
are expected to settle, with Government help, in the villages.

Dina Werth's own comments, confirmed on all sides, are
of interest: "We have about 300 girls who represent all the
tribes of the Ivory Coast (there are 64 racial groups).   Many
of them were incapable of understanding one another when they
first arrived here because of the variety of their dialects. Our
first task was to teach them French, which is the official language of the country.   And I mean everything from A to Z.
Here they learn to compose a well-balanced diet; they learn
how to knit and how to bring up children; they are taught the
rules of hygiene, the history of their country and of the colonies, and not to consider themselves as the slaves of men or

as the predestined victims of family or tribal prejudices.   In
short, they learn to be citizens of a state, the Ivory Coast,   to
recognize their rights and duties, and to have confidence in the
laws and institutions of the State.

"They are wonderful girls, very sweet and obedient, and
are extremely quick to learn. To obtain the same results with
our own Israeli girls, we should need ten times as many instructors and three times as much time. "

The course was not wholly successful, for about a third of
the girls left before the end--some, indeed, after a few weeks.
The second intake is an experiment with 300 totally illiterate
girls, few of whom can speak French.   The outcome of this
course in 1967 should be well worth studying.

With a large army and severe economic problems, Morocco is a natural subject of PUMF, and an enlightened government has made remarkable experiments in this direction. These efforts are unlikely to diminish, for the Army will not be reduced in the foreseeable future, or the economic problems speedily resolved.

The economic problems are fundamental. Morocco's budget had never balanced until 1966. Her production has only been rising by 1.6 per cent per year, while her birth-rate, at 3 per cent, is one of the highest in the world.

NATIONAL ADVANCEMENT

The King has grappled with this problem with an energy and imagination comparable to that of the Shah of Iran. One of his principal instruments has been the Plan for National Advancement, which is his own personal creation, and in which the armed forces have played a significant role. Since Morocco's problems are typical of many other developing countries, it is worth tracing the history of this institution.

The idea behind it was to mobilize the vast latent labour force believed to be available in the country; it had been estimated that for nearly 5,000,000 people of active age, living in the countryside, about 150 days in the year were economically unutilized. The other main object was to reform Morocco's agriculture.

The programme was triggered into action somewhat precipitately by the exceptional drought of 1961. Neither the central administration nor the local services had time to prepare for it, and several provinces were suffering from a shortage of administrators and technical experts. Some lacked engineers and works foremen, others were short of caids (local administrators). The King decided that the task transcended the sphere of any individual ministry and set up the High Council for National Advancement, with himself as president, and including all the ministers concerned.

141

Beneath this Council, a large measure of authority was delegated to the provincial governors, who were charged with working out and executing their own programmes.   The burden proved too great for some of them, and it is significant that, since a purge in late 1964, the majority of these governors are now serving officers.

While National Advancement has considerable funds at its disposal,   its personnel are seconded mainly from three ministries--Agriculture, Interior, and National Defence.   The numbers of personnel vary from province to province; a typical one--Rabat--has six members seconded from the Ministry of Agriculture, two from the Police, and two captains from the Ministry of National Defence.

EARLY PROBLEMS

The first year showed disappointing results, in terms of absorbing surplus labour.   A very serious shortage of technicians, particularly agricultural specialists, quickly manifested itself, while the caid proved often inadequate to fill the role of businessman, economist, and statistician that was expected of him.   Nevertheless, a great deal was achieved by sheer physical effort.   In one province alone, for instance-- Beni Mellal--450 acres of land were re-afforested, nearly 1,000 miles of road were repaired, over 125 miles of road were opened, and a considerable amount of irrigation was accomplished.   In another province, over 2,500 acres of land were cleared.

What chiefly surprised the organizers of the scheme were the fluctuations in labour available at any given time. Naturally, at harvest time there was practically no labour available in the countryside, and the projects were virtually suspended. Similarly, in the mountains during the rain and snow, it was practically impossible to achieve anything.   But aside from this, fewer workers were available than had been expected for a variety of reasons.   In some areas, particularly the better developed ones, it was found that workers would not come forward for the wages provided; in the south of Rabat Province, for instance, it was necessary to import workers from the Rif. Again, it was quickly clear that the shepherds in the Atlas area

had never held a shovel or a pickaxe, and had to be adapted
to this work gradually. Likewise, goatherds at first resisted
rather than cooperated in re-afforestation schemes.

OPERATION ECOLE

The Army's most striking contribution to this operation was
its part in a crash school-building programme. Engineer officers, together with specialists from the Police, the gen-
darmerie, and the auxiliary forces, were mobilized during September and October, 1961, to work with the local authorities
and the population as a whole. Over 1,200 schools and 700 additional buildings for teachers were constructed and equipped,
many of them in remote desert and mountain areas, making
possible the education of a quarter of a million new pupils.
The following year, a similar combination successfully undertook the construction of 130 community centres for the use of
rural townships. These generally comprised a conference hall,
administrative offices, and places where young people could be
educated and entertained.

The following year, the King decided to stiffen the administration of National Advancement by the introduction of young officers in the role of provincial assistants. A course for their
instruction under the direction of an engineer-agronomist was
given at Ifrane lasting four and a half months. Twenty-seven
Army officers, mostly captains and majors, attended this
course, which prepared them to become the right-hand men of
the governors in promoting this work. It comprised lectures
in economy, sociology, law, administration, and agriculture,
and the instructors included ministers, civilian professors,
and international technical experts. During the course, the
officers visited factories, hydroelectric schemes, and public
works projects.

PROVINCIAL ASSISTANTS

The assistants were charged with scrutinizing all National
Advancement projects, preparing the programmes for discussion in the provincial councils, examining the problems of pro-

viding the necessary cadres to supervise the workmen in these tasks, keeping the governor informed of their development, preparing all documents necessary for submission to the High Council, and generally supervising the economic use of men and material in their province. They were expected to undertake inspection of all these works and, in effect, to act as the governor's chief executive.

There is no doubt that this innovation has had a dramatic effect in short-circuiting hold-ups in the civil administration. The provincial assistant is in fact a direct heir to those resourceful officers of the French Service Indigène who, speaking Arabic and sometimes Berber, gained the confidence of local tribal government while at the same time keeping a sharp eye on the civil administration.

The High Council meets every year under the King to determine the needs and priorities of the National Advancement programme. It is at this meeting, attended by ministers, governors, provincial assistants, and labour representatives, that the governors receive their directives for the coming year. Priority is given to tasks that do not require a high degree of technical expertise, particularly levelling work for roads, anti-soil-erosion projects, and afforestation.

In addition to work specifically within the National Advancement programme, the Moroccan Army has a very considerable record of building villages, bringing medical help to remote areas, and distributing food. In this context, during the Ramadan fast the Army distributes thousands of evening meals to the needy.

DISASTER RELIEF

Morocco has had its full share of natural disasters in recent years. Most devastating have been the earthquake at Agadir and the flooding in the Gharb. In both, the Army played a decisive part. At Agadir, some 12,000 troops were engaged in rescue and first-aid work, burial of the dead, and relief for the survivors. The operation was directed by the Army Chief of Staff.

It is hardly surprising that the Moroccan Government was not altogether prepared for a disaster of this magnitude. It has since been suggested that a failure of coordination showed itself during the early stages. Governments all over the world offered help but did not always receive guidance, it is said, as to which type of help would be useful, and which only embarrassing. It is on the basis of this and other disasters that experts reporting to the United Nations Secretary General have concluded that the most urgent reform required in this field is the creation by every government of a high-level coordinating body that would be able, in the event of emergency, to state the country's needs when offers come from abroad. (This reform, they believe, would be of more practical value than, for instance, the establishment of a permanent United Nations Disaster Relief Corps.) (See Appendix E for a United Nations-ECOSOC discussion of this problem.)

The Moroccan Government has instituted a General Service of Civil Protection placed under the direct authority of the Ministry of the Interior. Apart from this, a Higher Commission for Civil Protection was created by Royal Decree No. 2.63-488, on May 16, 1963. This Commission, presided over by the Permanent Secretary General of the High Committee for National Defence, consists of one representative from each of the principal ministries likely to be concerned with disaster relief (Ministry of the Interior, Ministry of Public Works, Ministry of Health, etc.). The Commission, which is responsible directly to the King, meets automatically whenever grave disasters occur and plans over-all coordinated action. Due to the frequency of floods in the Gharb plain and pending the implementation of the "Sebou Project" for the construction of several dams on the Sebou, a Special National Anti-Flood Committee has been set up. It is headed by a general appointed by the Chief of the Army General Staff.

It can call on any units of the Army in emergency, and there is naturally now no shortage of troops experienced in this type of work. In particular, many officers, having experience of administrative work, have a better understanding of the problems involved than would their counterparts in other countries.

In respect of resettling ex-servicemen, Morocco suffers from widespread unemployment. As elsewhere, tradesmen have no difficulty in finding jobs; but for the others the picture is inevitably less cheerful, although National Advancement projects have been of enormous value. However, an important new step was taken in November, 1964, with the creation of an Under-Secretary of State at the Ministry of Defence, charged with looking after all ex-servicemen. This minister is currently looking into the whole question of resettlement, including the reservation of official jobs for ex-servicemen.

15

Nigeria has a first-class fighting force recruited voluntarily, led by some very fine officers, and is therefore among that group of countries on which the United Nations Secretary General would most readily call in case of emergency. Being fairly compact--some six battalions--it is well extended in a purely military capacity; apart from one or two road-building programmes, the erection of a few bridges, and channel clearance work in the Niger Delta, the Nigerian Army does not generally engage in development projects--though it is prompt and adept in emergencies. On the other hand, the Nigerian soldier has often found difficulty in transferring himself to a constructive place in civilian society after his release. The trouble, nine times out of ten, is lack of education, and here a programme of education is now being mounted that should transform the nature of the Army and greatly facilitate the adjustment of the serviceman to civilian life.

The most conspicuous "peaceful uses" of the Nigerian Army have been in the maintenance of law and order, at home and in United Nations operations. In both capacities, their conduct has been an example and an inspiration to other countries. At home they have benefited greatly, through their reputation for impartiality, by the recently introduced principle of quota recruiting, designed to prevent any of the four regions from obtaining undue predominance in the armed forces. It is true that, before this system was introduced, the more educated Southerner--very often--managed to get the edge on his brother in the North in the matter of advancement, but the application of the vital "melting pot" principle has ensured that no individual unit could be said to be biased in any direction in an internal security operation. One of the striking features of the January revolt was the way in which other ranks obeyed their officers, regardless of regional origin.

It may be argued that this revolt, in which Ibo officers were prominent, indicated a breakdown of the Army's regional impartiality. On the contrary, the officers in question were clearly concerned with restoring the principle of regional

147

balance, which they considered to have broken down and to have given way to a Northern hegemony. Plainly, the vast majority of the Nigerian people agreed with them; even the Northerners did not protest at the change.

That General Ironsi consented to take power does not betoken any political ambition on his part or that of the Army as a whole. History seems likely to judge them just as reluctant to take power as the Pakistan Army in 1958. What happened was that their ingrained loyalty to their political masters was overcome by their loyalty to Nigeria as a united country, when they conceived that the two came into conflict.

DISCIPLINE

The Army is respected in a way which even the Police is not, even though the Police must be among the most effective and honest in all Africa. In the Tiv region, for instance, it has been shown that only the Army could command the confidence of the troublemakers.

Elsewhere in Africa, their performance has been such that the only possible criticism might be regret that the Army is no larger than 8,000 strong. In the Congo, as during riots in Nigeria, the Nigerian soldier showed a rare gift for taking the heat out of a potentially incendiary situation. Asked what is the chief ingredient of this high standard of conduct, Nigerian senior officers will simply reply: "good discipline." It would seem that there is no short cut to the perfection of this art; other countries wishing to emulate the example of Nigeria must inculcate the same high standards of discipline. Only thus can a government ensure that its riot squads or its troops in aid of the civil power will not positively exacerbate a situation which is threatening to get out of hand, or will not prolong the coercive action after the need for it has ended. Nothing inspires greater respect for the instruments of law and order than the knowledge that they will never use more force than is absolutely necessary. This quality has shown itself time and again in the Congo operation. The Nigerian soldier could make his presence felt without firing a shot, simply by the authority of his bearing.

With this record, it is not surprising that it was to Nigeria that Tanganyika looked following the mutiny at the beginning of 1964. The Nigerian battalion that was sent there for six months did much to steady the situation in that country. Likewise, the Congo contemplated sending troops to Nigeria for training in 1964. This idea backfired for political reasons, but police were sent there for training.

It should be noted, incidentally, that the only special training which the Nigerian troops received was the normal instruction in riot drill and aid to the civil power.

EX-SERVICEMEN

The position of ex-servicemen in Nigeria is clearly less happy than in some other African countries. Certainly there is much to be done. Post-war arrangements have lapsed, while vocational training schemes are as yet only on the drawing-board. Following the war, an employment quota system was enforced under which all employers with over ten workers had to take on a certain percentage of registered disabled or able-bodied veterans. This is still in force, but the registration offices were closed in 1952 because of the negligible number of veterans reporting for registration. Likewise, vocational training was discontinued in 1951, after which the training centres were handed over to civilian training. Attempts were made to establish farm settlements by providing loans, but these were notably unsuccessful.

There is no pre-release training; no Government funds have been forthcoming. However, a vocational training centre is planned at Jos, which, it is hoped, will provide both types of instruction, starting as from 1965. The idea would be to train mainly infantrymen in four particular trades: carpentry, blacksmithy, turning, and welding. Fifteen places would be allotted for each trade, totalling sixty trainees. The premises for this centre already exist--a former barracks; the shortage, as usual, is of instructors. Advertisements for instructors from civilian life did not prove as successful as had been hoped.

As to resettlement, the picture is inevitably somewhat sad; the employment situation in the towns is bleak, and every year it is aggravated by the influx of some 150,000 young men from school * who prefer the bright lights to subsistence farming. The Government cites this situation as one reason for not restoring the post-war quota of reserved places for ex-servicemen; they say that it would only trigger off a further incursion of ex-servicemen to the towns, to little purpose, and that the best that can be done for them is to appeal quietly to business firms.

FARMING AND THE EX-SERVICEMAN

One of the most vigorous spokesmen for ex-servicemen, Mr. Rosiji (a minister in the Balewa Government), strongly believes that ex-servicemen could be the spearhead of a movement to place greater emphasis on agriculture in the nation's economy. He considers that ex-servicemen have the necessary discipline and energy to undertake this work; but with the post-war experiences behind him he does not believe that these schemes can be launched without an element of compulsion. If this should ever happen in Nigeria, the instrument for its execution would be more likely the Army than any paramilitary organization. For one thing, there is considerable interest in Nigeria in using the Army for peaceful purposes, and though it is fairly well extended at the moment, Government leaders seem ready to look for opportunities in the future.

Understandably there is widespread lamentation that the post-war proposals to introduce up to twenty-six ex-service industries fell largely by the wayside. The only one that was in fact set up--a firewood industry a few years ago--provides work for barely half a dozen ex-servicemen. The only other

---

*This tendency may have lately been reinforced by the findings of the Morgan Commission, which had the effect of accentuating still further the disparity in standard of living between town and country by raising the wages of urban workers.

ex-serviceman's industry is a factory for making Armistice poppies. Nevertheless, there seems a much greater need for schemes that would direct the ex-serviceman back to the land, and it would appear that the Government is ready to give a higher priority both to ex-servicemen and to the needs of agriculture than it has done in the past.

EDUCATION

For the future, as elsewhere, the main hope for employing the ex-serviceman lies in educating him while he is in uniform. Great emphasis is now being placed on this process, and the Nigerian Army has become even more of an elite than it has been in the recent past. During his first six months in the depot, the illiterate soldier is subjected to an intensive course of education, and by the end of this time most of them can read and write. This process is compulsory until the soldier can pass Stage 2--the ability to write simple letters and read simple orders in English. Stages 3 and 4--equivalent to third and fourth form in secondary schools--is voluntary and by selection. But those who cannot pass Stage 2 when they reach their unit are given intensive coaching during Army time. As yet it has not been possible exactly to correlate educational achievement with promotion to non-commissioned rank, but as of now there are very few corporals who have not passed Stage 2, or sergeants who have not passed Stage 3.

The results of the period 1962-64 indicate the progress made under this new regimen. In 1962, out of a total intake of 340, about 70 were totally illiterate and 270 semi-illiterate. At the end of six months, 20 were still at Stage 1, while 185 had reached Stage 3. In 1964, out of 390 recruits, 30 were totally illiterate (the Army has become more selective, but the quota system involving a basic minimum of Northerners ensures a certain number of illiterates). After six months, only 10 of these were still in Stage 1, 50 were in Stage 2, and 265 had reached Stage 3 intermediate.

For officers, the necessary qualification is either "O" level General Certificate of Education or the West African School Certificate. The aim at Kaduna Military Academy is to get the officer cadet up to the sixth form of secondary education. Here there are courses in current affairs, which form one of the examinations from captain to major, and doubtless help to equip an officer for service with the United Nations. As a result of this intensive educational programme, which is administered by an Education Corps, very few of the new ex-servicemen fail to get jobs.

A less energetic people than the Dutch would long ago have been overwhelmed by the elements which beset them; that they have survived at all is due in no small measure to the peaceful activities of their armed forces. Since the 1953 floods in particular, the Army, Navy, and Air Force have been integrated into an elaborate precautionary network that can move swiftly into action in the event of emergency.

The Defence Ministry has organized a "1,200-man arrangement" under which every chief engineer of the Provincial Waterways is allowed to ask a garrison commander to send some platoons at any hour of any day or night. The arrangement guarantees instant help for the civilian population. If troops normally stationed in the neighbourhood of a disaster happen to be away on manoeuvres, some of the earmarked contingents may have to travel some distance. But the arrangement works very efficiently, as was proved in the Groningen floods a few years ago. The men earmarked may come from any Army unit. They are not specially trained, on the grounds that it would be impossible to predict the exact nature of the catastrophe they might have to meet.

In the event of a flood, the Army contingent comes under civilian authorities. (In this connection, civilian authorities are: the Provincial Governor, Burgomasters, and the Chief Engineer of the Provincial Waterways.) They order the soldiers to fill sandbags or do whatever is most urgently needed. A civilian supervisor may take a couple of platoons of men to shore up a threatened sector. Communications will be supplied almost entirely by the Army's "walkie-talkies."

For other catastrophes, every man not earmarked for special duties is available. In the case of heath or forest fires, railway or other major accidents, every civil authority is allowed to ask the nearest military unit for assistance. It was used at the time of a multiple road accident near Utrecht involving some thirty cars.

The Engineers, who naturally play a vital part in emergency operations, are divided into three companies per battalion: the Pontoneers, who build bridges; the Pioneers, who build roads;

and the Electricians, who can help with the supply of public utilities. In order to facilitate the evacuation of the often threatened "Biesbosch" area in the Delta, a Pontoneer battalion and the Instruction School for Diving Personnel have been permanently designated for deployment here. These units practise their tasks every week. Another stand-by precaution is the provision of air communications for isolated areas, such as the Frisian Islands, when sea transport is blocked by heavy floating ice.

The Army also takes part in a wide variety of smaller tasks such as the Delta works, assistance with harvesting, transportation of cattle, food and, of course, bridge building. (Most bridges in Holland have a reserve structure--usually a Bailey bridge.)

Though it has to take care not to offend the susceptibilities of the trade unions by competing with civilian firms, the Army makes itself useful to the economy in a very wide variety of ways. For instance, in 1963 a bad accident spot was revealed in the South of the country, where three or four road accidents had taken children's lives within two weeks. Following a press campaign the local authorities grew extremely worried, but were aware that the remedy would take too long if they went through civilian channels. The Engineers were called on and duly put up a Bailey bridge for the children overnight. Such actions conform with the policy of the Dutch Government, in particular the Secretary for Defence, Mr. Haex, of improving the Army's image in the eyes of the people.

Formerly, the civilian authorities would have to go to the very top when seeking to borrow even a tent; today, they can go through the local commander. The latter must keep strictly within the policy laid down by the Government of never providing anything that can be obtained in the civilian sector. The Pontoneers in particular have to be careful not to compete with civilian firms. In the same context, the Army will be accepted as a legitimate instrument for doing casual work--for instance, levelling down the road leading to the paraplegics centre at Doorn. The local garrison of Marines has been helpful here, clearing snow whenever necessary and even providing male nurse replacements.

At sea, the Navy is naturally fully responsible for rescue work and also for fishery protection. One particular task of crucial importance is hydrography. As a result of the Delta dam, tidal streams are constantly being changed along the whole coast, and with them the water depth between the islands. The Netherlands Navy has the task of keeping watch on these developments. It also participates in overseas oceanographical projects. Like the Army, the Navy set up a new emergency organization following the 1953 floods. Local Naval officers-in-chief have comparable arrangements to supply so many boats, assault craft, tugs, etc., and clothing in emergencies.

For the Dutch forces, these functions do not impose an undue strain; the Netherlands defence commitments are not today so great as they were during the time of her Indonesian empire. One notable "peaceful use" in consequence has been--and it is practically unique in this survey--the earmarking of 300 Marines, formerly assigned to Indonesia, for permanent stand-by duty with the United Nations. No special training has been given them for this task. (Stand-by contributions are also, of course, being supplied by the Scandinavian countries, by Canada, and by the United Kingdom.)

The Air Force also undertakes massive weed-killing operations when there is a major outbreak and an urgent request is made by the Department of Agriculture. The Air Force likewise undertakes daily weather forecasts, which can obviously be of critical importance in the Netherlands.

One unusual "peaceful use" of the Netherlands defence forces is conscription for civil defence. Young men are conscripted for this purpose if they are ineligible for the Army for one reason or another: exempted university students, physical rejects, those in reserved occupations. They train one day a week for three years in such occupations as hospital work, fire fighting, and radio operating.

EDUCATION

Efforts to educate the Dutch servicemen have, as elsewhere in Europe, come up against the impediment of over-full employment. (A symptom of this situation, with its corollary of immigration from Southern Europe, is that one Dutch minister on the home front has been taking courses in Turkish.)

A range of over 2,000 different courses is available for a soldier to follow by correspondence course or evening class; he must study in his spare time, but the Army gets him special prices for these courses. (These concessions do not apply to officers.) He pays three-quarters of the normal price and receives one-third of it in return if he does well in the course. There is no Education Corps as such in the Netherlands Army, nor is there any compulsory education in the Netherlands armed forces. A welfare officer is attached to each barracks or unit. The soldier who wants to take a course approaches this officer, who sends his form on to The Hague where the Education Directorate forwards the request to a correspondence course institute. In mid-1964, over 11,000 other ranks were taking such courses. In addition, over 1,200 were attending evening classes, mostly in such subjects as languages, mathematics, and elementary education.

The results of these correspondence courses have been distinctly disappointing. A large number of servicemen start them, impressed either by their cheapness or by a talk from the welfare officer; but at least half abandon the course halfway through (the course is automatically suspended when the pupil is three months in arrears). Only about 18 per cent complete their course during the time they are in the Army-- although some continue it into civilian life. Language courses are provided for regular officers and NCO's--also on an incentive basis; though they have to pay, the money is refunded if they pass. Over 200 took these courses during 1965.

VOCATIONAL TRAINING

As to vocational training, courses are held at three different places in the Royal Netherlands Army and the Royal Netherlands Air Force; at 't Harde (started 1955), Eindhoven (1958), and Soesterberg (1951). At the last two of these the instructors are both military and civilian; but at 't Harde they are all civilians. Eindhoven, the RNAF centre, concentrates especially on technical subjects. A wide range of courses is available, from oxyacetylene welding to woodworking and radio engineering. The Military Welfare Section of the Defence Ministry is responsible for the administration of these courses.   Some 500 students take the trading-class courses every year; about 150 take welding courses and about 250 take longer vocational training courses. Up to November 1, 1962, these courses had been attended by 1,863 pupils, of whom 1,737 had completed them.   Of these, 716 received a certificate or diploma indicating success in the course, while others received a record of their level of proficiency attained during it.   This records how many hours of practical and theoretical training the man has undergone. In all three centres the latest available figures were: number of pupils, 2,480; finished the course, 2,209; received certificates, 881.

These students are nearly all conscripts doing their period of national service (twenty to twenty-four months). The courses are available to volunteers, but few of them are interested; those who wish to improve themselves normally make use of the facilities at high schools and universities.   The entire cost of this vocational training falls on the Ministry of Defence.

Under an Air Force scheme introduced in 1961, all officers and NCO's who have completed their initial service training can follow lectures at a university during service hours.   Permission is normally given for two days a week or the equivalent, though the air base commander can suspend it in emergencies.   The same facilities--2 days a week--are available to NCO's who wish to bring their educational attainments up to grammar school standards.

Professional courses are available for short-contract volunteers (those who do not wait to be conscripted but sign up for four years, or sometimes six) and also for conscripts who have signed on after they were due for release and have served for four years.   The Government foots the whole bill for these courses, though these too must be conducted in the serviceman's spare time.   Those who have served for less than four years can get these facilities for the same period of time out of uniform as they have served in uniform.

RESETTLEMENT

The Dutch serviceman's transition to civilian life is generously facilitated by the Government.   The short-contract volunteer receives 25 per cent of his monthly salary for every month he has served.   Likewise, the man who has signed on at the end of his conscription period can, on release, apply for an allowance to tide him over in civilian life when he is unable to find a job. He receives, in effect, special unemployment pay at a graduated percentage of his military salary. He is allowed 80 per cent of that salary if he is the head of a family, 70 per cent if he is living alone, 60 per cent if he is merely one of a family, etc.

Again, the short-contract volunteer who has served at least four years may, after leaving, apply for an interest-free loan up to the equivalent of $1,500. He must use this to establish himself by buying a shop or some similar enterprise. The Government will carefully check his case to ensure that it is a good business proposition and retains the right to inspect his books at the end of each year for as long as it deems necessary.

Technicians will find their diplomas in most cases interchangeable with those of civilian life. Those who have passed their electronic courses since 1957, for example, can apply for an equivalent civilian certificate; an electronics corporal will get a diploma enabling him to open a shop for electronics. Likewise, a radar corporal is given a certificate of radio and TV technician, and can open a radio or TV shop.

The Dutch programme for educating servicemen has the full backing of the State at the highest level. It stems from the creation some fifteen years ago of a National Committee of Military Welfare under Prince Bernhard, who has taken a personal interest in these activities. On it are represented all the big industrial concerns and Government officials connected with the welfare of armed forces. Under it a Central Advisory Committee has operated for the last ten years, similarly composed of leading industrial and official representatives, and charged with the task of improving the standard of education in the Royal Netherlands forces. This programme has gathered momentum in recent months; and already the Government's desire to improve the armed forces' image, coupled with the native genius for improvisation, has made The Netherlands one of the more active countries in the peaceful use of armed forces.

17

The Pakistan Army has made a contribution to the defence of the country's economy that at times has been absolutely decisive. Without its benevolent interventions, Pakistan would almost certainly have gone bankrupt. The country has developed well from the most unpromising beginnings. When it was created, many of its enemies believed it would founder in a matter of weeks, and it was all hands to the pump. One might indeed more aptly say that it was "every man a bucket"; for it was the almost total absence of machinery that was the most striking feature of the newly created country. In East Pakistan, which is dependent upon high-grade jute for its economic survival, there was not a single jute-baler at the time of Partition; all of them were across the Partition line around Calcutta.

It was in East Pakistan that the Army's most spectacular contribution to the economy was made. This was nothing short of a rescue operation without which the province would have been plunged into economic catastrophe and the country very probably split in two.

East Pakistan is no stranger to disaster even when the jute crop is bringing in a proper revenue. As embarrassed by excess of water as West Pakistan has been by the lack of it, it is the target of frequent merciless floods intensified by cyclones. A predominantly rural economy, it must nevertheless support a population slightly larger than that of West Pakistan on an area barely one-seventh the size. Thus, when smuggling in jute became rife in the early 1950's, the danger of a collapse in the East Pakistan economy appeared imminent. Over 700,000 bales of the 1951-52 jute crop had been smuggled across the border into India. In consequence, Pakistan was losing revenue at an appalling rate, and the Pakistan rupee threatened to nosedive. The only hope was to bring in the Army.

On the Government's instructions, General (now Field-Marshal) Ayub Khan, as Commander-in-Chief, ordered General Mohamed Musa, then G. O. C. 14th Division, to take charge of anti-smuggling operations. The East Pakistan Rifles were authorized to arrest anyone engaged in smuggling. Control of the operation remained in the hands of district magistrates, but officers and JCO's were authorized to use whatever force they considered necessary for the success of the operation.

The Army went into action on September 12, 1952. This was a colossal undertaking involving supervision of a thousand-mile border. It meant searching all country boats using the numerous river routes into India and bullock carts and any other means of land transport. The troops were virtually on twenty-four-hour duty at the climax of the monsoon season. Much of their work was done knee-deep, often neck-deep, in water. No other organization could have begun to tackle such an assignment.

It was an astonishing success and widely applauded by the public. Though authorized to shoot smugglers on sight, the Army was able to report that it had put a stop to smuggling without firing a single shot. In the first month, about 500 smugglers were captured, most of whom had either not heard of the Army's intervention or wrongly imagined that the troops were susceptible to bribes. Within four months the leak had been stopped. The Pakistan rupee rallied.

Three years later, the country was plunged into the threat of a severe famine compounded by food-hoarding such as has occurred in recent months in India. As in several Indian provinces, scarcities were created deliberately and, by the middle of 1956, the food situation was critical. It is notable that, following its success in preventing smuggling, the Army was popularly regarded as the only possible source of salvation. On June 30, the Governor announced that food distribution would be handled by the Army through the civil channels. This was a new and unfamiliar task for the Pakistan soldier. Not only had he to control the movement of food, but also to enforce the exceedingly complex regulations governing its distribution.

Simultaneously, new steps had to be taken to revive anti-smuggling measures; a headquarters Army Food Control was set up in Dacca in charge of three sector headquarters at Comilla, Jessore, and Dacca. Subordinate headquarters were set up corresponding to those of the Civil Government.

Within a month remarkable results had been achieved. Above all, hoarded food came out into the open market. Large quantities of rice were impounded as they were being smuggled out of the country. Three hundred thousand false ration cards were seized in swoops on ration shops. Above all, public confidence was restored. But exactly a month after the operation began, the Army was abruptly withdrawn. No doubt the politicians feared that they were being replaced in the public favour by the military--a very reasonable fear. At all events, for whatever reason, it was not long before the black marketeers came out of their burrows again.

In their wake came the smugglers, now better organized than ever. These were the months immediately preceding the collapse of the Civil Government and the final military take-over by General Ayub Khan. Already, the economy of East Pakistan was tottering. At a top-level meeting in the closing weeks of 1957, the Chief Minister of East Pakistan told the Prime Minister, Mr. Chundrigar, that only the Army could save his province and asked that it should be allowed to resume anti-smuggling duties.

It was only the need to save his country from the total collapse of law and order that caused Ayub Khan to intervene. Now, in December, 1957, he was more anxious than ever to avoid civil involvement. But the failures of the politicians had created a hopeless situation. On December 18, the Army again took over in East Pakistan. Once again public confidence was rapidly restored--the vital precondition of capturing and eliminating smugglers. A leak estimated at Rs. 400 million worth of currency over the previous year was stopped dead within a fortnight. Four hundred smugglers were tried and punished. Once again the rupee revived.

Unfortunately, the smugglers had their friends and accomplices in high places. As before, they called off the military on January 5, 1958, to the dismay of press and public. But this was the last time they were able to play ducks and drakes with the fortunes of the Pakistani people. Unable to work efficiently and honestly and unwilling to utilize the Army sensibly, the Civil Government fell to a military coup d'état.

Considering the extent of their commitments, it is astonishing how much the Pakistani Army has been able to contribute to the development of the country. Apart from the normal emergency work undertaken by nearly all armed forces, it has engaged in road construction, house-building, an anti-locust campaign--which virtually eliminated the locust in West Pakistan--and boar hunts to rid the country of a serious scourge to farmers. Perhaps the most conspicuous individual feats have been the erection of the Wali Tangi Dam at Quetta and the construction of the spectacular Gilgit Road into the mountainous North of the country (see Appendix G, Part I).

Besides using servicemen to assist the country's development, Pakistan is also outstanding among developing countries for the lengths to which it goes to assimilate ex-servicemen into the economy. This is not altogether surprising. There is basically a very pro-Army feeling in Pakistan society.

There is an almost universal belief that the country would not survive a day without a first-class army. The defence budget is large in relation to the country's economy.

Hence the acceptance of a special status for returned ex-servicemen which, to all intents and purposes, does not exist in India. Its most striking feature, however, it does share with India: the Post War Services Reconstruction Fund (see Appendix G, Part II). The Fund was begun in April, 1942, when a sum of two rupees per month was set aside for every combatant soldier who served in the ranks and one rupee for every non-combatant. Until recently, it was confined to 1939-45 veterans, but in Pakistan it has lately been extended to all ex-servicemen. India received around £8 million all told, while Pakistan received less than £2 million.

The money was transferred to all provinces according to the strength of their service personnel to be used for their integration into civilian life. It was required that provincial trusts should be set up and administered in accordance with the Charitable Endowments Act of 1890.

This fund is administered in Pakistan by Committees of Administration in each of the two main provinces.

A word is in order here about the Pakistan Armed Services Board, a national organization with responsibility for looking after all problems of ex-servicemen. This agency is a reorganized version of the old Soldiers', Sailors', and Airmen's Board set up by the Government of India in 1932.

The four provincial boards taken over at the time of independence failed to function effectively, and the early years were not good ones for the ex-servicemen. However, in 1958, General Ayub Khan, then Commander-in-Chief, got them reorganized. There is now a central board composed of the Minister of Defence (Chairman); the Ministers of Education, Finance, Labour, and Law; the three Commanders-in-Chief; the Financial Adviser to the Ministry of Defence; and the Secretary of Defence. The main functions of the PASB are to give all possible help in administrative matters connected with the serviceman and his family, to circulate information regarding educational and other facilities available for servicemen, to investigate cases of disability and allot pensions, to help in the resettlement of ex-servicemen, and to promote better military-civilian relations.

All policy matters are referred to the Secretary, Pakistan Armed Services Board, by the Services Headquarters and the provincial boards, and the decision of the PASB is issued through him to all concerned for the implementation of the policy relating to the welfare of ex-servicemen, their dependents, and that of service personnel in their civil capacity. (For excerpts from the annual report of the Pakistan Armed Services Board, 1964-65, see Appendix G, Part III.) The latest Five-Year Plan (1965-70) has stressed the need for close cooperation between the Labour Department and the Armed Services Board's district offices in the placement of ex-servicemen.

The PWSR likewise suffered during the post-independence years, but General Ayub Khan was able to force through reforms several years before he became President. Most notable was the investment of a large proportion of the PWSR funds in the Fauji textile mills at Jhelum.[*] This concept of the Fund gave

---

[*]The PWSR's prize project is now the Fauji sugar mill, which in 1966 was expected to make a profit of Rs. 10 million.

it two advantages that it lacks in most parts of India. It is expanding far faster than it would if invested in Government securities and supplying much more income for training ex-servicemen for civilian life, and it also provides the place to train them. In due course, other big undertakings were acquired or started: the Cereal Manufacturing Products at Rawalpindi, the Khyber Tobacco Company at Mardan, two flour mills--at Rawalpindi and Chittagong--a rice mill at Rangipur, and a radio and bulb factory at Dacca. The Fund now has a net worth of nearly £3.5 million, having trebled itself in the last five years. It spends over £160,000 a year. Of this, some £80,000 goes on stipends and scholarships for educational training of servicemen and their sons. A hospital has been built at Rawalpindi that provides for ex-servicemen the only surgical treatment for TB in the country. In addition, funds are used to maintain and build rest houses in the bigger towns--since, of course, most servicemen come from the country.

VOCATIONAL TRAINING

Post-release vocational training is at once one of the successes and one of the headaches of the Pakistan Army. Twenty-five per cent of the seats in six technical training centres are reserved for ex-servicemen and their sons. The courses last for ten to twelve months, during which time the PWSR supplements the Government's monthly payment of 15 rupees with an additional stipend of 40 rupees a month. Free hostel accommodation is provided.

The scheme is excellent as far as it goes though, like most vocational training schemes, it has its shortcomings. Most conspicuous is the fact the 25 per cent quota is not fully taken up. Only some 4 per cent of the reserved seats are taken up by ex-servicemen. The PWSR Fund tries to make up the number by detailing their children, who are also beneficiaries. (The figures are: seats reserved, 502; seats taken up by ex-servicemen, 21; seats taken by ex-servicemen's children, 282.) The reasons for this lack of enthusiasm by the ex-servicemen themselves are probably endemic to the problem of resettling ex-servicemen in the developing countries, though perhaps exaggerated by the special circumstances of Pakistan.

First, the Pakistani jawan's first idea upon release is to get home. Since most of the country's martial stock comes from the countryside, this means he will gravitate back to his village, most likely in the northern and northwestern part of West Pakistan.

Second, it is, therefore, extremely difficult to get him to leave home for an industrial training centre. Apart from family ties, there is the cost of the rail fare and the ever present possibility of sickness in the family which might require his recall.

Thus, post-release industrial training still requires several adjustments. Most particularly, more effort should be made to ensure that the soldier, on release, is fully informed of the opportunities available to him and the prospects that would be open to him if he mastered the art of machinist, welder, turner, or fitter. Also, some further thought should be given to the inexorable fact that in Pakistan--as in most countries in the world--though it may be hard to get the job to the man, it seems practically impossible to get the man to the job.

The difficulties of post-release training, however, only highlight the value of pre-release training. Here the soldier's interest is captured before he leaves the service. He is not sacrificing any time with his family. And he should be in full possession of the facts relating to his prospects on release. Compared with most developing countries, Pakistan is strong on pre-release training. The operative order stemmed from the Ministry of Defence, August 31, 1957, to the Adjutant-General and states:

> I am directed to convey the sanction of the President to the free pre-release training of Junior Commissioned Officers and other ranks in the Government Vocational Training Centres and private industrial institutions for a maximum period of six months prior to their release from the Army. This training will be treated as bona fide duty, and the personnel will not be replaced in their units.

It has been successfully carried out in cotton mills, woollen mills, silk mills, sugar mills, and rubber, cement, and shoe-making factories. The work falls under the supervision of the Welfare and Rehabilitation Directorate, General Headquarters,

Rawalpindi. Over 1,000 soldiers a year complete these courses. The 1963 figure was 1,164; that for 1964 was well over 1,500. Altogether, some 7,000 people have been trained in this way.

Recently there has been a diversification to include farming. Over 700 servicemen have been trained in dairy farming and bee-keeping and over 300 in tractor driving. Also of benefit to farming is the emphasis on the training of tube-well operators--152 in all. The latest development is that the Welfare Directorate has asked that 25 per cent of all seats in the six vocational training centres shall be reserved for serving soldiers. Meanwhile, the Ministry of Defence has agreed to extend the pre-release training period from six months to a year if necessary. Vacancies are obtained from factory owners and allotted to Regiment/Corps centres which seek bids from their respective units and place them before General Headquarters.

Much of this training is, of course, done in the PWSR Fund's factories but, it could be argued, not enough. Some would like to see the factories exclusively manned by ex-servicemen. This is perhaps less important than a concentrated effort to provide more pre-release training.

Of all forms of industrial training, this is undoubtedly the most helpful to the ex-servicemen and beneficial to society. The advantages of training and employment in the same factory are self-evident. If there is to be more pre-release training, however, the method of selecting candidates might well be tightened up. There is no doubt that applicants are genuine volunteers, but many of them have proved incapable of benefiting from the course. They have not been sufficiently screened through aptitude tests or interviewing boards as they are in some Western countries. Meanwhile, the Government is pressing ahead with pre-release training and has laid it down that two centres should start operating in 1967 exclusively for this purpose; one is in the Islamabad area (1,000 places) and one in Dacca (500).

Where so much has been obviously achieved, it seems helpful rather than otherwise to be frank. It is no good blinking the fact that supposedly trained ex-servicemen have arrived at factories only to find that, for one reason or another, they are not up to the job. This is discouraging for industrialists who voluntarily make places for ex-servicemen. They are watching the progress of a parliamentary bill which would make it compulsory for public organizations to absorb a certain percentage of ex-servicemen. This bill, if it becomes law after the completion of the presidential election, will undoubtedly be the envy of ex-service organizations in Asia. But it will call for a tightening up in the training of ex-servicemen.

Likewise, there is a case for regulating the training courses with reference to the needs of the labour market. At the moment, the facilities for acquiring information about the success of trained ex-servicemen in finding a job are less than adequate. Machinery for this does exist, but it does not provide adequate guidance. In the past, employment exchanges have not shown too much zeal in the rehabilitation of ex-servicemen. This, of course, was originally due to the enormous concentration of effort required to accommodate the influx of refugees. But the fact is that, although some 500,000 servicemen have been demobilized since independence and under Government instructions each of them should have been registered at the employment exchanges, these exchanges have hardly registered 45,000 of them, let alone provided them with employment.

Since registering is voluntary, the blame for this theoretically lies with the ex-serviceman, but it could also reflect his lack of confidence in the employment exchanges. These have failed to indicate in advance the fields of employment in which ex-servicemen can be absorbed. This may not be the most important link in the chain, but it is in a sense the first one; without full knowledge of what is required by the civilian economy, the whole machinery of training and resettlement can be dislocated. Among ideas put forward to rectify the situation is that of a cell within employment exchanges, headed by an ex-serviceman and specifically authorized to help ex-servicemen. It has also been suggested that a bulletin should be issued on the lines of the one published by the Ministry of Labour in Britain. More employment exchanges are needed in areas where there is a concentration of ex-servicemen. Most important of all, employment exchanges should notify the armed forces of the likely number and nature of future vacancies.

The new emphasis placed on agriculture in Pakistan's pre-release training programme is interesting. For it is in the field of modernizing agricultural methods that the ex-serviceman could make a unique contribution to his country's economy. In large parts of West Pakistan, the village leader is a retired serviceman. If more of them were pre-release trained in modern farming methods, the effect on the country's economy could be dramatic. It is regrettable that in their pursuit of skilled industrial labour--certainly a legitimate pursuit--some Asian governments are guilty of downgrading the profession of agriculture.

Besides introducing this training, Pakistan operates land settlement schemes for ex-servicemen and those within five years of retirement. These involve allocations of land which are "brought in" by the Army itself. Unlike the industrial training schemes, they are immensely popular; the number of applicants vastly exceeds the number of openings. Under the previous regime, the selection often owed much to favouritism, but nowadays strict account is taken of such factors as length of service and number in family.

Unfortunately--as with industrial training--the selection methods do not always seem to pay due attention to aptitude or suitability. Only about 60 per cent of those who have been allocated land actually farm it. The remaining 40 per cent are absentees, many of them living in their original villages or deriving a second income from working in the towns. Here again, there would seem to be scope for closer screening of applicants.

All in all, the Pakistanis are well justified in claiming, about their attitude to ex-servicemen, that "Well begun is half done."

CHAPTER 18   PERU

The opening up of the fertile jungle lands on the eastern slopes of the Andes has long been a logical ambition of the Peruvian peoples; but it has required the vision and vigour of President Belaunde, harnessing the energies of the Army, to give effect to these hopes. A prerequisite is the colossal task of driving roads through the mountains to connect the eastern seaboard with the Amazon basin. This area comprises just over 60 per cent of all Peru but contains only 12 per cent of the population; much of it is rich land, but most of it has not even been completely explored. A major penetration road construction and maintenance effort is being carried out by Government forces consisting of six Army Engineer battalions and one Engineer company, reinforced with Ministry of Development civilian personnel. Other Army units provide logistic and training support.

In the North, two Engineer battalions and one Engineer company are at work on three projects: one of them—Jean-San Ignacio—is already in operation, opening up the prospect of 350,000 acres for cultivation. Two others in the Marañon region offer the gradual opening up of 3.25 million acres by 1970. One of the two battalions—the 6th Engineer Battalion—was organized and equipped in 1958-61 as a divisional combat battalion for a hemispheric defence mission, but since then has been completely reorganized for a civic action internal security mission. All units, with the exception of the single company referred to above, are supported by the U.S. Military Aid Program. Fifteen tractors received under MAP greatly increased the capability of these two battalions. By November, 1964, advanced elements of the 6th Battalion reached Rio Imaza, its objective. The 1st Battalion advanced into the Nazaret colonization area, a major immediate objective. The company continued to keep open the road to San Ignacio. This "trail" will be redesigned and upgraded as the Ecuador-Peru connecting link of a new highway, which will lie to the east of the main Andean Range, and will provide the first integrated highway system in the Upper Amazon basin. It will open to agriculture the rich land of the high jungle regions of Peru, Colombia, Ecuador, and Bolivia.

Another battalion--the 2nd Engineer Construction Battalion--continues the maintenance of 200 miles of the vital central highway. In due course, the Government hopes to utilize this battalion on the proposed Peru-Brazil Highway between Pucallpa (Peru) and Cruzeiro Do Sul (Brazil). The 3rd Engineer Battalion has made excellent progress in the vicinity of Cuzco--an area troubled by disturbances from land-hungry peasants in recent months. Just below this overpopulated area lies the Manu region containing half a million acres of excellent land. In late 1963, the President directed the Army to initiate construction of a sixty-five-mile highway to provide access to this important area. The project was initiated in 1965 by a company of the 3rd Engineer Battalion.

The 4th Engineer Battalion has been employed in constructing a difficult project near the Bolivian border in southeast Peru. Its work is of particular interest as the first Army-sponsored "Food for Work" project. Initiated in 1964, this provides food for civilian workers of the battalion and their families, as well as for volunteer workers. In the first nine months, approximately 90,000 rations were issued. The results of this programme are reported to be excellent.

The goals assigned for 1964-65 were 80 miles of road construction and 475 miles of road maintenance work.

One of the most striking by-products of this road programme has been the spontaneous colonization of the adjacent land. This is particularly facilitated by the Army's practice of leaving behind old construction camp sites, into which colonists move the moment they are evacuated, and form them into the nucleus of new towns.

U.S. HELP

In all these operations, U.S. participation is important. It includes equipment and technical assistance through the Military Aid Program, funds and equipment from the Agency for International Development, and loans from the Export-Import Bank. Technical advice is provided in the form of either mobile training teams or, more frequently, individual

Engineer officers with NCO assistance. These advisers help in the vital task of training Peruvian Engineer units in the maintenance and operation of new projects. Naturally this training is of an eminently practical kind. Recently, in the space of thirteen weeks, one Engineer officer and two NCO's were able to train 53 officers, 288 other ranks, and 91 civilians in construction techniques and the operation of equipment. This was, of course, on-the-spot training without sophisticated aids. But it paid remarkable dividends in terms of the rate of road construction.

Likewise, at the highest level of national planning, the U.S. Army Corps of Engineers is helping the Peruvian Government to organize an inventory of its natural resources.

COMMUNITY PROJECTS

In addition to this long-term development work, the Peruvian Army carries out large numbers of community projects. Examples include: a mobile medical and dental team in Piura; repair of 400 school desks in the slums of Lima; levelling and straightening of streets in the slums of Lima; dental services in Lima; a cultural centre for students of Cuzco University.

This programme is largely within the scope of the military regional commanders and local individual units.

HEALTH

The Army Health Assistance Plan aims to bring medicine to areas which the Ministry of Public Health does not reach-- including outlying suburbs as well as isolated communities. Many Army units provide basic medicine free of charge, including instructions on preventive medicine, baby care, and hygiene measures. In 1964, the target was the provision of medical care for 72,000 patients and 60,000 dental patients through the operation of 20 medical posts--13 fixed and 7 mobile.

SURVEY

The President has set a goal of five years for completing a national survey of Peru. The responsible organization for this work is the Military Geographic Institute. Its long-range goals include the survey of 320 national charts to cover all of Peru on a scale of 1:100,000. Late in 1964, only 17 charts had been produced, the annual production capacity being 12 maps. It is urgently hoped to obtain further help to accelerate this programme.

COLONIZATION

The Army is destined to play a crucial part in land colonization, a project vital to the future of Peru. The problem is, of course, that while millions of Indians live in terrible hardship in the Sierras, there exist on the other side of the Andes, in the high jungle region along their eastern slopes, large expanses of good agricultural land. There has been talk of colonization for at least twenty years. Since the arrival of President Belaunde, this has been translated into major acceleration of activity. The problems are colossal. Even granted the successful opening up of communications, the obstacles to colonization as such must be as awesome as they are anywhere in the world. It cannot be assumed, for instance, that because a better life awaits them on the other side of the mountains, the Indians will migrate to it or stay there when they get there. For one thing, the climate is dramatically different; in some ways it is unhealthier. Many have doubts whether the immigrants will eventually come from the Sierras, believing that they are more likely to be recruited from the poverty-stricken barriadas around the bigger towns. Even this would be a double achievement, however, relieving the terrible pressure of population on these towns and also helping to offset the country's imbalance of food trade.

President Belaunde is under no illusions about the magnitude of the task. Forethought is the order of the day. Early in 1964, ten selected officers were sent to Israel to receive specialized training, and on their return an Army Colonization Office was set up. Detailed on-site studies have been made of three colonization areas assigned to the Army: Nazaret-Marañon-Nieva in the North, Pucallpa-Central Region in the East, and Manu Region in the Southeast.

Method

The method will be to use military units of some 300 specially trained troops, all of them volunteers. Projects will vary from 150,000 to 200,000 acres. It is planned to keep the Army in these areas for not longer than six to ten years. Their role will be essentially limited to initiating the settlement. Thereafter, the Civilian Land Reform Agency (Oficina Nacional de Agra Reforma) will take complete control and the Army will move on. The Army will establish itself in the centre of the settlement and develop four quadrants in turn. Each will be settled by some 300 families. Members of the Army will be allowed, indeed encouraged, to stay on as civilians in these settlements after release. They will receive equipment, loans, etc.

One among many problems here is that the troops from the Sierra region are frightened of the unfamiliar jungle, not altogether without reason. It is hoped to overcome these fears by mixing Sierra troops with others from the jungle. This initiation will be helpful at least in inducing the Sierra ex-serviceman to settle in the jungle areas. Experience in Bolivia has shown that in the first place voluntary workers will come only for two or three months at a time, but after repeating this procedure they often decide to settle with their families.

The aim was to have two colonization nuclei in operation (Pucallpa and Nazaret) by 1966.

Plan of Campaign

The Peruvian Army's plan of campaign has been lucidly analysed by Doctor Milton Jacobs, Special Operations Research Field Office, Fort Clayton, Canal Zone. It consists of three stages:

1. The collection of basic information: high-level recon-
    naissance (ten days); decision on zone; reconnaissance
    of technicians (55 days);   decisions about setting up
    nucleus, access roads, etc.

2. Planning project: formulation (140 days); further recon-
    naissance (15 to 30 days); develop preliminary project
    (1 month); develop final project (3 months); acceptance
    of final project.

3. Execution of the project: headquarters: commanding
    and planning (both military and civilian); contracting
    (with free enterprise or Army); implementation (equip-
    ment); first steps for recruiting colonists and training
    them;   coordination, administration (supply, etc.);
    norms and regulations;   information, education, and
    training plans; commercialization of products.

Under the tentative schedule, four and a half years will be
required for the soil preparation of 5,000 acres; the initial
settlement, involving working up to 30,000 acres; development,
working up to around 70,000 acres;   and transfer to civilian
control.

VOCATIONAL TRAINING

The Peruvian Army's pre-release training arrangements
are unquestionably among the most remarkable in the whole of
Latin America. By early 1965, there were four centres training
750 soldiers and this has since been increased to five.   Most
of the courses are of three months' duration, covering the
closing period of the conscripted soldier's service.   In all,
some 3,800 servicemen have been trained in this way during
the last two and a half years. It is planned that within the next
two years the Army will be discharging semi-skilled workers
to civilian life at the rate of 6,000 to 8,000 a year.

The programme was inaugurated in April, 1962, with the
opening of the centre at Lima.   Courses included carpentry,
masonry, electricity, iron work, plumbing, and painting.   It
was initially financed by $2,000,000 of Peruvian Army funds

plus $5,000 from AID for the purchase of hand tools. Under the direction of civilian instructors employed by the Peruvian Army, the students themselves constructed their own centre, including concrete paving, roof construction, installation of utilities, work benches, cabinets, tables, etc. This practical work was a valuable complement to the instruction in the theory of the various trades, plus education in rights and obligations under labour laws, community development, etc.

Meanwhile, AID had agreed to support a five-year programme with tools, equipment, and technical assistance. Under this agreement, which is renewed annually, the Peruvian Army provides land, buildings, utilities, administration, civilian academic staff, and logistical support. AID provided $150,000 in 1963 and again in 1964. This was all in the form of grant or donation funds.

In July, 1963, a centre was opened at Cuzco with 100 students, and the following January a third was set up at Arequipa with another 100. In October, 1964, the centre at Piura was opened with 150 students; the fifth centre at Iquitos was due to be opened in May, 1965. Each military region of Peru will then have its own training centre.

Initially, each centre concentrates on the same five or six construction trades in order to establish its own installations. Thereafter, the trades taught are adapted to the needs of local industry.

FREEDOM FROM MILITARY DUTIES

The Army's willingness to relinquish three months out of the conscripts' twenty-four months' service is a remarkable manifestation of civic action, representing an important contribution to the country's development. Students are selected for training by a series of aptitude tests coupled with their educational level and record of conduct. Once selected, they remain at the centre for three months, during which time they are relieved of all other military duties. They are instructed by an academic staff of civilians, who are journeymen in their trades with over ten years of experience. They are supervised

by technically qualified shop-supervisors and academic directors. At least 80 per cent of the instruction is practical work.
In each centre, a public relations section carries out instruction on resettlement into civilian life and also provides liaison
with industry and helps in the employment of the soldiers on
their discharge.

In addition to these industrial training centres, a new departure in 1965 was the establishment of an agricultural training
centre in the Cuzco area. This is training up to 900 students
a year in four cycles of six months each.   Subjects include
farm equipment operation and maintenance, animal husbandry,
fruit- and vegetable-growing, and the preservation of food of all
descriptions. Instruction concentrates on small farm methods,
but there is also tuition in cooperative farming. The centre is
open to local civilians.

Another new centre will be the Heavy Equipment Training
Centre, which will train operators of engineer road construction equipment in support of the Army's road programme.
Here, too, it is planned to accept civilians.   The centre will
undoubtedly do much to curb the abuse and neglect of valuable
machinery.

Considering the size of the Peruvian Army--around 30,000--
the proportion involved in this form of training is remarkable.
Already the four initial centres have an aggregate annual training capacity of 3,200 students.   The ultimate target is 10,000
students a year.

EX-SERVICE TEACHERS

Besides technical training, there has been an interesting
campaign in the Army to educate each soldier to become, at
the end of his military service, an instructor in his home
community or town in the simpler arts of economic and social
development.   Similarly, a new programme is afoot to train
servicemen on their release to instruct their communities in
literacy.   This programme is supported by the Ministry of
Public Education. It is early yet to tell how many ex-servicemen
will take up voluntarily this unpaid work; at present, their only

inducement is the receipt of a prize for training ten illiterates. But if it does not work, it seems probable that further inducements will be found to make it work. A course for literacy instructors, already operating, contemplates the training of 6,000 such instructors every year. It is hoped that each of these will train an average of five persons to read and write, thus contributing to the instruction of 30,000 Peruvians a year. This programme will be completely financed by the Agency for International Development.

Besides the training of instructors there is an important programme for training illiterate soldiers. Conscripts are on the average from humble origins, and there is a considerable illiteracy rate. A literacy school has as annual objective the training of 6,000 men through the operation of 90 primary instruction units.

TWO PROBLEMS

This ambitious programme inevitably creates new problems. In the technical centres, the worst is the shortage of instructors. The journeymen appear to be adequate, but lacking in adaptability to new techniques; there are no graduates of polytechnics at these centres. There would seem to be a need for new methods of training instructors, and one suggested idea is to recruit Peace Corps-type engineers from overseas. A move has been made to hire U.S. Army personnel, but AID finds this too costly. Those on the spot would like to see in every centre half a dozen retired Army personnel, e.g., from the Army Corps of Engineers.

A second problem is the use made of this training. There is absolutely no difficulty about obtaining employment on the part of anyone who has completed one of these courses, especially since they are orientated to the demands of industry. On the other hand, it is sometimes difficult to persuade them to accept employment. Some of them, particularly Indians, will drift back to the villages from which they came, making no use of their technical training.

It is indeed notable that, as in many parts of Asia, the returning serviceman prefers to stick to agriculture; hence the importance of the new agricultural training centre. Agricultural and livestock training was initially considered to be part of the training programme for industrial training centres. But it was later decided to classify it as an independent programme on its own. In due course, training is to be done at the existing Army Farming and Livestock Centres in Lima, Cajamarca, Caraz, and Tacna. At a later stage, use will be made of the military farms at Tumbes, Lambayeque, Talara, Piura, Arequipa, and Cuzco. As yet the numbers involved in these courses are small.

NAVY

The Navy also does considerable educational work, notably at the Miguel Grau Nautical School under the Naval School of Peru, which has been created specially for the training of future officers of the merchant marine. It has been in operation for several years. But as far as general education goes, the Navy's problems compared with those of the Army are negligible. Retired Naval personnel seldom have trouble in gaining employment. Recently, General Motors Corporation, which has been installing an assembly plant near Lima, asked the Navy through its Public Relations Department to provide up to 180 names of qualified technicial personnel who were trained in the Navy.

Another feature of the Navy's educational programme is that during 1964 each unit of the Fleet in the Pacific sponsored a public school in one of the ports. This has naturally gained the Navy a great deal of goodwill.

In a move to conserve Peru's large ocean resources, the Peruvian Navy and the National Fishery Society approved an agreement in the summer of 1964 in which the two will contribute financial help to the Instituto del Mar del Peru, which was created by Supreme Decree No. 7 of March 20, 1964. A converted Navy ship, operated by the Navy, has been undertaking scientific observations of marine life off the Peruvian coast. An important part of the programme has been the study

to determine fluctuations of the anchovy population, which is
used for Peru's vast fishmeal industry.   Other programmes
include studies of edible fish, whales, and guano birds.

Perhaps even more remarkable than its sea-going role has
been the Navy's riverine civic action programme.   Direction
of the drive to bring civilization to the Amazon region is in
fact under the over-all supervision of the Navy.   In 1964, a
gunboat, the "Marañon," completed the second stage of the plan,
consisting of visits to the river towns of the Amazon, Yavarí,
and Yavarí-Mirin.   In collaboration with the Ministries of
Education, Health, and Agriculture, this ship gave medical,
sanitary, educational, agricultural, and veterinary assistance
and courses in literacy.   Motion pictures, both recreational
and instructional, were shown in these towns.   The medical
personnel of the gunboat provided immunization services
to all the people of the towns visited and gave free medicines.   Four other ships also took part in the operation in
this enormous area.   During 1964, a total of 15,772 medical
and dental consultations were provided. One widely publicized
achievement of the "Marañon" was the rescue of survivors of an
expedition that had been attacked by the Cocomas Indians. Also
involved in this operation were U.S. helicopters from Panama.

In the field of scientific investigation, besides its work
with the Instituto del Mar the Navy plays an important part in
hydrography and oceanography through its hydrographic and
lighthouse service. Six meteorology stations are to be set up
to provide a weather prediction service for shipping.   The
service is also extending its operations to the river basins of
the Amazon, where it is advising on the location of ports to
provide terminals for penetration roads.   The Navy has also
provided transport for heavy vehicles for the construction of
these penetration roads.

AIR FORCE

The Peruvian Air Force plays a vigorous role in civic action,
especially in the Amazon basin.   There it provides air transport, helps to build landing fields, is establishing new air
routes to aid in colonization and development, and is provid-

ing medical and dental help by means of a specially equipped aircraft. Apart from this programme in the Amazon basin, the PAF is collaborating directly with the various Government agencies for the almost daily transport of personnel and equipment needed for the operations of the Ministries of Public Health, Development, Agriculture, and Public Education.

SATCO (Servicio Aereo de Transportes Comerciales) is the commercial air transport unit of the PAF and, together with the military air transport units, it is extending its present air routes and opening new ones in areas where civil air transport is not feasible. Its main emphasis has been on three air routes, all of them connecting Iquitos with the larger townships between the Andes and Peru's eastern borders. Two services run weekly, one bi-weekly. Transport has been provided since July, 1964, for passengers and cargo at prices that barely cover fuel consumption. The greatest benefit is derived by the small farmer and businessman. In addition, the PAF provides unscheduled flights covering the entire Amazon basin, utilizing amphibian and Catalina aircraft based at Iquitos. Helicopters are also in constant demand to carry technical personnel and cargo to inaccessible areas. They also transport mail, support the Ministry of Public Health in immunization projects and the Ministry of Agriculture in surveys for agrarian reform and colonization.

The PAF runs a mobile air dispensary (C-47) based in Iquitos. Its schedule is fixed, and patients can therefore count on it. This operation is closely coordinated with the Ministry of Health to provide preventive medicine, tackle epidemics, and effect evacuations.

By the start of 1965, four airstrips had been completed, or nearly completed, in the Amazon jungle region, and eight others were in process of construction. This constitutes, in fact, the first stage of opening up the Amazon basin. The PAF provides technical assistance, equipment, and some of the necessary funds. Each community provides the labour, together with the balance of the funds. Some of the airfields will be incorporated in the mobile dispensary routes.

The PAF is active in performing aerial photographic surveys, while its General Directorate of Meteorology carries out a direct programme of support in the work of agriculture, air navigation, public health, and industrial development.

As its Government well understands, Thailand is under permanent threat of infiltration from across the Laotian and Cambodian borders. Whether disaster can be prevented depends on action now, and action adopted by the Thai Government will undoubtedly command the interest of many governments. So important is the concept of the Mobile Development Unit, in fact, that considerable attention is devoted to it below.

Meanwhile, it is of interest that, though the MDU's employ only servicemen and specialist civilians, a role is developing for the ex-serviceman in these border concepts. The latest of the ex-service land settlements is, in fact, situated right up against the Laos border, in the province of Udorn-Dhani; with some 400 families, this will be the biggest such project yet initiated. It is planned to establish 8 villages of about 50 families each, and to grow rice, sugar-cane, and corn in an area which has been largely jungle.

A further land settlement was planned, also for 1965, at Klong-Man-Sai, on the Cambodian border. It is, in fact, situated in between the border and a Civil Development project under the Public Welfare Department. Thus situated, it will be in a position to protect the CD project, a task for which the ex-serviceman will receive additional training from the Army. The ex-serviceman will not be permanently supplied with arms, but it is intended that the Army will supply them as necessary. This is a brand new concept in Thailand.

SOLDIERS AND EX-SERVICEMEN

Unlike the Klong-Man-Sai project, the one at Udorn-Dhani falls within an MDU area. The cooperation of the ex-serviceman with the local MDU should be extremely fruitful. At any rate, that is the hope of the War Veterans' Organization, which looks after ex-servicemen in Thailand. As this is a classic example of the use of ex-service settlers to guard frontiers, the project is of some interest. It is intended that the settlers shall undergo special training to support military and administrative activities in times of emergency. Unlike four earlier projects, the ex-serviceman will be screened for honesty, reliability, and patriotism. (In the previous schemes, the only criteria were that the veteran must come from a farming area and be homeless and jobless. As elsewhere in the world, there have been many unsatisfactory settlers.)   Settlers will periodically undergo training in defending the border by unconventional and guerrilla tactics.   Close cooperation will be maintained with the Military Command at Udorn-Dhani.

The initiation of the project is planned to take three years. It will be the biggest of the WVO's land settlements.   But an earlier one at Muek Lek, some ninety miles from Bangkok along the Friendship Highway, has shown that these land settlements can be a success, depending on how much money is available for the project and the quality of the ex-servicemen. The latter should not be a problem, providing selection is done intelligently.   Out of a huge number of ex-servicemen issuing into society every year, the vast majority come from farming regions, and it seems certain that a large majority of these would prefer to return to the land.   However, while Thailand is comparatively a very rich country, there is a definite shortage of land available for these ex-servicemen so that, as in India, many of them end up on the street corners of the larger towns. If properly selected, ex-service farm settlers could be of a high calibre.

MOBILE DEVELOPMENT UNITS

While this is all in the future, the Mobile Development Unit has already been tried in the balance and found well worth following up.   It is a mixed Army and civilian body under Army command, whose exclusive purpose is civic action.   First units were operated on the Laos border and later ones are being moved into the Cambodian, Burmese, and Malayan borders.

Recognizing the threat to Thailand in the Laotian situation, the Government in April, 1962, set up a National Security

Command whose chief function was to combat subversion.   It
is composed of civilians as well as soldiers. This body ordered
a considerable number of suppressive and preventive measures;
the MDU is the most conspicuous of the preventive measures.
The first was set up in August the same year, after consultations between the armed forces and the civilian agencies.

A typical MDU consists of a headquarters and 3 mobile teams.
The headquarters comprises 60 personnel; half of them will
be from the armed forces, 10 men from the Ministry of the
Interior, 4 from the Ministry of Health, 4 from the Ministry
of Agriculture, 4 from the Ministry of National Development,
6 from the Ministry of Education, and 2 from the Public Relations Department.   A mobile team consists of 9 members of
the armed forces, 2 from the Ministry of Interior, 2 from the
Ministry of Health, 1 from the Ministry of Agriculture, and 3
from the Public Relations Department.   With 3 teams of 17
men and a headquarters of 60, the full complement of an MDU
is 111.

Nine MDU's were in operation by the end of 1964; some of
their achievements are worth recording.   The first accomplished 7 irrigation projects, 50 miles of rural road, 15
artesian wells, 1 model village, the distribution of 5,200
articles of clothing, the erection of 2 small electric power
plants, 5 small dams, the rebuilding of just over 100 schools,
and the supply of 15 radio receivers.   They also gave 14,000
medical treatments and evacuated 49 people by helicopter.   In
addition, they erected a public health nursing station.   The
second MDU's accomplishments included: 5 irrigation projects,
65 miles of road, 38 artesian wells, 5 model villages, the
erection of 4 small electric power plants, distribution of 14,000
fish for breeding, 2,700 veterinary vaccinations, 4 small dams,
reconstruction of 327 schools, handout of 18,000 schoolbooks,
provision of 50 radio receiver sets, and erection of 3 public
health nursing stations.

"Hearts and Minds"

So much for the surface results. But one of the most crucial
features of civic action, not always fully appreciated in places
where decisions are made, is that the provision of material
welfare is only one factor in the winning over of the hearts of

the people concerned; in fact, the experience of the MDU's has been that while these material gains are keenly appreciated, the greatest gain from the point of view of the average villager has been the feeling that for the first time in his life or that of his forefathers, somebody in Bangkok cares about him. This is of profound importance to those concerned with the problem of counter-insurgency.

The specific objectives of the MDU are to strengthen local confidence in the Thai Government and to provide information-- hitherto virtually non-existent--on which the civilian author- ities can build development plans. Each of the three teams in the unit has a forty-day mission allowing it about two days per village. Experience has shown that while a great deal can be achieved in two days, anything less is liable to leave the village in a state of psychological confusion. One procedure that has proved effective is that immediately on arrival, the team leaders acquaint themselves with the village and the peo- ple, particularly the elected headman and the schoolteacher. A meeting of the village is called, usually by means of broad- casting from a car, and the team leader explains what he is trying to do. Where requests come from the villages, there is no problem as to which projects to undertake; sometimes, however, the ideas have to be sold by the team leader. It is notable that welfare personnel on the team are invaluable at assessing the genuineness or otherwise of individual hardship claims.

Self-Help

Apart from instruction by the team's experts and the hand- outs of gifts and the evening film shows, the main work of the team centres on the particular construction project it is decid- ed to carry out. Choice of the project depends on demand by the villagers and feasibility of completion in one day. An essential part of it is self-help by the villagers. But leadership invariably has to come from the MDU side. The technique of getting the villagers to work requires tact, and apparently the most successful method is for the team leader to ask the vil- lagers directly--and not through the headman--what they would like to see done. It seems pointless, if not worse, to undertake a job which nobody asked for. In fact, if a team comes across a village in a bad mood--resentful, perhaps, over the Government's failure to protect them against banditry--to make the villagers work on a project they have not requested could have a very adverse effect. Where this has happened, indeed, a change of tactics has been found appropriate; instead of action, there is talk, in which every member of the team is mobilized to meet as many members of the village as is practicable to explain to them what the Government is trying to do and to assure them of its concern in their lives. Here the greatest effect is obviously achieved if the maximum number of the team have mastered the local dialect. In such cases, the team's mission becomes social rather than developmental. The broadcasting of folk music from a team van is a great solvent.

In any case, as noted above, the social communications achieved as a result of the MDU's work may well be even more striking than the economic benefits. What impresses the villagers is the simple appearance of officials from Bangkok, listening to them on terms of equality. An important by-product of this mutual respect between villager and MDU man is the example set by the MDU to the local leadership. The headman realizes that this informal respect is what is expected of him, and the villager comes to expect the same from his headman. Since the vital problem of MDU's is the question of what happens after they have left, this example may be among the most important legacies of all.

Criteria

Success in these operations depends on a number of obvious general criteria. The quality of leadership must be extremely high--though this is not asking for the impossible in view of the very small numbers engaged. There should be an element of versatility comparable to the dual training of every member of a STAT (the U.S. Sea Bee Teams) inasmuch as experience has shown that experts in one subject are constantly being called on at short notice to perform in another. More specifically, a number of proposals were made to improve the MDU's performance by Dr. Lee Huff, one of the world's foremost experts in the subject, after they had been going on for rather under a year, as follows: road-building projects using village labour, he felt, are in general not the most rewarding type of work. Civilian government agencies should conduct surveys of resources to provide a more accurate background against which the MDU can operate. Hygiene should not be neglected in the promotion of medical treatment. A balanced diet should be encouraged by greater cultivation of gardens, a process requiring instruction. (On this point, the omission of an agricultural expert on the MDU could be changed, but only if it is felt he could impart the necessary information in the brief period available.) Villages might in some respects be made competitive and awards made to those with the greatest enterprise--in the form, perhaps, of vehicles or implements. Closer attention should be given to adapting films to the villagers' particular requirements, especially instruction in hygiene and gardening. MDU officials should be trained to a high standard of proficiency in holding public meetings. Local officials should work closely with the MDU's, but attempts to include them in the chain of command have not been successful, partly because they have not the time to spare; they should instead be used to the full as advisers. A high degree of discretion should be left to the mobile teams, within the compass of a plan laid down by headquarters. The lowlier members of the team should be brought up to a minimum level of enthusiasm and responsibility. (One man, even a cook or a driver, can undo good work by the rest of the team.) This requires special attention during training. Team leaders should be in a position to request replacement for unsatisfactory members, and these should be forthcoming from field headquarters.

Reinforcing Success

In general, as Dr. Huff points out, there are some fundamental questions about subversion that the Thai Government has still to answer. The MDU concept is spreading steadily; but the great majority of the Thai Army is still in the vicinity of Bangkok. Like many another government, no doubt, the Thai Government might well be asking itself more urgently what its military priorities should be. Should there not be greater emphasis on training in counter-insurgency and civic action? And if there is a case for training more troops in these techniques, should this not also embrace ex-servicemen? A large proportion of those recruited from the Northeast, for instance, would be happy to return there, and many do; apart from the concept of land settlements, there may be a case for training these men while they are still in the Army for functions that would be useful in civic action after they leave--including positions of responsibility in the villages. There being no record of what becomes of ex-servicemen, it is hard at present to make such use of those who have already left. But steps might be taken to find out where some of them have gone, particularly those with specialist training.

One outstanding feature of this scheme has been the cooperation between the Army and civilian departments, no doubt facilitated by a militaristic government. This close relationship might well be fostered so that the MDU headquarters in Bangkok would obtain greater access to the resources and experience of civilian ministries.

Follow-Up

Above all, the Government faces the problem of having the civil ministries take over effectively from the MDU's after they have moved on. This question of follow-up is the crucial problem of MDU's, and it has still not been solved in Thailand. For the truth about the MDU's is that what was intended to be a purely catalytic mission has become a permanent one. MDU's are remaining in situ. Keeping the pot warm in this way is of the greatest value, providing, as it does, an assurance of continued interest by Bangkok. But the "multiplying factor" is obviously lost if teams cannot keep moving on to open up new ground.

There have been recriminations at the failure to provide for follow-up in the initial 1962 plan. It has been alleged that this was, after all, an almost unique operation and as such would absolutely require some systematic forward planning. On the other hand, the planners can fairly reply that they had only the sketchiest information about life on the northeast frontier and therefore on how far the MDU's would succeed and what the requirements would be after they had left. So slender was this information, in fact, that it appears to have been a deliberate decision to "play it by ear." MDU field commanders were to provide the data on which future planning was to be based. Granted this decision, it was acted on with intelligence. The field commanders were, in fact, given wide discretion in recommending solutions and were listened to with respect.

Though the MDU's have never been fully withdrawn, some qualified transfer of authority has taken place in the earlier ones. MDU field commanders were replaced by local officials-- in one case the Governor. Under him an MDU headquarters in Bangkok agreed to provide a deputy commander and a staff of up to ten people for an unspecified period. The staff included a doctor, road adviser, and two communications men and their equipment to link the deputy commanders in their headquarters' villages with the new commanders. It was then decided to concentrate community development workers to bear the burden of follow-up operations. Thereafter, however, the process of transfer seemed to stall. The Governor in question delegated his authority to the Deputy Governor and the local officials who had been made deputy commanders showed no greater inclination to shoulder their new responsibility. Likewise, the ministries in Bangkok sent few new personnel to the area.

Unexpected Benefits

Mention has been made above of the villagers' reaction to these operations. The MDU's reaction and conclusions, analysed by Dr. Huff, are also of interest. The chief benefits of these operations, in the eyes of the MDU, are a clear understanding of the nature of the subversion in these areas, the cleaning up of crime, and an improved standard of efficiency by the local officials. On the first point, much is being learned here for the first time about the true impact of the Communist appeal; by the same token, a great deal has been done to end the practice of bogus threats of Communism manufactured by local authorities for their own gain or glory. It is now much easier for Bangkok to identify these false charges, so that a very unhealthy and demoralizing practice is now on the decline.

The second by-product, the reduction of crime, is primarily an outcome of improved communications. News of banditry, of which the most common example is buffalo and cattle thieving, now travels much faster, and the authorities can respond more quickly. In addition, of course, the very presence of Bangkok representatives in the form of MDU teams is a form of deterrent, and the success of these teams ensures a considerable volume of intelligence. Moreover, since the MDU's started operating, Army patrols have been brought in to suppress banditry, often with dramatic effects in terms of crime. The Army has a special advantage denied to the local police in that it is able to operate across district boundaries. These boundaries had previously been a great source of comfort to the bandits. One district official declared that this development had been his principal benefit from MDU operations. Clearly, where a man's livelihood depends on one or two head of cattle, the suppression of thieving could be of even greater value than more constructive civic action benefits.

Local Authorities

Not surprisingly, these successes have kept the local police on their toes. They have also greatly improved the degree of initiative in local authority offices. If for no more public-spirited motives, these officials have been quick to associate themselves with MDU projects and the kudos that attaches to them. Their standing is obviously increased if they can provide villages with new projects and the MDU headquarters with new ideas. Inasmuch as these men will have to carry most of the burden when the MDU leaves, this achievement is clearly of scarcely less importance than the suppression of crime.

It is notable that the chief anxiety of the district official is the impending departure of the MDU. This is not because of the cut-off of material assistance; that represents a serious blow since he knows that any further development is dependent on programmes in Bangkok over which he has no influence. His real fear is that the MDU will take with it his only instrument for getting things done. He knows that the MDU commander will accept ideas that are both practicable and worthwhile, and is in a position to act on them at once. Projects that would otherwise take months to arrange, through traditional channels to Bangkok and back, can be set up within days with help from the MDU. Even if the commander has not the resources or the authority to act on a particular project, he has direct telephone access to Bangkok. The presence of the MDU, in short, means that local officials' initiative can be speedily rewarded. Its withdrawal threatens the reverse. This state of affairs must be recognized as a remarkable tribute to the MDU's, whose relationship with local authorities might have been marked by friction.

Vital Machinery

The departure of the MDU would, in fact, mean the end for the vital interdepartmental coordinating machinery at local level. The MDU commander directs and coordinates provincial and district officials from the Ministries of Agriculture, Public Health, etc., in a way that the district commissioner could never achieve by himself. Thus as long as he has the MDU, the district commissioner is in a position of strong influence. Hence there is a case for retaining at least a handful of MDU personnel to guide follow-up operations. For the virtue of the MDU is that its field commanders can funnel the requests for assistance prepared by local experts up to a high-level headquarters that enjoys the confidence and support of the Prime Minister. This short-circuits interdepartmental wrangling. Ultimately, of course, this function might be fulfilled by an overseeing civilian ministry; but the time for that is clearly not yet, granted the security threat.

The MDU follow-up arrangements embody three valuable and related features. First, an impartial coordinating official in each MDU field operations area who can look at the requirements of his region as a whole and adjust the contribution of each ministry accordingly. Secondly, a headquarters staff in Bangkok, which performs much the same function at a higher level. Thirdly, a headquarters unit with sufficient authority to ensure that contributions required of each ministry are fulfilled.

An important task now for the MDU headquarters in Bangkok is to persuade the civil ministries to pull their weight in the follow-up operation. Happily, it has received full support from the Government at the highest level, without which the whole project would collapse. It would also be in a bad way but for the high quality of the MDU's staff, which is on excellent personal terms with most ministries. Again, MDU headquarters commands funds that can make the difference between departmental cooperation and obstruction. Shortage of funds can always be used as an excuse by the civil department, who naturally have other responsibilities elsewhere; it is indeed one of the genuine limitations on the expansion of MDU's.

RESERVOIR OF MANPOWER

But it should not be overlooked that another comparably serious limitation is the reluctance of the Thai Army to commit a greater proportion of its forces--easily the biggest reservoir of organized manpower in the country--to this work. Efforts to enlist a greater number of troops have so far foundered on hoary obstacles like the claims of training requirements, unit integrity, etc.

Again, as noted above, there is a strong case for imparting instruction to national servicemen that would be useful to them on their return to civilian life. Pre-release training, whether industrial or agricultural, is relatively embryonic in Thailand. It could be introduced with special emphasis on those hailing from, and about to return to, the sensitive border areas. The step might lead to something of more general benefit to the economy as a whole, but it could hardly fail to be of immediate impact on the security problem. Though instruction would concentrate on agriculture, it could surely include a wide range of activities connoted by civic action. In a way, indeed, it is curious that the Thai Government, which has blazed such a trail in the promotion of MDU's, lags behind some other countries in this respect. Nor need such training be simply "pre-release." In a counter-insurgency situation, the arts of economic development can be as useful in the hands of the soldier as they are in the hands of the ex-serviceman.

It seems that only when the question of military priorities has been answered can there be a breakthrough to the problem of the MDU follow-up. The MDU, in sum, has proved itself to provide non-material as well as material benefits, and the former would be jeopardized if it were not followed up. Its role as leader, coordinator, and watchdog appears too effective and valuable to be abandoned without causing distress and dislocation.

Thanks to a very low unemployment rate--less than 2 per cent--Britain has had little difficulty in finding jobs for its ex-servicemen. Of the 350,000 who left the services after redundancy had begun to take its toll in mid-1957, only 757 were still registered as unemployed by 1964, and less than 300 of these had been out of work for more than six weeks.

Though the task has been easy by the standards of developing countries, considerable credit must go to the Government's highly effective resettlement service. If this has lately become as good as any in the world, as it has, one of the spurs has been the need to attract an all-volunteer army, with the ending of conscription. It was felt that a decisive inducement to recruits was the assurance that they could obtain a good job when they left.

Even before the ending of conscription, the machinery for resettlement was fairly comprehensive. In 1950, an Advisory Council had been set up under the chairmanship of the Ministry of Labour's Permanent Secretary to advise the Minister, and also the Minister of Defence, on the best means to bridge the gap between service and civilian employment. Under the aegis of this council, agreements were negotiated with various industries, including the nationalized ones, securing concessions on behalf of ex-servicemen, and special arrangements were made to facilitate the entry of ex-servicemen into the Civil Service, the Police and Fire Services. The service departments negotiated agreements with a number of trade unions whereby recognition was accorded to service training and experience in a wide range of trades. These measures worked well. In 1956, of the scores of thousands who had left the regular forces the previous year, there were only about 150 who had registered as unemployed for more than six weeks.

1957 was the crucial year, inaugurating as it did major reductions in the armed forces. To meet this situation a Resettlement Advisory Board was set up, as well as resettlement committees of leading local industries throughout the country. This was the start of what is now known as the Regular Forces

Resettlement Service.   On the Board's advice, special attention was given to making employers aware of the pool of talent
that would shortly become available.   Steps were taken to increase the pre-release advice given to regulars shortly before
discharge, and the scope for pre- and post-release training
available.

Today, the Regular Forces Resettlement Service links together the three services, the Ministry of Labour, and the voluntary organizations that advise servicemen on opportunities
in civilian life. Their respective roles are:

1. The Services:

These provide a Resettlement Information and Advice
Service, including a monthly bulletin.

2. The Ministry of Labour:

This provides comprehensive advisory and placing services, of which the foremost are the Employment Exchange
Service and the Professional and Executive Register (the latter
chiefly used by officers). Every one of the 900 local offices in
the country has on its staff someone entrusted with the special
task of helping ex-servicemen.   In 38 of them a Professional
and Executive Register is maintained to help those interested
in executive posts.

3. Voluntary Organizations:

The Officers' Association, the most important of whose
tasks is to provide employment for officers on leaving the active
list.

The National Association for Employment of Regular
Sailors, Soldiers and Airmen (commonly known as the Forces
Employment Association). This has forty-nine branch offices
at each of which there is a job-finder, and any regular with at
least three years' service may consult the Association about his
civilian prospects. It is approved by the three service ministries and financially supported by the Royal Navy Benevolent
Trust, the Army Benevolent Fund and Corps and regimental
associations, and the RAF Central Fund. Recognized as part
of the Regular Forces Resettlement Service, it receives a grant
from Government funds.

In 1963, the Association placed 12,444 men and women of
the three services out of 16,060 who registered.* The breakdown of these placements was as follows: About a quarter
were placed in Government employment;   of these, a large
majority took advantage of the preference accorded to the ex-
servicemen by the General Post Office.   Three thousand two
hundred and sixty-nine went into private industries--1,301 as
skilled workers, 1,210 as semi-skilled, and 758 as unskilled.
Five hundred and forty went as trainees to private firms, and
51 to Government organizations. Among other main categories
were:

Security, works police	385
Salesmen, representatives	358
Nationalized industries	350
Admiralty establishments	318
Commissionaires, messengers	292
War Department establishments	224
County and municipal offices	199
Shops, distributive trades	190
Supervisory	183
Hotels and catering	148
Radio, radar, and TV	145
Air Ministry establishments	137

Established in 1885, the National Association for Employment of Regular Sailors, Soldiers and Airmen feels a special
responsibility towards long-service men and women.   It has
a particularly good record of success in finding first-class jobs
for the older man.   In fact, statistics show that it is slightly
easier to place the long-serviceman, a measure of the confidence employers have in the reliability of older servicemen.
The Association takes no fees from either applicants or employers.

In 1964, more than 70 per cent of ex-regulars registered
with the Association. Incidentally, one proof of success of its
activities is the fact that building societies will now accept a
firm promise of employment when a member of the Associa-

---

*Most of the rest either found jobs for themselves or went
to the Ministry of Labour's Resettlement Division of the Employment Department.

tion applies for a loan, whereas previously, the serviceman had to wait until he was actually established in a civilian job.

The Officers' Association has found work for some 12,000 officers since 1945. In one recent year, jobs were found for 642 of them. The Association also gives advice or practical assistance on such subjects as pension claims, grants towards education of children, and relief of distress caused by sickness. It works closely with the British Legion and other service charities and runs a number of homes for elderly and impoverished ex-officers. Since it was inaugurated in 1920, the Association has spent more than £5.5 million in cash grants. During 1962-63 alone, more than £100,000 was spent on relief of distress; nearly a third of that went to officers' widows.

Failure to obtain a job, by either officers or other ranks, can no longer be attributed to lack of information. Of particular value here is the Services Resettlement Bulletin, compiled from material which has been approved by an editorial committee comprising representatives of the three service ministries with a representative of the Ministry of Labour in attendance. Its object is not only to help all ranks towards resettlement, but also to provide a source of reference for service officers responsible for giving resettlement information and advice. The bulletin normally contains a general section consisting of articles of interest to the serviceman about to enter civilian life; a reference section, which also includes opportunities offered by employers; and a services information section giving information on matters applicable to each of the services.

The Ministry of Labour in conjunction with the three services has issued brochures advising "What to Do on Leaving the Service and How to Do It."

ADVICE FOR EX-SERVICEMEN

What in fact is the procedure for the ex-serviceman--for instance a soldier--leaving the service? First, all regular soldiers and airmen must appear before a Preliminary Resettlement Board eighteen months before discharge. Attendance is voluntary in the Royal Navy, although the well-advised majority do attend.

Some three months before his service is due to end, the serviceman is invited to a Resettlement Board interview.   At these interviews, representatives of the Ministry of Labour and the Regular Forces Employment Association are normally present. If the soldier already knows what job he wants, they will advise him on how to go about finding it. If not, the interview may give him some ideas.

He will be told what kind of work is available in the area in which he wants to live, or in other parts of the country. After the interview, the employment exchange in his home area and the local branch of the National Association are told about the kind of work he is looking for. The employment exchange will write to ask him to call to discuss his prospects with a member of the staff whose special duty it is to help ex-regulars.   He is advised to do this in good time; otherwise, if he waits till the end of his release leave, he may land himself in a spell of unemployment.

If he cannot find work in his home area, he may be eligible for financial assistance under the Ministry of Labour Transfer Schemes designed to help workers to take jobs in other areas. The serviceman will be told of certain forms of employment in which special arrangements have been made to help ex-regulars.   Chief among these is the Civil Service, where ex-servicemen have for many years had a special claim to jobs such as postmen, office messengers, and employment in the Royal Dockyards and Royal Ordnance Factories.   For almost all posts in the Civil Service that are filled by competitive examination, an ex-regular can deduct his period of regular service from his actual age so as to bring himself within the age limits.   For some Civil Service grades, a proportion of vacancies filled by examination is reserved exclusively for ex-servicemen and, in the clerical and executive classes, at whatever age they leave the service they can take a special examination designed to test general intelligence and education rather than book learning.

Likewise, there are special arrangements for those who wish to enter clerical employment under local authorities. The Army Certificate of Education, First Class, exempts ex-servicemen from the usual qualifying examination for clerical employment. Nationalized industries also give special consideration to the ex-serviceman. The London Transport Executive reserves them a quota of its posts in the basic grades, while other public bodies either give them preference for engagement or relax the normal recruiting age limits in their favour.

PRE-RELEASE TRAINING

Any serviceman who has completed five years' service or more is eligible to take a twenty-eight-day pre-release course either at a higher education centre or by attachment to a civilian firm.   There are two other main centres for pre-release training: Ministry of Labour training establishments for potential supervisors in industry, and technical colleges, where courses of six-weeks' business training are provided under arrangements made by the Ministry of Labour.   The governmental structure under which this programme is administered is an interdepartmental committee comprising representatives of the Ministries of Labour, Education, and Defence.   Some 5,000 officers and other ranks make use of these facilities every year. As with post-release training, these pre-release courses are given on a basis of forecasts made by the Ministry of Labour of the skills that are most likely to be needed in the immediate future (see Appendix H).

The serviceman applying for a pre-release course must state his service qualifications (trade, occupation, and experience), educational attainments, civilian qualifications (including membership of trade union, etc.), and proposed civilian occupation. He must sign a statement recognizing that he will not be entitled to any allowance other than ration allowance, where appropriate, for the period of the course, and that he will be required to pay any expenses or fees incurred.   It is then up to the Resettlement Board to decide whether he is recommended for the course--or, where a Resettlement Board interview has not been held, the recommendation of a Royal Army Educational Corps officer is valid. His application must also be signed by his commanding officer.

The main pre-release training centres are at Catterick and Aldershot, both run by the RAEC.   Number 1 Resettlement Centre at Catterick provides an introductory commerce course;

Number 2 Centre at Aldershot gives particular attention to
manual skills and concentrates on trades introductory courses.
These are principally valuable in initiating the ex-serviceman
in a skill that he will pursue further, on release, in a Government training centre. About 150 students take these courses
monthly. Many of them have only the most tentative idea of
what profession or skill they intend to adopt and may change
their minds in the middle of the course. They, are indeed,
encouraged to circulate round a wide range of workshops in
order to help make up their minds. At present, the choice is
not a very wide one--the courses are mostly in engineering
trades, plus wood machining--but others may be added shortly.

Members of all three services are eligible to study at these
centres, and among the thirty-four students on the household
maintenance course recently were an air vice-marshal, a
group-captain, a wing-commander, two major-generals, a
padre, a colonel, and a WRAC major. (This particular course
includes bricklaying, plastering, concreting, painting, decorat-
ing, glazing, French polishing, soldering, and sash-cord
repairs.) The centre also has a General Studies department
designed to help students to pass civil and public service
examinations. English, arithmetic, and general knowledge are
covered at various levels, and the centres' record of success
in the relevant examinations is well above the national average.
Altogether, some 5,000 officers and other ranks pass through
these pre-release courses annually.

POST-RELEASE TRAINING

After his release, the serviceman is helped to increase his
specialist skill by post-release training. The enabling legislation for this falls under the Employment and Training Act
of 1948, empowering the Minister of Labour to provide training courses to assist people to fit themselves for suitable employment. For ex-regulars, it is provided mainly under the
Ministry of Labour's Vocational Training Scheme, operated
under that Act. It is open to any ex-regular of good character
who has completed three years in the service. It is provided
in a very wide variety of trades at Government training
centres, technical and commercial colleges, and sometimes
in employers' premises.

Under the Employment and Training Act, the following courses are also provided:

1. A six-week business training course at commercial colleges for ex-regular officers and suitable other ranks. This course is designed to ease the transition from service to business life.

2. Courses in the duties and methods of supervision in industry for regular warrant officers and senior NCO's.

During 1962, 732 ex-servicemen were provided with training under the Ministry of Labour's Vocational Training Scheme. Since 1958, when the accelerated outflow from the services began, 4,920 have completed industrial training courses under this scheme; 3,625 officers and 135 other ranks have completed business training courses; and 380 warrant officers and NCO's have completed the supervisors' course.

Education or resettlement officers in the services are kept informed by the Ministry of Labour of post-release training courses available. Application for these courses may be made three months before, and normally not later than twelve months after, discharge from the services, through the local offices of the Ministry of Labour. For some courses, a selection panel (on which is included a representative of the trade) interviews all applicants to determine their suitability.

EDUCATION

It has already been noted that an important prerequisite of successful assimilation to civilian life is an energetic educational programme during service, and here again the British Government has been particularly active since the ending of conscription. A great deal of attention is paid to general education nowadays; Britain must be one of the few countries in the world with an all-officer Education Corps. Courses of preparation for examinations for Army Certificates of Education, Third, Second, and First Class, are established by the War Office (Directorate of Army Education) and administered by the

RAEC*.   Besides these essentially military programmes, courses are also provided in preliminary education to enable soldiers who are backward in basic subjects to reach a level of attainment at which they can benefit from normal courses for ACE, Third Class, and, on a voluntary basis, for GCE and other civilian examinations. Wide facilities for voluntary education include the provision of university assistance, evening classes at technical colleges, etc., correspondence courses, and courses and activities at Army education centres.

In the Navy, all ratings are required to pass or gain exemption from an examination in English and arithmetic before they can be advanced to Leading Rate. Facilities are also provided in all ships and establishments for ratings to study for higher educational examinations (including GCE), which allow them to become candidates for the Special Duties List of officers, or for promotion from the lower deck. As with the other services, the technical training given to artificers and mechanics is aligned with the syllabi and examinations required by the civilian Ordinary National Certificate or City and Guilds of London Institute. Engineer officers at the Royal Naval Engineering College are trained in degree and diploma courses in mechanical and electrical engineering. In addition to these educational opportunities, correspondence courses are also provided for both service and civil examinations and for commercial and academic qualifications.

Similar arrangements exist in the Air Force; the RAF Educational Test is intended to provide an objective for systematic study in a group of subjects at an elementary level, which will serve both as an opportunity for revising education received at school and, for those who wish it, as an introduction to more advanced study, and to provide serving airmen with an opportunity of attaining the educational standards required for promotion to corporal or corporal technician, sergeant or senior

---

*All soldiers attend courses for ACE, Third and Second Class, and these examinations are linked to promotion. All candidates for promotion to warrant officer must pass ACE, First Class.   A corporal requires a Third Class certificate, and a sergeant requires a Second Class Certificate. First Class is about a year below GCE in standard.

technician. An airman needs to pass Part 1 of the test before he can be promoted to corporal or corporal technician. He must pass Part 2 for promotion to the substantive rank of sergeant or senior technician. All airmen who have passed two subjects, including English, in GCE or equivalent examinations are exempt from both parts of the test. Airmen born before January 1, 1921, are exempt from Part 2 of the test. Within the service, an educational standard connoted by a GCE with a suitable range of subjects at "O" and/or "A" level is a requirement for selection for commission, for entry to aircrew training, and for advanced training in some trades. Moreover, the possession of GCE in an acceptable range and standard of subjects is an important qualification for resettlement. Special arrangements have been made with the University of Cambridge Local Examinations Syndicate for servicemen to take the examinations for GCE at "O" and "A" levels at stations at home and overseas. Candidates are not required to pay examination fees. Officers and airmen may also take subjects in GCE under any of the other recognized examining bodies. Instruction in citizenship and current affairs is arranged wherever possible. Facilities are also provided for practical activities such as handicrafts and hobbies of educational value for the encouragement and cultivation of music, art, drama, and other cultural subjects.

As in the other services, airmen are trained to standards that are recognized by most trade unions as sufficient qualification for employment in civil life (see Appendix I). The RAF Education Test and the subsequent GCE are, where possible, geared to the appropriate trades. Each man on discharge is given a certificate of service that records the service and civilian examinations he has passed, the service trade in which he has qualified, and an assessment of his proficiency as a tradesman, including his ability to supervise. Selection for trade and specialist training in the services is based on a system of educational aptitude testing and interview assessment procedure. This is carried out by specially trained officers and men.

Nowadays, of course, a higher proportion of servicemen than ever are already qualified for a trade long before they approach retirement. This is particularly true in Britain, which formerly relied heavily on national servicemen for its technicians, but now has to train many of them from scratch.

A recruit can start learning a trade immediately after his preliminary military training, which normally lasts eight weeks.
Trade training is on the whole more concentrated than in industry, and qualification comes quicker. There are over 200
trades open to the soldier today, and over 100 of them get full
trade union recognition in civilian life. In the Army, under the
Trade Training Scheme, a soldier automatically becomes a
lance-corporal as soon as he has completed a course of training as a technician; this is not true, however, of a tradesman,
which the British Army strongly distinguishes from a technician.

After successfully completing a year's service in a technician trade, he is promoted to the rank of corporal. A total of
five years' service in a technician trade entitles the technician
to promotion to the rank of sergeant, provided he has the necessary educational qualifications.

THE ROYAL ARMY EDUCATION CORPS

Since the RAEC is almost unique in the world, a word may
be in order about its structure. All major policy is formulated at the War Office. The Director of Army Education is a
major-general. His Directorate consists of five branches,
three of which are headed by a colonel, the other two by
lieutenant-colonels. All are staffed by majors and captains.

The Institute of Army Education, which is located at Eltham,
London, relieves the Directorate of purely executive matters
connected with the administration of Army education. It is
commanded by a colonel and has three wings; one, the In-
spectorate, is headed by a colonel who also carries out advanced research in Army education and is staffed by lieutenant-
colonels and majors; the other two, the Technical Wing and
the Children's and Young Soldiers' Wing, are each headed by
a lieutenant-colonel and are staffed by majors and captains.
The Army School of Education and Depot is responsible for the
training of RAEC officers. The commandant is a colonel, and
he has a chief instructor who is a lieutenant-colonel, and a staff
of majors and captains.

The United Kingdom and Territories Overseas are divided into Commands. The principal duties of a chief education officer at Command Headquarters and his staff are to advise the commander on educational matters, to supervise and administer Army education in the Command in accordance with War Office and Command policy, to organize such Command central activities as are necessary, and to maintain liaison with the civilian authorities. The educational staff at the headquarters of a Command usually consists of a chief education officer, who, according to the size of the Command, is a brigadier, colonel or lieutenant-colonel, assisted by majors and captains.

Apart from the considerable task of educating boys at the rate of 12,000 a year, the RAEC may well claim to have more experience of adult education than any body in the country. At any rate, it is constantly experimenting, with impressive results. One example may be cited: the new method of teaching troops to converse in German in just two weeks. This ambitious task was entrusted to Major George Brewer, RAEC, with the object of teaching soldiers in the Rhine Army sufficient German for them to make friendly contact with the local population. He began tackling the problem with two fundamental decisions: to teach oral German orally, and to ignore the intricacies of German grammar.

Because of the shortage of qualified teachers, Major Brewer decided to undertake the training of instructors from all over Germany, who could then return to their units and run courses. He allowed five weeks to train instructors and only two weeks for the instructors to train the troops. Many believed he could never do it, but he succeeded. He started by visualizing a number of everyday situations in which soldiers would be likely to find themselves. He then analysed the words used in these situations and wrote them all down on a huge sheet of paper. From these situations, he formulated 191 sentences, which form the backbone of the course. The final vocabulary worked out at 637 words. This he rightly judged to be more than sufficient to "break the ice"; the soldier himself could take it from there in his contacts with the German population.

The instructors are trained at the Higher Education Centre, Hohne. Each instructor is given a set of tapes recorded by German officers and their wives with several regional inflections. (Much of the time in this course is spent in perfecting accents, and great stress is laid on correct pronunciation. The tape-recorder figures prominently in this five-week course; students record passages and have their pronunciations corrected when they are played back.) Between thirty and forty potential instructors are constantly being trained on this course.

The results of the unit courses have amply vindicated Major Brewer's theory. Indeed, it seems certain that the very concentrated intensity of the course has its advantages.

An analysis of the Hohne course results showed clearly that high attainment in the academic field is not necessarily related to high marks in the colloquial examination. The student with a background of academic training and experience of the classical methods of language teaching often finds himself consciously drawn towards formalized grammatical study, as a result of which his oral fluency is impaired. The average number of marks obtained in this analysis was highest, it is true, at the Honours Degree level, but the next category was the GCE "O" level, followed equally by the GCE "A" and ACE (2) levels. The entry of students with a General Degree level came lowest of all. It must be noted that some of these entries were confined to a very small number of students and do not represent a fair cross-section. Nevertheless, this method of teaching clearly opens up a whole new range of principles in the teaching of languages.

MILITARY-CIVIL ACTION

The peaceful uses of the British armed services, both at home and even more abroad, are considerable. But they are on what might be termed an ad hoc basis. At home, the services do not undertake any major projects to help the economic development of the country. But they render minor assistance when requested to undertake tasks that conform with the following requirements: the work must be done for a public authority or non-profit-making concern and must constitute good military training; the agreement of the trade unions and employers associations must be obtained; the civilian authority must agree to pay for the hire of equipment and any extra costs over and above what is essential for military training.

Within this framework, examples of the routine peaceful uses of the British armed forces include:

1. Construction of temporary equipment bridges for use while permanent bridges are being constructed under civil arrangements, e.g., heavy girder bridges at York in 1960 and Bath in 1961.

2. Construction of short reinforced-concrete bridges and metalled roads for the Forestry Commission, e.g., construction of four miles of metalled road and a sixty-foot pre-stressed concrete bridge and culverts in the area of Otterburn in 1960.

3. The attachment of regular Royal Engineer officers to civil engineering firms working on the Medway bridge between 1960 and 1963, and the Scottish hydroelectric projects in 1950.

4. The attachment of regular Royal Engineer officers to the Ordnance Survey.

5. The use of aerial surveys carried out by RAF aircraft to bring maps and charts up to date.

6. A project for the creation of a common system of air traffic control in the United Kingdom intended to cover both civil and military air traffic. The RAF is cooperating with the civil authorities on this.

An impression of the smaller-scale routine activities of the armed forces may be gained from the following list of undertakings by the Royal Engineers in a single Command--Southern-- during 1964.

Plymouth	Extension and improvements of club sports ground.
Weymouth	Preparation of the site for the new Weymouth Boys' Club building.
Brixham	Extension of a slipway at the Brixham Seamen's Boys' Home.

Exeter	Construction of a Bailey bridge over the railway at Pinhoe, near Exeter, to provide an additional access route to the Devon County Show Grounds.
Niton, Isle of Wight	Demolition of four mast bases for the GPO.
Stonedown Wood, Cranborne Chase	Demolition of a derelict house for the Forestry Commission.
Calne	Emergency water main. Laying of three and one-half miles of PVC piping in five days for the West Wilts Water Board.

At home, the armed forces are always available for first aid in emergencies, most notably during the East Coast floods in 1953, most recently in the Welsh floods in the winter of 1964-65.

Overseas

British armed forces have done a full share of emergency relief work overseas. A notable example was the operation in the wake of "Hurricane Hattie" which devastated Belize, capital of British Honduras. Within forty-eight hours the garrison on the spot was reinforced from Jamaica, and within a fortnight 1,300 British troops--more than half of them flown from Britain in the Army's biggest-ever mercy airlift--were re-establishing public services, fighting disease, and guarding warehouses against looters. The Royal Navy's frigate H.M.S. "Troubridge" sailed at full speed from Jamaica, negotiating unmarked channels into Belize harbour, and landed forty-five men from the Royal Hampshire Regiment, a captain, sergeant, and corporal from the RAMC, and the ship's surgeon-lieutenant. The United States sent two destroyers, an aircraft-carrier and tankers with helicopters, as well as medical supplies. Together they inoculated the whole population against typhoid. These doctors were soon reinforced by the 19th Field Ambulance from Colchester, the 51st Field Surgical Team from the Cambridge Military Hospital, Aldershot, and from the Army School of Health at Mytchett, a light hygiene section, which used over 300 gallons of insecticide to prevent contamination of food by flies.

The operation was a test of the British soldier's versatility. Infantrymen found themselves controlling food queues and cooking the food at one of the emergency feeding centres. Over 2,300 people a day were fed by two Army cooks. In Stann Creek, twenty miles to the south, the Hampshires in cooperation with the town's Disaster Committee evolved a system of allocating food, in return for a day's work, to the able-bodied section of the population.

But more help was urgently needed and the First Battalion of the Worcestershire Regiment, a Sapper field squadron, and small specialist units were flown out from Britain together with sixty tons of supplies. They were transported by a shuttle service of fourteen RAF and five BOAC chartered aircraft. (The Worcesters were chosen partly because the battalion had just spent three years in the Caribbean, and many of its men were old friends to the people of British Honduras.) Having stabilized the situation in Stann Creek, they moved into Belize to relieve the Hampshires. By then, it had become possible to reduce guard duties considerably, and with more men available, goodwill parties were organized to give local people special assistance. Each section was allotted its own area and, guided by the parish priest, set to work helping those most in need. The soldiers found this particularly congenial work. They cleared rubble and mended rooms, floors, walls, and furniture and put up the framework for a new school building outside Belize.

Meanwhile, Sappers of the 12th Field Squadron, a unit of Strategic Reserve of the 38th Corps Engineer Regiment, flew in and quickly settled down to restoring the public services in Belize. They set up a public water point, pumping twenty-four hours a day from a reservoir that had not been completely destroyed, relit the docks and reinstated power poles destroyed in the disaster. The squadron's Plant Section brought in bulldozers to cope with the rubble. Relief supplies sent by the Red Cross, and from Britain, the United States, and other countries were handled at Stanley Airfield by a forward air supply organization. A captain and nine men of the RASC unloaded aircraft and transferred supplies to American helicopters, or sent them to civilian distribution centres. Also working with the forward air supply organization were a detachment of Royal Military Police, and the 468th Courier and Postal Unit, Royal Engineers, which dealt with military mail and also helped Belize General Post Office to clean up its flooded premises.

For much of the time, the joint Army and Navy Command controlled all military operations. Soldiers worked closely with sailors from the frigates H.M.S. "Troubridge" and H.M.S. "Londonderry," while sailors from the survey ship H.M.S. "Vidal" worked with the Sappers in delivering building materials to villages along the swampy coastline.

Throughout the operation the policy was to return the responsibility to the civil authorities as quickly as possible. The Worcesters came home after just over a month and were followed soon after by the remainder of the force.

A measure of the operation's success was the comparatively low casualty rate. In the much less fierce hurricane of 1931 there were 2,000 deaths; in 1961 the figure was a little over 300.

The Skoplje earthquake again found British Engineers on an errand of mercy. Once the initial catastrophe was over, taking with it 1,500 lives, the city's chief problem was the rehousing of over 100,000 people. Just a fortnight after the earthquake, a party of one Sapper officer and six NCO's arrived in the city to supervise the erection of twenty-four Nissen huts. The function of the NCO's was to supervise the conversion of the huts into schools by Yugoslav labour. On August 13, eighteen days after the disaster, Britain offered another twenty Nissen huts. This meant that five schools in all could be built, though it imposed a heavy strain on the Sapper contingent. (It should, of course, be borne in mind that the British contribution was but a small element in an enormous international effort in which Germans, Swedes, Russians, and Danes played at least as great a part.)

The following month, after an appeal by "War on Want" that raised nearly £400,000, no less than 200 more Nissen huts were despatched and the Royal Engineers were called for further assistance. This was provided by a party of 43 men from the 35th Corps, Royal Engineer Regiment. By the time they left at the end of November, 86 huts had been erected, 1,000 metres of road works had been prepared for surfacing, a water tower had been built and the beginning of a water supply had been laid. As a result of their efforts, 2,000 people were accommodated for the winter and 7,000 children were furnished with schoolrooms.

One of the happier features of this reconstruction was the friendly rivalry between national contingents. At one point it looked as though a British Nissen hut would be the first foreign-built structure to go up since the earthquake, but the West German Red Cross managed to complete a house on timber piles while the Sappers were still waiting for their concrete to set. Enthusiasm became infectious; as the final screw was driven home on the first Nissen hut, a great cheer went up from the local population. In the evenings, West German and Yugoslav workers joined in singing English songs, the Sappers tried to reciprocate in German, while British and German soldiers tried gallantly, but unsuccessfully, to master the songs of their hosts.

Less spectacular, but just as important, have been the Army's successful efforts to avert disasters overseas. After a series of forest fires in Hong Kong, there was an urgent need for water storage tanks high in the Jubilee Reservoir area of the New Territories; this could only be provided by moving tons of sand, gravel, and cement over miles of difficult ground. The Army was called in--in this case, the 29th Company RASC (pack transport), "the men with the mules." The convoys covered 30 miles a day with temperatures in the 90's, each mule carrying 150 lbs. Thus, ten tons of material a day were moved, enough for one 2,000-gallon tank. Also in Hong Kong, it became urgently necessary to relieve a water shortage in the island of Kat O. British Engineers provided a 6,000-ft. underwater pipeline assisted by sampan fishermen working without pay.

In East Africa, Royal Engineers saved Nairobi from a serious water shortage after a landslide had broken two large water mains. Requested by the city for help, the Sappers forced their way through dense bamboo forests and swamp in heavy rain and thick mud. They were able to mend the rupture with a twenty-four-inch pipeline.

A less successful bid for water in the same area was an attempt by members of the 16th Company RASC (Air Despatch) to create rain over the parched grazing lands near Nairobi. At the urgent request of the Kenya Government's Meteorological Department, they tried to seed the clouds with salt to make moisture coalesce over an area that had had virtually no rain for six years. Immediately after the first sortie, half an inch of rain did fall. But the second effort was a total failure.

Many and varied are the Army's "peaceful uses" overseas. In Kenya alone, they have included the building of an all-weather airstrip, sixty miles of track for security operations, a bridge over the River Melawa of great value to local farmers, and a climbers' hut on Mount Kilimanjaro; they also helped the Game Department to conserve the Harters Hartebeest, assisted the Kenya Government and the United Nations in discovering the source of Lake Chala, and blasted away dangerous rocks overhanging a railway line.

Such activities have been even more intense in theatres of war. A valuable analysis of engineering projects in Aden and the South Arabian Federation has been made by Brigadier R.L. Clutterbuck, R.E. He points out that up till 1958 there was only one road connecting Aden with the fertile highlands fifty miles inland--the road through Lahej; apart from this, the only access to Aden was either by air or by mule, camel, or foot. This meant that the highlands' exports could only reach market at great cost either in money or time.

In 1959, an independent troop of British Royal Engineers was sent to develop mountain tracks in the area. Their first job was to open a lateral road along the highlands to enable troop formations to move quickly against raids. Initially, the tribesmen were hostile. But when, the following year, a new project was set afoot to link this track with a pass up a sheer 4,000-foot escarpment, the local population began to see that the new road would make an enormous difference to their sales in the markets of Aden.

The Engineers engaged on this work became very popular. The tribesmen realized that the rebels who were soliciting their support could not provide them with such opportunities for advancement. In the last five years, the extent of these road operations has rapidly expanded, and the area has experienced a prosperity never known before.

The British prototype for such operations was, perhaps, Malaya. As Brigadier Clutterbuck also points out, the problem was to root out the Communist guerrillas who were battening on the primitive aboriginal communities. The guerrillas had won their hospitality by helping them to grow more food.

The only way of enlisting their loyalty was by extending to them the benefit of Government services--education, trade, and, above all, medicine. The Special Air Services Regiment, in groups of about fifteen, landed by helicopters and lived in the jungle for thirteen weeks at a time before being relieved; they offered the aborigines an outlet for trade through helicopter and airdrop contacts. Army medical men arrived and were quickly surrounded by patients. Shortly afterwards, engineers would build an airstrip, and this would be followed by a considerable extension of trading, educational, and medical services. The terrorists soon discovered that they were no longer welcome, and their collapse is now part of history. (For the "Do's" and "Don'ts" as formulated for the Hearts and Minds Campaign in Brunei, see Appendix J.)

Shortly after Malayan independence, an operation on similar principles was carried out against the Communist fall-back position near the Thai border. This involved driving a sixty-four-mile road into the region occupied by the Sum-Sums, a half-breed Thai-Malay tribe. The operation, which was followed by a steady flow of trading, educational, and medical services, proved a complete success.

This success is sometimes compared invidiously with the situation in Vietnam. Several factors exist in Vietnam, however, which did not apply in Malaya. It has a common frontier with the Communist bloc that sustains the Vietcong. Identification of guerrillas is much harder than in Malaya, where most terrorists were Chinese. There is practically no civil administration outside the larger towns that is worthy of the name. The National Government also had a more solid base than appears to be the case in Vietnam. But to identify the difficulties of Vietnam is not to minimize the effectiveness of the formula applied to Malaya, which embodies important lessons for the growing number of countries faced with insurgency problems.

It may be of interest that, for all her success in this field, Britain still possesses no organization comparable with the U.S. machinery for civic action, or even France's Special

Administrative Service, which did similar work on a massive scale in Algeria. There is no section of the Defence Secretariat specifically charged with this task. As to financing these operations, there is no vote sub-head for them under the defence appropriation. Accounting is entirely in the hands of local command secretaries. Judged on its record, this ad hoc system seems to work remarkably well. On the other hand, it can raise difficulties. One distinguished officer, during the Honduras disaster related above, bought some equipment, including a water purifier, from the U.S. forces on the scene. He was well outside his authority; he "got away with it" on the strength of being a good officer who had done the sensible thing. Again, the lack of system precludes the establishment of anything resembling the U.S. Civic Action Mobile Training Teams; this would require coordination with the overseas ministries, and joint budgeting. It might be no bad thing if this were done and, at the same time, some of the U.K.'s overseas military training missions were given a "civic" slant.

CHAPTER 21   UNITED STATES OF AMERICA

The United States of America, as a developing country in the eighteenth and nineteenth centuries, was a vigorous exponent of PUMF; much of the opening up of the West was done by U.S. Army Engineers, and this tradition is continued today in flood control and the maintenance of some of the country's major riverworks. With this tradition, it is not surprising that in the 1960's the U.S. has sought to recommend PUMF to her friends overseas. In a way, it is surprising that she did not do so earlier.

The sequence of events was broadly as follows. During the 1960's, in response to the threat of Communism, the U.S. helped to build up considerable armies around the world in the interests of her allies' security. This was in part a reaction to the Korean War. It was felt that other countries might be threatened with a similar experience and that the only safeguard against it was the establishment of a large army capable of deterring that threat.

Whatever the logic of this policy, it had two side effects. One was that this defence effort weighed heavily on these countries' resources, both in money and skilled manpower. The other was that it took little account of the fact that the basic threat to the security of nearly every developing country is that of disaffection and subversion--often owing nothing to outside interference--from within its own borders.

Thus, this policy not only diverted vital energy away from young and tender economies into purely inflationary channels of defence spending. It also produced defence establishments that were unsuited--actually too large, some experts would contend--to meet the challenge with which they were most likely to contend: insurrection. Over-large armies are often liable to fall into the grip of a kind of Parkinson's Law; when organized on a divisional basis, they tend to create ambitions within their ranks that can only be satisfied by the supply of considerable numbers of tanks, bombers, and similar strategic weapons. Just how much use these are in an insurgency situation has recently been demonstrated in Iraq, where tanks have been proved useless for dealing with the Kurdish rebellion. It has also been shown in Vietnam, where quality rather than quantity was the urgent need in the initial stages five years ago.

It is understandable that Korea should have dominated the thinking of Washington in the 1950's. Yet even while Korea was being fought, the U.S. was successfully engaged in a form of warfare that was to prove much more typical of the military problems of the future: the insurrection in the Philippines. It was here, in fact, that the doctrine of civic action in an insurgency context was patiently and pragmatically evolved-- just as the "hearts and minds" technique was simultaneously being evolved by the British in Malaya. The lessons of this operation, coupled with the evident dangers of over-emphasis on large defence establishments, were by no means lost on Washington. In the middle 1950's, a group of State Department experts under Herbert Hoover, Jr. began to ask themselves whether the large armies being built up could not be put to some constructive use. An important subsequent development was the appointment of the Draper Committee in 1958. This committee's report the following year included the recommendation that consideration be given to the use of indigenous forces in the social and economic development of their countries. The idea was incorporated in the basic statute of the U.S. Congress on economic and military assistance the same year. It was carried over and included in the new Foreign Assistance Act of 1961, which, as amended, has governed administration of the U.S. Economic and Military Assistance Program. Section 505 of this act was amended in 1965 to elevate civic action to be one of the purposes of MAP (see Appendix K).

In the light of this act, the Army recommended that a definite programme be undertaken to encourage other countries to adopt measures similar to the programme already being implemented in Korea, under which the armed forces were building hundreds of schools and churches and providing massive medical aid. This recommendation, approved by the Department of Defense on May 9, 1960, formed the basis for the Army's civic action programme.

Ten months later, in a special message to Congress, President Kennedy declared: "To the extent that world security conditions permit, military assistance will in the future more actively emphasize internal security, civil works, and economic growth to the nations thus aided."

The following year he elaborated this doctrine. "Pure military skill," he said, "is not enough. A full spectrum of military, paramilitary, and civil action must be blended to produce success. The enemy uses economic and political warfare, propaganda, and naked military aggression in an endless combination to oppose a free choice of government and suppress the rights of the individual by terror, by subversion, and by force of arms. To win in this struggle, our officers and men must understand and combine the political, economic and civil actions with skilled military efforts in the execution of this mission."

Meanwhile, in late 1961, he had defined three types of situations where civic action would be helpful. These were (1) the subversion situation, where civic action is indispensable to strengthen the economic base and establish a link between the armed forces and the people; (2) even in countries threatened by external aggression, armed forces should undertake civic action so long as it does not impair the performance of their primary mission; (3) countries threatened neither by subversion nor attack should use selected indigenous forces to further economic and social development.

FUNDING MILITARY ASSISTANCE

Initially, when the Department of the Army developed a concentrated programme of encouraging Military Assistance Advisory Groups to promote civic action, it was felt that the cost of this programme must be kept to a minimum and that the project should be capable of being financed by the host government. This principle was soon abandoned for two reasons: (1) some countries simply had no funds available; (2) it was soon evident that an extremely small U.S. outlay could achieve disproportionately large results. A formula was worked out between the Department of Defense and the Agency for International Development for financing these programmes. The Military Assistance Program is authorized to provide funds for equipment and its maintenance (e. g. , bulldozers) and for any training connected with its use. AID is authorized to provide material costs (e. g. , cement for roads) and consumable items (petrol, etc.) used by the military while actually engaged in civic action.

Though the sums of money involved are small in relation to Washington's massive overseas expenditure, this arrangement is of interest. Without some such formula, local civic action initiatives can be completely stultified. (If, for example, a British officer wishes to bequeath the engine of a defunct motor vehicle to a village, where it would be useful for operating a well, he may have difficulty in accounting for the transaction.) Under the U.S. system, civic action programming and funding are heavily influenced by the U.S. Country Team (civilian and military officials under the ambassador). They will propose which portion of the funds for a project should come from AID or MAP, who will furnish the technical advice, and what method of operation to emply.

MOBILE TRAINING TEAMS

To provide this technical advice, a new instrument was developed: the Civic Action Mobile Training Team (CAMTT). This consists normally of anything from one to four people, though if the situation requires it, it may reach platoon strength. It comprises experts in one or more of the following fields: governmental affairs, civic action, engineering, medical and/or public health, sanitation, psychological operations, agriculture, education, and public relations. Its task is four-fold: (1) to keep the Country Team informed of civic action operations; (2) to identify areas where civic action could be useful; (3) to develop a civic action programme; (4) to provide training and guidance for local forces and specific technical assistance.

CAMTT specialists occupy themselves with the following tasks:

The civil affairs officer advises on civil-military relationships, governmental organization at all levels, public administration, and public relations.

The engineer advises on construction and repair of road-, rail-, and waterways, bridges, building of all kinds, water utilities, fire protection arrangements, mapping projects, insect and rodent control.

The medical/public health and sanitation member advises on hospital and dispensary needs, preventive medicine programmes, requirements for medical supplies, vaccines and equipment, instruction in basic sanitation, first aid and hygiene, and food inspection.

The agricultural expert advises on crop improvement, pest and wild game control, irrigation and water storage needs, fertilizer needs and harvesting needs.

The educational expert advises on training programmes that the military services could initiate in order to give their own members basic education and technical training useful in civilian occupations, and requirements for school buildings, school equipment, and instructors.

These teams are themselves advised before leaving the U.S. to find out what civic action is being done and how the local population is reacting to it. In preparing a civic action programme, they are instructed to consider the following factors: what the military high command needs to do in the way of instructing the lower echelons; what organization would be required to carry out a civic action mission; the training required to accomplish civic action projects or prepare servicemen for civilian life; the basic needs of the area; specific projects that the military forces can undertake at little experience; whether it would be useful to establish joint military-civilian local councils.

A number of criteria for civic action are also laid down as follows:

1. A few small projects done well will be far more effective than a broad effort that will overtax the ability for the available resources.

2. CAMTT men must be prepared to work alongside local labour, and not just direct.

3. Good listening is of the essence. (This point recurs again and again as one of the foremost lessons of civic action experience around the world.)

4. Work through the channels.   It is a grave mistake to acquire the image of a special unit that answers only to headquarters.

5. Start slowly.

6. The team should know when to step out of the act.   The local people should be encouraged to "go it alone."

As already indicated, some CAMTT's may be as large as platoon strength.   One, which recently went to advise Guinea, consisted of about twenty-five men.   It was led by a major, with a captain under him as Executive/Operations Officer. The rest of the team was made up of one sergeant-major;   one administrative NCO; a maintenance officer plus motor maintenance sergeant and two enlisted men;   a three-man team specializing in bridging, demolitions, and field constructions; another three-man team specializing in permanent construction--buildings, utilities, and roads;   and a third such team specializing in engineering equipment. In addition, there was a supply officer, a food service supervisor, and a medical specialist.   To this last group and to each of the other subunits was attached an interpreter. But in addition to this special expertise, the commander and ten team members had acquired proficiency in the French language.

Some teams are more heavily accented in the direction of counter-insurgency than this one. The supply of experts in this field presents fewer problems than that of experts in civilian skills, some of the most valuable of which are relatively scarce in the military services. Specialists in education, agriculture, and economics are not normally numerous outside active Army civil affairs units.   A move is afoot to sift out those whose training or educational background includes these skills and second them for this type of work.   Those whose military skills lend themselves readily to adaptation to civilian purposes--men in medical, signals, engineer, transportation, and other technical units--are receiving training in such adaptation.   The Civil Affairs School at Fort Gordon, Georgia, operates a six-week course on a quarterly basis.   This has become the focal point for formal civic action training within the Department of Defense.

By the end of the financial year 1964, the U.S. Army had despatched 76 CAMTT's to more than 20 different countries. It also provided instruction at Fort Gulick, the Canal Zone, known as the School of the Americas, where over 400 troops at a time from 19 Latin American countries study civic action techniques integrated into courses lasting from 2 to 40 weeks. The school has graduated 15,000 Latin Americans and 10,000 U.S. servicemen in every kind of military skill including, in part, those in the civic action field.

LOW COST OF PROGRAMMES

As noted above, the cost of the U.S. investment in civic action programmes is small. Between 1961 and 1964, in programmes involving more than 30 nations, the cost was no more than U.S. $100 million. Its biggest single MAP civic action outlays in Latin America for the fiscal year 1965 have been U.S. $2.4 million each in Peru and Brazil. (On the record of past years, the AID appropriation here would be smaller.) In the financial year 1965, Colombia was programmed at just over a half-million U.S. dollars (MAP) and just under that through AID. In Argentina, Brazil, Chile, Colombia, Korea, Paraguay, Peru, Thailand, and Vietnam, the MAP civic action appropriations exceeded U.S. $1 million in a single year prior to the financial year 1966. The same applies to the AID appropriations in Bolivia, Brazil, Korea, Thailand, and Jordan. Just over a million dollars covers the MAP appropriation, and less than a million dollars covers the AID appropriation, for the whole of Africa, South Asia (Malaysia to India), and the Near East combined. In this category the biggest--indeed, the only considerable--effort has gone into Iran and Jordan and, to a lesser extent, Senegal and Liberia.

President Johnson is a supporter of civic action. In August, 1964, he addressed this statement to a conference of U.S. and Latin American army chiefs of staff: "It is not sufficient that the military protect our lands from outside interference or attack. In addition, it is the responsibility of each of us to contribute to the security and well-being of our fellow citizens by working together for military and civic progress." He has followed this up with a strong affirmation of his faith in civic action in his 1966 Foreign Aid programme.

COMMUNITY RELATIONS

The U.S. Defense Department is responsible for well over a million Americans, including some half a million dependents, living in about ninety countries throughout the world. They are performing a military function at the request of the host government--but this obviously does not automatically give them a passport to the hearts and minds of the local community.

Washington makes no bones about the fact that good community relations are a facet of the military function. An Army manual states: "Community relations is that command function that appraises the attitudes of the civilian community toward the command, as well as the attitude of the command toward the civilian community, and initiates programs of action to aid community respect and confidence."

This takes many forms throughout the world. In Germany, a major technique for cooperation is the German-American Advisory Council. There are more than fifty such councils in Germany, in which the local Army Commander, his provost-marshal, his chaplain, special-service officer and others meet with their counterparts in German civilian life. Among the many issues that come up for discussion, traffic accidents are inevitably a perennial subject--as, of course, they were in the Congo. Agreement is reached on a uniform code for recreational facilities and arrangements are made with retail associations.

These Advisory Councils, though highly successful in Germany, do not seem to be universally applicable. They are evidently disliked in France, for instance, where they appear to revive memories of the German occupation. In Italy, things are handled more informally, simply through a provost-marshal and the head of the local police, without reference to any larger body.

Community relations can embrace a wide range of activities: football and judo matches, a joint conference of professional men, concerts, support for local orphanages, help in emergency situations, and even children's tea-parties.

One particularly American difficulty, though equally applicable to many United Nations contingents, is the disparity
in standards of living between the visiting contingent and the
host community. In the past, of course, this has caused
friction as between different contingents of the United Nations;
but the local community itself can feel "occupied" if visiting
servicemen should happen to spend their money in an ostenta-
tious fashion. Every effort should clearly be made to prevent
the visiting serviceman from queue-jumping on the strength of
his superior income; this probably leads to more slogans on
walls than most other causes of friction put together.

But individual incidents of crime can also be disproportionately damaging. The Americans rightly insist on the highest
standard of law-enforcement; they also find that crime
prevention may be facilitated by pairing with local police on
highways, in dance-halls, or in red-light areas.

Simple good manners are correspondingly important, though
harder to enforce. If troops cannot be inducted into the customs of the local country, they should at least be warned to
make allowances for them in advance. In a word, they should
be made to realize that this is not their country. A visiting
contingent can very easily behave as if it owned the place;
this is the one sin to avoid at all costs. Every country has
features that may strike the visitor as odd, or even ludicrous,
but only those who live there have the right to point them out.

The American Government takes considerable care to
prepare men for life abroad. This is done through special
Community Relations Officers and, as far as possible, men are
given specific orientation on the country they are to visit.
They will be given general background on vocabulary, history,
culture, and customs. The base Community Relations Officer
may be the same person as the Public Information Officer, or
may work under him. In the past, these posts often attracted
the second best, but now training and selection has become
increasingly careful. Sometimes the Army overseas will call
in an experienced newspaperman to act as a civilian community
relations worker; he will have acquired special knowledge of
the country over a period of years, and will probably speak the
language with a fluency which no visiting serviceman could
rival.

So successful have such civilians been in this post that it has been suggested that troop service educational programmes should be based on a different kind of specialist than at present is the case. He would be a counsellor, not a commander--an expert in the political and social sciences. The idea, however, has so far been rejected on the ground that it could smack of political indoctrination.   But whatever form the community relations guidance takes, this is a vital function of overseas service of any kind.   It deserves the fullest support of commanding officers.

APPENDIXES

The main study lists the advantages and pitfalls of PUMF and, on examination, these are also present in costing. The central issues are: availability of private sector contractors, and accessibility. The normal mobility of armed forces provides them with lower cost accessibility to remote projects. Private contractors will perform in almost any part of the world--but the costs would be prohibitive in many sectors.

Two cost-favourable examples of contractors--PUMF versus civilian--are listed below.

MILITARY-CIVIL COMPARISONS

Where they do compete, however, comparisons are of interest.

In Peru, a local contractor and military civic action units each completed a six-mile section of road through mountainous rainforests as part of a project to open up a colonization area. The local contractor charged U.S. $132,000. Civic action units did their section for U.S. $33,454. (The breakdown for the civic action job was as follows: materials, $18,560; troop pay, including food and uniforms, $5,202; depreciation of equipment, $7,035; U.S. mobile training teams (two), $2,657. No civilian labour was used in this project.)

A breakdown of comparative costs (civilian contractor first, military unit second) are as follows: (1) excavation (per cubic metre), $0.60 against $0.46; (2) structural excavation (per cubic metre), $1.06 against $0.79; (3) reinforced concrete (per cubic metre), $100 (both); (4) cyclopean concrete for foundation, 50 per cent rock enlarging (per cubic metre), $15.67 against $14.67; (5) installation of cement pipe (per metre), $10.00 against $0.25.

As category (5) clearly shows, this was a labour-intensive concept. With civilians earning up to a dollar a day, and conscripts a mere ninety cents a month, civic action for a labour-intensive project is unquestionably cheap.

A second example from another continent: the famous Gilgit Road in West Pakistan up to the Himalayas would not have been achieved at all without PUMF. Until 1958, the only land route was a mule track, just negotiable by jeeps, built by the Army Engineers in 1948-49. As this traversed a 14,000-foot pass that was open for only three months of the year and had to be reinforced by an air route, the Gilgit Agency was inaccessible for commercial purposes. In 1956, the Central Public Works Department prepared a plan reportedly costing around 60.6 million rupees. This was far too expensive, and to cut down costs the Army's assistance was sought. In 1958 it was decided to entrust the project to the Army Corps of Engineers. The revised estimates came to 30.5 million rupees, thus releasing resources for other development projects. Work began in January, 1959, and it was due for completion by the end of 1965.

It was a cooperative effort between the Army Corps of Engineers and the Public Works Department. The Army undertook the 158-mile stretch from Karora to Chilas, where not even a proper footpath existed. The estimated cost of this sector was 20.4 million rupees. The PWD undertook the 87-mile stretch from Chilas to Gilgit, where a jeep road already existed and the work principally involved widening it. Estimated cost of this section was 8 million rupees. Even here, however, it was expected that the Army Engineers would have to help in order to speed up the work.

The Corps of Engineers had deployed some 750 of their troops, and they hired about 1,000 local civilian labourers. The project was one of the most arduous of its kind in the world. Every foot of the new road had to be blasted with explosives. The Corps of Engineers benefited greatly from previous experience in hill road construction, but this was their toughest assignment yet and more than 20 lives were lost.

The Gilgit Road is a good example of an army helping to pay for itself. For it was estimated that its use would save the Pakistan Government large sums of money spent in subsidizing the transport charges for food that had to be imported into the Gilgit area, either by air or through the 14,000-foot pass. It is PUMF at its best.

BELGIAN EMERGENCY USE CONVENTION

CONCLUDED BETWEEN the Departments of Finance, Interior,
Public Works, Agriculture, Industry, Middle-Class Af-
fairs and Interior Trade, Communications, Labour and
Social Protection, Transport, National Company of
Belgian Railways, Concessionary Railway Companies, the
National Company of Regional Railways

ON THE ONE HAND

and the Department of National Defence

ON THE OTHER HAND

with a view to ensuring the aid of troops to Administrations of
Communes, Civil Engineering, Water and Forests, Mines,
Post-Telegraph-Telephone, to the National Company of
Belgian Railways, to the Naval Administration, to the
various Railway Companies, etc., in cases of emergency.

CHAPTER ONE

CASES WHEN THESE EVENTS
DO NOT AFFECT PUBLIC ORDER

I.   Apart from cases of employing military manpower for
the maintenance of public order, which are governed by other
regulations, and with a view to meeting unexpected emergencies, namely, extraordinary events and accidents such as:
floods, landslides, snowfalls, repairs of electric lines damaged
with malicious intent, hurricanes, frosts, fires in State forests
or communal or public establishments, breaches in dams or
causeways, etc., the Department of National Defence authorizes the Lt. Governors of Provinces or, in case of urgency,
the Commanding Officers of Districts or the Detachment Com-

manders, to place troops at the disposal of the National Company of Belgian Railways, the National Company of Regional Railways, the Concessionary Railway Companies, the Postal, Telegraph and Telephone Administrations, the Naval Administration, the Water and Forests, and the Civil Engineering Administrations if, after having exhausted the facilities at their disposal, these Administrations or Companies have no other means of meeting the situation.

II.   The officials listed below are solely qualified to address to the Lt. Governor of the Province and, in case of urgency, to the Commanding Officer of the District nearest to the place where the assistance of the troop is recognized as absolutely indispensable, or to the Detachment Commander, a request specifying the number of men required and, as far as possible, the equipment, the amount and nature of tools required, the place to which they should be transported, as well as the event motivating the operations:

a) for the Société Nationale des Chemins de Fer Belge (National Company of Belgian Railways): the chief engineers, the principal engineers, the principal inspectors, the stationmasters, the engineers running workshops and sheds, technical inspectors, chiefs of section and technicians acting as chiefs;

for the Société Nationale des Chemins de Fer Vicinaux (National Company of Regional Railways): the Director of regularly operated lines or the Administrator-Delegate for a line or group of lines on lease (concessionary companies);

for the Compagnie du Chemin de Fer du Nord (Railway Company for the North)--Northern Belgian Lines: the Inspector General and his assistant, the principal inspector, the engineer of the traffic department, the railway track engineer, the chiefs of sections and stationmasters;

for the Compagnie du Chemin de Fer de Chimay (Railway Company of Chimay): the Director of the Company and the Inspector of Operations;

for the Compagnie du Chemin de Fer de Malines (Railway Company of Malines), at Terneuzen: the Administrator General Director;

for the Naval Administration: the Director General, the piloting director at Antwerp, and the assistant director of liners in Ostend;

b) for the Postal Administration: the regional postal directors or their assistants, or, in their absence, the postal collectors;

c) for the Telegraph and Telephone Administration: chief engineers, regional directors or their assistants, chiefs of technical sections and, when necessary, the telegraph and telephone officials;

d) for the Water and Forest Administration: the principal inspectors, inspectors, sub-inspectors and general keepers;

e) for the Civil Engineering Administration: the chief engineers directors, engineers and foremen of Civil Engineering, architects in general service or their substitutes.

The request in case of need may be made by telegram, which shall be confirmed immediately in the customary way.

III.   The above officials shall not address their requests to more than one Lt. Governor of the Province at a time. If the number of men required exceeds that which the nearest garrison can provide, or if it lacks skilled manpower, the Lt. Governor shall promptly take steps to secure the necessary reinforcements or men from the garrisons nearest to the spot where the troops are to be sent. If these reinforcements there belong to the garrison of another province, he shall reach an agreement on this matter with the Lt. Governor of that province.[*]

The Lt. Governors shall report without delay to the Department of National Defence (Army Headquarters, 1st Section).

---

[*]He can, for instance, upon the request of the Chief of Section of the National Company of Belgian Railways, despatch the troops in such a way as to clear the railway line promptly by effecting operations from both ends.

In case of extreme urgency, requests may be addressed:

a) to the Commanding Officer of the District, who shall take the necessary steps along the above lines;

b) in localities where there is no Lt. Governor or District Commanding Officer: to the troop Commanders stationed near-by who are in a position to meet requests for assistance.

In either case, the Commanding Officer of the District or the Detachment Commander shall notify the Lt. Governor of the Province, direct or by telephone or telegraph and shall confirm his notification through the official channels by an explanatory report regarding the steps he was obliged to take himself and on his own responsibility.

The Lt. Governor of the Province shall report immediately to the Department of National Defence (Army Headquarters, 1st Section).

If the troops coming under "b)" above are in transit--marching to camps or drilling--or if their services are needed for more than one day, the Lt. Governor of the Province receiving the request shall take the necessary steps to have the troops in transit duly relieved by barracked troops, so that the programmes of marches or drilling are not seriously disrupted.

If there is no great urgency, the requests received by the Commanding Officer of the District or the Detachment Commanders shall be transmitted by them, at the cost of the administration employing the troops, to the Lt. Governor of the Province.

In no case shall troops on their way to maintain or restore public order (strikes, disturbances, riots, etc.) be spared to meet requests for assistance, since, under the circumstances, any delay would result in grave damages to persons and property.

Neither may troops of educational institutions or paid military workmen be called upon for assistance.

IV.   The troops shall travel in the uniforms determined by the Commanding Officer or the Detachment Commander, according to circumstances and the nature of the operations; they shall bring camping equipment and all necessary and readily transportable tools; they shall be admitted to passenger or merchandise trains of the lines run by the National Belgian Railway Lines, the Concessionary Railway Companies or the Regional Railway Companies that can transport them with the greatest speed to the place where they are awaited; the stationmasters shall receive from the Lt. Governor of the Province, the Commanding Officer of the District, or the Detachment Commanders all the information necessary to organize the transportation of the troops required.

For the Regional Railways, this information shall be addressed to the Director responsible for the lines regularly in operation or to the Administrator-Delegate in the case of lines run by Concessionary Companies.

Transportation expenses shall be borne by the Administration having applied for Army assistance.

If this assistance was requested by the National Company of Belgian Railways, the troops shall be transported free of charge on all the lines of that Company, on regional lines, as well as on concessionary lines, there and back, upon presentation of a duplicate copy of the application for manpower; this copy shall be annexed to the request and shall serve in this particular case as a travel voucher.

On a reciprocal basis, free transportation shall be granted in identical conditions to troops placed at the disposal of the National Company of Regional Railways or of Concessionary Railway Lines, when they travel on lines of the National Company of Belgian Railways to reach a regional or concessionary line.

The military authorities shall specify, on the duplicate copy of the application, the number of officers, non-commissioned officers, corporals, privates, and vehicles to be transported. The duplicate copy, duly completed, shall be endorsed by the stationmaster upon departure and collected by him on the way back for his accountancy records.

Troops whose assistance was requested by an Administration or agency not specified in the present Article (paras. 4 and 5) are transported at the expense of the said Administration or agency at half price, upon presentation of Form 33 annexed to the Regulations for Military Railway Transportation.

The statements made out for this purpose shall be marked clearly, in red ink, as follows: "On behalf of.....employing body..." If transportation (equipment or troops) is effected by motorized Army vehicles, the Corps shall present invoices based on the official scales for lease and by addressing these invoices, with an accompanying memorandum, to the Department of National Defence (Service of Motorized Vehicles and Fuel), who shall do the needful.

V.   If the troops placed at the disposal of the assisted Administration are unable to bring all the necessary tools and equipment, additional supplies shall be shipped as rapidly as possible, at the expense of the Administration concerned; this will also be done if in the course of operations additional tools are found to be indispensable.

The Lt. Governor of the Province, the Commanding Officer of the District, or the Detachment Commander may, upon the request of the above officials or agents, apply in writing for the necessary tools and equipment to the Commanding Officer or the Head of the Engineering Detachment, the Engineering Commander, the Technical Assistant of Military Buildings, or the Accountancy Officer for Artillery Equipment (or, in his absence, to the adjutant in charge of equipment) in their own or in a neighbouring region.

These officers and the technical assistants of Military Buildings are authorized in urgent cases, to deliver, in a temporary capacity, the tools, etc. for which a request has been made, in writing, by the said officials or agents.

VI.   The senior official or agent present on the spot shall notify the Lt. Governor of the Province or the Commanding Officer of the District of the return of the troops.

VII.   The servicemen shall remain under the authority of their immediate superiors.

VIII.   The assignment of men and the distribution of labour shall be effected by mutual agreement between the Chief of Detachment and the senior officer or agent present.

IX.   For the execution of operations, the military shall conform to the directions of the official or agent representing the Administration that applied for assistance.

He shall report to the Chief of Detachment, when necessary, regarding any serviceman giving rise to serious complaints.

X.   Any sick or injured servicemen who can be transported shall be sent to a military hospital; those who are not transportable, in default of a military hospital, shall be cared for on the spot in a civilian hospital, when available.

The employing authorities shall pay direct for the hospitalization of servicemen receiving treatment in a civilian hospital or with private persons.   They shall also pay for medicines provided to non-hospitalized servicemen.

With regard to servicemen admitted for treatment into military hospitals, the amount due for hospitalization shall be claimed from the authorities employing the military manpower and paid to the Department of National Defence, General Civilian Administration, Claims Office.

XI.   The Department of National Defence is not responsible for any expenses incurred for the period during which the troops are placed at the disposal of another Administration.

Therefore, if a serviceman is the victim of an accident, or if he contracts an illness, resulting in disability entitling him to a pension under the provisions of the laws governing military pensions, this pension shall be settled by the Department of National Defence, and the amount shall be refunded to the Treasury by the Administration employing the troops.

If an accident or illness leads to the death of a serviceman, the same procedure is applied with regard to pensions, if any, to his widow, orphans, parents, or dependents, payable under the provisions of the laws on military pensions, or to expenses for funerals and the return of the body to the family.

These pensions, allowances or compensations constitute a minimum for reparations. Consequently, the employing Administration shall be directly responsible for paying not only the above pensions and expenses but also for any other forms of compensation which may be granted either by the Court or out of Court, to servicemen or to their dependents, under the provisions of Common Law.

If the deceased serviceman has won Front-Line Service Stripes ("chevrons") but not yet reached the prescribed age for the allowance therefor, the Administration concerned shall refund the State for any extra expenses incurred from the premature payment of a pension to the widow and orphans, if any.

The Administration shall fulfil all the obligations resulting from accidents befalling any other persons in the performance of the operations.

The amounts due for pensions, allowances, funerals, and expenses for the transfer of the body to the family, for expenses resulting from the premature attribution of allowances for Front-Line Service Stripes or from pensions due to the Widows' and Orphans' Fund, shall be claimed by the Department of National Defence, General Civilian Administration, Secretariat and Claims Office.

XII.   Allowances shall be paid by the employing Administration to the servicemen of the detachments concerned from the day on which they march out to the day inclusive of their return.

They are established as follows:

a) In the case of remuneration for the assistance of troops to the Administrations specified in Articles I and II of the present Convention as well as to Communes:

Senior Officers	53	francs
Subaltern Officers	45	"
Non-Commissioned Officers	15	"
Corporals	11	"
Privates	7.50	"

b) In the case of remuneration for the assistance of troops to private enterprises (Article XVIII):

Senior Officers	85	francs
Subaltern Officers	60	"
Non-Commissioned Officers	30	"
Corporals	20	"
Privates	15	"

These allowances can be subjected to no reductions or deductions.

Servicemen who are heads of families (married, widowers, legally separated or divorced with children of under twenty-one years of age exclusively dependent on them) shall further receive, at the expense of the relevant Administration, the daily allowance for "separation" provided for in the Regulations defining the rights to various allowances and benefits.

The present scale of allowances is the following:

Senior Officers	15	francs
Subaltern Officers	10	"
Non-Commissioned Officers	8	"
Corporals	6	"
Privates	6	"

When the work requires the assistance of experts (divers, etc.), they shall be remunerated at the expense of the employing Administration, in accordance with the scales established by the Department of National Defence.

Allowances are paid daily to servicemen of lower ranks; those due to officers are paid on Saturdays or on the last day of participation in operations when they are not concluded at the end of the week.

XIII.   The payment of allowances under Article XII shall be ensured by the military authorities, and the Administration employing the services of the troops shall refund these expenses direct to the body concerned, upon receipt of nominal statements (weekly or daily, as the case may be) specifying, in addition to the working days, the ranks, the civil status of dependents, and the various allowances due to each.

XIV.   If the length of service, from the date of departure from the barracks to the date of return, is less than six hours, the above allowances are reduced by half.

XV.   The Administration concerned shall also ensure the billeting of the troops placed at its disposal in localities devoid of garrisons.   These premises may be ensured by means of requisition, at the expense of the said Administration.

In garrison towns the troops shall be housed in State barracks whenever possible.

The Administration concerned shall also cover the cost of any drinks and additional food which may be provided to staff on guard, staff cooperating in operations at night or, generally speaking, of any additional expenses resulting from the services rendered by the troops.

Officers shall be responsible for their own housing and meals and shall cover the cost thereof out of the allowances provided for under Article XII.

XVI.   Any compensation for clothing, equipment, tools, camping articles and, subsequently, for any special work for which the servicemen are employed shall be effected at the cost of the Administration having applied for the troops.

Any replacement of articles lost or destroyed in the course of operations, as well as damages incurred by motorized vehicles having been put to abnormal use, shall be borne by the above Administration.

After the return of troops to their garrisons, the units concerned shall transmit to the employing authorities the necessary statements of expenses specifying all the items listed in the preceding paragraphs.

The Commanding Officers shall first of all apply to the Department of National Defence (Quartermaster General, Administration and Supplies, Service of Armaments and Ammunition, Technical Engineering Service, or Service of Motorized Vehicles and Fuel, as the case may be) to ascertain:

1. The value of the objects lost or damaged;

2. The amount due for clothing, equipment, material, etc. ;

3. The assignment of the sums claimed for the above.

XVII.   Five days after their return to the garrison, the Detachment Commanders shall submit to their immediate superiors a detailed report on the mission they were called upon to accomplish.

In conformity with the duties and procedure laid down for military authorities in case of accidents, this report shall be accompanied by a nominal statement regarding any servicemen who died, were injured, or fell sick in the course of their mission, and relating in each instance the circumstances of the death, injuries, or illness.

A similar report shall be submitted if, after returning to his garrison, a serviceman is stricken by an illness the causes of which can be attributed to any special duty he was called upon to perform in the course of operations.

When necessary, a detailed list of damages undergone and reparations due (Article XVI) shall be annexed to the report.

This report and this list shall be transmitted to the Department of National Defence with the comments of the responsible chiefs.

XVIII.   The above provisions shall be fully applied to the troops placed in the circumstances specified in Article I at the disposal of communes or companies exploiting public services (gas, electricity, water, etc.), as well as of private enterprises.

The employment of military manpower on behalf of communes, enterprises, etc. mentioned in the preceding paragraph is subjected to a written statement on the attached form signifying that the employers have taken due note of the present Convention and commit themselves to comply with all the provisions specified in Articles X, XI, XII, XIII, XIV, XV, and XVI.

CHAPTER TWO

EMPLOYMENT OF MILITARY MANPOWER FOR
THE MAINTENANCE OF PUBLIC ORDER

I.   Cases When the Army Is Appointed to Supply
a Deficiency in Civilian Manpower

The Army may be appointed to supply a deficiency in civilian manpower for the maintenance of order, namely:

a) To ensure the operations of establishments and services indispensable to the daily life of the Army and the population, such as gas or electric power installations with the fuel they require, telegraph and telephone centres, water installations, railway lines, food industries, and so forth.

b) To ensure certain urgent and indispensable operations to protect those who are called upon to guarantee the integrity and safety of mines, such as pumping, ventilation, upkeep of outlets, and so forth.

Nevertheless, the assistance of the Army, whose means are always limited, can only be extended to the extent that it is needed to protect public interests and order and when there are no other means to meet the situation. In case of shortage in military manpower, priority shall be given by the responsible authorities to the establishments and services specified in paragraph "a)" above.

II.   Conditions Determining Authorization for
           Employment of Military Manpower

Authorization for the employment of military manpower may
only be granted to meet requests addressed by Governors of
Provinces.   These requests shall be accompanied by written
statements from the authorities concerned certifying that the
establishments are indeed of public utility and specifying the
purpose for which the manpower is required: to protect the
establishment or to ensure the daily life of the Army and the
population.

The employment of military manpower on behalf of civilian
bodies is subordinated to a written declaration made in accordance with the attached form stating that the applicants have
taken due note of the present Convention and commit themselves to cover all the expenses specified in Articles IV, V,
and VI.   This declaration is transmitted to the Commander of
the detachment of workers immediately upon his arrival on the
spot.

The authorities making the request and the military authorities shall both see to it that the military manpower provided
and the duration of employment are fully justified by requirements.   The requisition is made for a maximum period, but
may be renewable for another ten days, if necessary.

III.   Method of Establishment and Transmission
           of Requests for Military Manpower

The requests of the public administrations and the conces-
sionaries of services of public utility and private enterprises
shall be addressed to the Governor of the Province.

Requests for assistance to guard against an imminent danger
in mines shall be addressed by the engineers of the mines concerned to the Governor of the Province. These requests shall
specify the nature of the work to be effected and the number of

men required. They shall state the purpose for which the manpower is needed, whether solely to safeguard the mine, or to
safeguard the mine and at the same time ensure the daily life
of the Army and the population. The Governor of the Province
shall transmit the requests, if necessary, to the Lt. Governor
of the Province together with the statements specified in
Article II, paragraph 1.

IV.   Methods of Execution

a) Uniforms and Transportation.

The troops shall travel in the uniforms decided upon by the
Commanding Officer or the Detachment Commander according to circumstances and the nature of the operations.

They shall bring camping equipment and all necessary and
readily transportable tools.

They shall be admitted to passenger or merchandise trains
of the lines run by the National Belgian Railways Lines, the
Concessionary Railway Companies, or the Regional Railway
Companies that can transport them with the greatest speed to
the place where they are awaited.

The stationmasters shall receive from the Lt. Governor of
the Province, the Commanding Officer of the District, or the
Detachment Commanders all the information necessary to
organize the transportation of the troops.

For Regional Railways, this information shall be addressed
to the Director responsible for the lines regularly in operation,
or to the Administrator-Delegate in the case of lines run by
Concessionary Companies.

Transportation expenses shall be borne by the company having applied for Army assistance.

If this assistance was requested by the National Company of
Belgian Railways, the troops shall be transported there and
back free of charge on all the lines of that Company, on re-

gional lines, as well as on concessionary lines, upon presentation of a duplicate copy of the application for manpower; this
copy shall be annexed to the request and shall serve in this
particular case as a travel voucher.

On a reciprocal basis, free transportation shall be granted
in identical conditions to troops placed at the disposal of the
National Company of Regional Railways or of Concessionary
Railway Lines when they travel on lines of the National Company of Belgian Railways to reach a regional or concessionary
line.

The military authorities shall specify, on the duplicate copy
of the application, the number of officers, non-commissioned
officers, corporals, privates, and vehicles to be transported.
The duplicate copy, duly completed, shall be endorsed by the
stationmaster upon departure and collected by him, on the way
back, for his accountancy records.

Troops whose assistance was requested by an Administration
or agency not specified in the present Article (paras. 7 and 8)
are transported at the expense of the said Administration or
agency at half price, upon presentation of Form 33 annexed to
the Regulations for Military Railway Transportation.

The statements or travel vouchers made out for this purpose
shall be marked clearly, in red ink, as follows: "On behalf
of ... (employing body) ..." If transportation (equipment or
troops) is effected by motorized Army vehicles, the Corps shall
present invoices by applying the official scales for lease and by
addressing these invoices with an accompanying memorandum
to the Department of National Defence (Service of Motorized
Vehicles and Fuel), who shall do the needful.

If the troops placed at the disposal of the employing body are
unable to bring all the necessary tools and equipment, additional
supplies shall be shipped as rapidly as possible, at the expense
of the employing body; this shall be done also if, in the course
of operations, additional tools are found to be indispensable.

The Lt. Governor of the Province, the Commanding Officer
of the District, or the Detachment Commander may, upon the
request of the officials or agents of the above body, apply in

writing for the necessary equipment to the Commanding Officer or the Head of the Engineering Detachment, the Engineering Commander, the Technical Assistant of Military Buildings, or the Accountancy Officer for Military Equipment (or, in his absence, the adjutant in charge of equipment) in their own or in a neighbouring region.

These officers and the Technical Assistants of Military Buildings are authorized, in urgent cases, to deliver, in a temporary capacity, the tools, etc. for which a request has been made, in writing, by the said officials or agents of the employing body.

b) Distribution of labour and discipline.

The assignment of men and the distribution of labour shall be effected by mutual agreement between the Chief of the Detachment and the senior official or agent present.

For the execution of operations, the military shall conform to the directions of the official or agent representing the Administration or enterprise that applied for assistance.

He shall report to the Detachment Chief, when necessary, regarding any serviceman giving rise to serious complaint.

The military shall remain under the authority of their immediate superiors.

c) Evacuation of the sick or injured.

Any sick or injured servicemen who can be transported shall be sent to a military hospital; if they are not transportable, and in default of a military hospital, they shall be cared for on the spot or in civilian hospitals, when available.

The employing bodies shall pay direct for the hospitalization of servicemen receiving treatment in a civilian hospital or with private persons. They shall also pay for medicines given to non-hospitalized servicemen.

For servicemen admitted for treatment into a military hospital, the amount due for hospitalization shall be claimed from the authorities employing the military manpower and refunded

to the Department of National Defence, General Civilian
Administration, Claims Office.

V.   Expenses and Allowances

a) <u>Pensions, allowances, aid in case of accidents, sickness,
   injuries, etc.</u>

The Department of National Defence is not responsible for
any expenses incurred for the period during which the troops
are placed at the disposal of another Administration.

Therefore, if a serviceman is the victim of an accident, or
if he contracts an illness, resulting in disability entitling him
to a pension under the provisions of the laws governing military pensions, this pension shall be settled by the Department
of National Defence and the amount refunded to the Treasury
by the Administration employing the troops.

If an accident or illness results in the death of a serviceman,
the same procedure is applied with regard to pensions, if any,
to his widow, orphans, parents, or dependents, payable under
the provisions of the laws on military pensions, or for expenses
for funerals and the return of the body to the family.

These pensions, allowances, or compensations constitute a
minimum for reparations. Consequently, the employing
Administration shall be directly responsible for paying not
only the above pensions and allowances, but also for any other
forms of compensation that may be granted either by the Court
or out of Court to servicemen or to their dependents under the
provisions of the Common Law.

If the deceased serviceman has won chevrons on the front but
has not yet reached the prescribed age for his annuity, the
Administration concerned shall refund the State for any extra
expenses incurred from the premature payment of the said
pension to the widow or orphans of the deceased.

If the deceased was a regular soldier and married, the above
Administration shall refund the Widows' and Orphans' Fund to

which it belongs for any extra expenses incurred for the premature payment of a pension to the widow and orphans.

The Administration shall fulfil all the obligations resulting from any accidents befalling any other persons in the performance of the operations.

The amounts due for pensions, allowances, expenses for funerals or the transfer of the body to the family, for expenses resulting from the premature attribution of allowances for Front-Line Service Stripes, or from the pensions due to the Widows' and Orphans' Fund, shall be claimed by the Department of National Defence, General Civilian Administration, Secretariat and Claims Office.

b) Daily Allowances.

Allowances shall be paid by the employing bodies to the servicemen of the Detachments concerned from the day on which they marched out to the day (inclusive) of their return.

These allowances shall be equivalent to the average wages of workmen whom the servicemen are called upon to replace.

For corporals, non-commissioned officers, subaltern officers, and senior officers, they shall be based on the indexes 1.5, 2, 3, and 4 respectively.

These allowances can be subjected to no deductions.

They are paid daily to the lower ranks and to officers every Saturday or on any other day on which the operations are concluded.

If the length of service, from the date of departure from the barracks to the date of return, is less than six hours, the above allowances are reduced by one half.

The payment of daily allowances is ensured by the military authorities.

The Administration or agency employing the troops shall refund these expenses direct to the body concerned upon receipt of statements (weekly or daily, as the case may be), specifying, in addition to the dates of operations, the ranks, civil status of dependents, and the various allowances due to each serviceman.

c) Compensations for clothing, equipment, tools, and camping articles.

Any compensation for clothing, equipment, tools, camping articles and subsequently for any special work for which the servicemen are employed shall be effected at the cost of the Administration or civilian body employing the troops.

Any replacement of articles lost or destroyed in the course of operations, as well as damages incurred by motorized vehicles by having been put to abnormal use, shall be borne by the Administration or the above bodies employing the troops.

After the return of the troops to their garrison, the units concerned shall transmit to the authorities having employed the troops the necessary statements of expenses specifying all the items listed in the preceding paragraphs.

The Commanding Officers shall first of all apply to the Department of National Defence (Quartermaster General, Administration and Supplies, Service of Armaments and Ammunition, Technical Engineering Service, or Service of Motorized Vehicles and Fuel, as the case may be) to ascertain:

1. the value of the objects lost or damaged;

2. the amount due for clothing, equipment, etc.;

3. the assignment of the sums to be collected for the above.

VI.   Housing--Drinks--Additional Food

The employing bodies shall also ensure the billeting of the troops placed at their disposal in localities devoid of garrisons. These premises may be ensured by means of requisition, at the expense of the above bodies.

In garrison towns the troops shall be housed in State barracks whenever possible.

The said employing bodies shall also cover the cost of any drinks and additional food which may be provided to staff on guard, to staff cooperating in operations at night or, generally speaking, of any additional expenses resulting from the services rendered by the troops.

Officers shall be responsible for their own housing and meals and shall cover the cost thereof out of the allowances provided for under Article V.

At the end of the operations, the Detachment Commanders shall address to the Lt. Governor of the Province or to the Commander of the District a detailed report on the accomplished mission.

In conformity with the duties and procedure laid down for military authorities with regard to accidents, this report shall be accompanied by a nominal statement concerning any servicemen who died, were injured, or fell sick in the course of their mission and relating, in each instance, the circumstances of the death, injuries, or illness.

A similar report shall be submitted if, after returning to his garrison, a serviceman is stricken by an illness the causes of which can be attributed to any special duty he was called upon to perform in the course of operations.

When necessary, a detailed list of damages undergone and reparations due (Article V) shall be annexed to the report.

This report and this list shall be transmitted to the Department of National Defence (General Army Headquarters, 1st Section), with the comments of the responsible chiefs.

BRAZILIAN DECREE (No. 37.148 A of April 5, 1955) REGARDING HIGHWAY AND RAILWAY WORKS AND ANTI-DROUGHT WORKS

Draft of Agreement between the Ministry of War and the Ministry of Communications and Public Works for the construction by Military Commissions and Units of highway and railway works and anti-drought works.

The President of the Republic of the United States of Brazil, empowered by Article 87, Number 1, of the Constitution, resolves:

Article 1

To approve the agreement for the construction by Military Commissions and Units of highway and railway works and anti-drought works in the Northeast. The list of such works will be specified, to all intents and purposes, in the text attached to the Agreement.

Article 2

This Decree will come into force on the date of its publication.

Article 3

All dispositions to the contrary are cancelled.

Rio de Janeiro, April 5, 1955, 134th year of the Independence and 67th year of the Republic.

(Signed) João Café Filho
Henrique Lott
Rodrigo Octavio Jordão Ramos

Agreement between the Ministry of War and the Ministry of Communications and Public Works for the construction by Military Commissions and Units of highway and railway works and anti-drought works in the Northeast.

First Clause

The Ministry of Communications and Public Works will delegate to the Ministry of War the construction by Military Commissions and Units of highway and railway works and anti-drought works in the Northeast.   The list of such works will be specified, to all intents and purposes, in the text attached to the Agreement.

Second Clause

The works to be carried out within the framework of this Agreement must first be agreed upon between the two Secretariats of State, and its volume must be in accordance with the construction capacity of the referred Military Units.

Third Clause

The works, which will be entrusted to the Ministry of War, including the facilities of the Military Commissions and Units, will be defrayed by resources of the Ministry of Communications and Public Works, or financed by the respective Departments.

Fourth Clause

The Ministry of War will supply military personnel and matériel, within its strength and regular budget allowances, which will be completely devoted to carrying out the entrusted works without causing prejudice to its main military activities.

Fifth Clause

The contents of the Order (Portaria) No. 1,200, of December 13, 1954, from the Ministry of Communications and Public Works applies to the Military Commissions and Units used for the construction of works in the Northeast.

APPENDIX C253

Sixth Clause

Taking into account the particular nature of the military system, the same technical and administrative methods and processes used by the Departments of the Ministry of Communications and Public Works will be adopted in the delegated constructions.

Seventh Clause

The Districts of Construction of the Departments of the Ministry of Communications and Public Works will entrust to the Military Commissions and Units the construction of works already undertaken with a detailed descriptive report in which will also be specified the commitments made with third parties. The revision of these commitments, if found necessary, possible, or advisable, could be made upon request to the Ministry of Communications and Public Works by the body in charge of the work.

a) The facilities, equipment, and materials used in the administration and services being carried out will be transferred to the Military Commissions with a definition of the terms of responsibility.

b) The Military Commissions and Units will absorb, as soon as possible, the personnel already under contract for the construction of the delegated works.

And, being in agreement, Major General Henrique Baptista Duffles Teixeira Lott, Minister of War, and Colonel Rodrigo Octavio Jordão Ramos, Minister of Communications and Public Works, have signed the present special Agreement.

Rio de Janeiro, April 5, 1955.

(Signed)   General Henrique Lott

Rodrigo Octavio Jordão Ramos

Additional text to the Agreement made between the Ministry of War and the Ministry of Communications and Public Works on April 5, 1955, for the construction of anti-drought works in the Northeast by Military Commissions and Units.

First Clause

On the general basis established by the Agreement made between the Ministry of War and the Ministry of Communications and Public Works on April 5, 1955, there will be delegated to the Ministry of War the construction of the following works designed for protection against droughts in the Northeast:

a) To be carried out by the 3rd Railway Battalion:

Curimatã public dam and irrigation system;
Curimataú public dam;
Highway branch to Picuí;
Highway Mark Zero-Taperoá.

b) To be carried out by the 4th Railway Battalion:

Irrigation works of the Várzea do Boi public dam;
Ceará Central Highway.

c) To be carried out by the 1st Highway Battalion:

Marshal Dutra public dam;
Highway Catolé do Rocha-Patu;
Highway Catolé de Rocha-Alexandria-Pau dos Ferros;
Highway Patos-Santa Luzia-Parelhas;
Highway Grejo da Cruz-Patu;
Highway Caicó-Jucurutu;
Highway Caicó-Patos;
Road Jardim do Seridó-Ouro Branco;
Highway Branch to Carraúba dos Dantas-Picuí;
Bridge over the Seridó River.

Second Clause

The construction of the works specified in the First Clause will be financed by emergency budget allowances and special credits, which are assigned to them by means of advance pay or supply of funds furnished directly to the Commanders of Battalions in charge of its execution by the Director-General of the National Department of Anti-Drought Works.

Third Clause

The Battalions will carry out the works of construction in accordance with the programmes and sequence orders previously approved by the Director-General of the National Department of Anti-Drought Works.

Fourth Clause

The financing of the works and the control of the sums involved will be made in accordance with procedures, instructions, and Orders (Portarias) issued by the Director-General of the National Department of Anti-Drought Works.

Fifth Clause

The Director-General of the National Department of Anti-Drought Works can carry out technical and administrative inspections of the services under the responsibility of the military units. The recommendations that may be deemed necessary during the inspections will be communicated only to the Commander of the Battalion.

Sixth Clause

For the reciprocal interest of efficiency of the Services, the Chiefs of Sectors of the National Department of Anti-Drought Works will, without other formality, give information and technical assistance when requested by the Commanders of Battalions.

Seventh Clause

The officers and non-commissioned officers of the military units are allowed to take apprenticeship in the laboratories and services under the responsibility of the National Department of Anti-Drought Works, on the proposal of the Commanders of Battalions and the approval of the Director-General of the National Department of Anti-Drought Works.

Eighth Clause

The Director-General of the National Department of Anti-Drought Works can assign to the Battalions the drilling and fitting of wells, and also the study and inspection of construction of dams and irrigation to be done in cooperation with the States and Counties.

Ninth Clause

The Battalions will organize, under the guidance of the Agricultural and Industrial Service of the National Department of Anti-Drought Works, courses that will be given to soldiers; these will have the object of educating the men for living in a drought zone and teaching them the means of defence against the irregularity of the climate, absence of natural resources, and the technique of irrigated farming.

Tenth Clause

During periods of climatic crisis, the Battalions will be entrusted with the assistance and protection of the populations of the zones where their works are taking place. They will have the responsibility of preparing and submitting in advance to the Director-General of the National Department of Anti-Drought Works emergency plans and proposals of preliminary measures considered necessary for their execution, such as the construction of lodging houses, warehouses for tools, etc.

Rio de Janeiro, April 5, 1955.

(Signed) Henrique Lott

Rodrigo Octavio Jordão Ramos

(Diário Oficial de 12-4-1955)
(Boletim de Exército No. 16, de 16-4-1955, páginas 944-47)

EXTRACTS FROM FRENCH MINISTRY OF DEFENCE
NOTE FOR COMPANY COMMANDERS REGARDING
THE ESTABLISHMENT OF GENERAL AND TECHNICAL
TRAINING COURSES

The following principles have been accepted by the Ministry of Armed Forces:

> The training offered to young soldiers will be given them by the appropriate ministries in close collaboration with the armed forces. This training will be directed only towards those who wish for it. Training will be given after hours at the base. It will be given at times arranged by the Company Commander to suit the exigencies of duty and requirements of the training.

These principles allow the deduction of an average of 240 hours from the period of military service for further education (Promotion Sociale). The 240 hours will be spread over ten months at the rate of six hours a week, in principle.

This provides an opportunity for additional training that will allow conscripts to:

> acquire additional or technical training;

> prepare for entrance examinations giving access to the courses given by Vocational Training of Adults;

> prepare to re-sit an examination they failed before being called up;

> maintain, thanks to a refresher course, their skill and professional knowledge.

TYPES OF TRAINING POSSIBLE

Conscripts can benefit from four types of training:

evening classes, internal or external;

correspondence classes;

courses preparatory to the Vocational Training of Adults (FPA);

classes of agricultural instruction.

Each of these types of training has its own special features and is thus aimed more particularly at a certain category of conscripts.

Evening classes may take place within the company, or outside in training schools for the general public. (Note: Generally under the direction of the Ministry of Education but also of the Ministry of Labour and Agriculture.) The organization of external courses depends on the existence, near to the unit, of a centre, school, college, or high school. The variety of courses that might be available to conscripts is a function of local conditions (existence of a college of technical training or a technical high school, an institute for the improvement of work skills, a centre associated with the National Conservatoire of Arts and Crafts, a centre of the Vocational Training of Adults.)

The pattern of evening classes is aimed primarily at young men with a poor level of primary education (illiterates, semi-illiterates, middle-school courses) for whom oral instruction is indispensable, and at candidates for technical and vocational certificates whose complete training cannot be provided by a correspondence course.

Soldiers wishing to attend evening classes will be accepted into the further education courses already organized in most areas. When the number of soldiers enrolling justifies it, special courses can be arranged for their benefit.

The correspondence courses, in contrast to evening classes, may be followed everywhere and offer an extremely wide
range of possibilities at every level of education. But they
demand of the student a considerable and continuous effort.

Each week, the student receives a work programme and a
set of homework; this is sent back to the centre and returned,
corrected and annotated, two weeks later. The enrolment fees
are low (27 francs per student), but one must add to this the
purchase price of books on which the course is based.

Agricultural training - Correspondence courses organized
by the Departments of Agricultural Services of certain regions
offer, at the moment, courses preparing only for the Certificate of Professional Aptitude in Agriculture (CAP) and the
Certificate of Agricultural Apprenticeship.

The general training courses preparatory to the Vocational
Training of Adults set up by the National Interprofessional Association for the Rational Training of Labour in collaboration
with the Ministry of Labour are only designed for candidates
for FPA courses. They are placed at the level of the Certificate of Primary Studies (CEP) and are orientated towards
artisan skills.

Courses (lessons and homework) are sent to the units by
ANIFRMO (National Interprofessional Association for the
Rational Training of Labour). Army instructors go through
the lessons and correct homework with the aid of an answer
sheet.

For the entrance examination to the FPA courses, the board
places great importance on the marks (grades) obtained by
students in the preparatory courses.

Classes of agricultural information are aimed at farm
workers and members of agricultural clubs. Organized in
close collaboration with the Regional Departments of Agricultural Services, they have as their aim the awakening of
young rural workers to the problems of their profession and
of initiating them into modern methods of management and new
agricultural techniques. The programme varies according to
local possibilities and the level and interests of participants.

Soldiers who are organizers of agricultural clubs will attend, once or twice a year, superior courses of information, organized in each region on the request of the Ministry of Armed Forces or the Ministry of Agriculture.

ORGANIZATION

General Information

This should be begun from the period of communal basic training and intensified at the time when the young men are leaving the instruction centre.

Its aim is to make known to the conscripts the opportunities for improvement that are offered them and draw their attention to the advantages and profit they would derive from it if they are willing to make the necessary effort.

The information will be given by means of:

Posters stuck up in the halls and units--one poster prepared by ANIFRMO was circulated recently. Others are in preparation. Company Commanders should also get themselves informative pamphlets from the heads of institutions where further education classes are organized.

Films. Five films devoted to the vocational training of adults have been made by ANIFRMO and are available to Company Commanders in the regional depots of the Film Unit of the armed forces. Films can be obtained from the film libraries of public education and through the Departments of the Agricultural Services, from the Film Library of the Ministry of Agriculture.

Lectures will be given by the representatives of the ministries concerned. Four lectures at least should be envisaged: an introductory lecture on Promotion Sociale, its organization and aims--this lecture preferably should be given by the Company Commander, who would thus demonstrate on this occasion the importance he attaches to the work of social promotion--and lectures given by representatives of each ministry concerned and dealing with the opportunities for improvement which they offer to young men.

This general information could be usefully completed by talks between officers and their men.

Particular Information

This will be given in the month preceding the beginning of the courses and will consist of:

Individual discussions between officiers-conseil and conscripts.

Visits to FPA centres, technical colleges, technical high schools, and institutes of further education of labour.

Specialized lectures given by particularly qualified persons (director of an FPA centre, technical college, technical high school, institute of further education of labour); officers giving advice on the conditions of the courses (voluntary nature, timetables, levels of different courses, means of enrolment, etc.).

Organizational Phase

Consists of:

Establishment of liaisons.

Division of pupils into groups according to their level and their preparation.

Practical organization of courses.

Establishment of Liaisons

The Inspector of the Educational District, the Director of Labour and Manpower, and the Director of Agricultural Services direct at departmental level the services of the three ministries. On them are dependent the heads of the different educational establishments operating in the department.

In order to avoid unwelcome requests, the Subdivisional Commander will first call on each of these officials in order to ensure, at every level, collaboration between the armed forces and the civilian ministries.

The Army Commanders will subsequently make contact with the heads of institutes indicated by the Inspectors, the Directors of Labour and Agricultural Services to arrange further education courses.

For correspondence courses, the Company Commanders will apply directly to the heads of teaching centres by letter. The contacts to make are detailed below:

<u>Military Authority</u>
Subdivisional Commander
(or failing him, Army Commander)

Person to Contact	Type of Contact
Inspector of Educational District.	Briefing. Help of the Education authorities in providing places and staff for the setting up of evening classes.
Director of Regional Centre of the University Bureau of Statistics (at each Educational District headquarters).	Briefing. General information on careers and new opportunities.
Inspector of Labour responsible at regional level for employment and the experimental sections of Vocational Guidance.	Briefing. Guidance by the Services of Vocational Guidance.

Military Authority
Subdivisional Commander
(or failing him, Army Commander)
(continued)

Person to Contact	Type of Contact
Departmental Director of Labour and Manpower.	Briefing. Psychotechnical tests of ANI-FRMO. Preparatory courses for FPA.
Departmental Director of Agricultural Services.	Briefing. Help in meetings on agricultural information.

Army Commander

Head of institution of education (technical college, technical high school, etc.).	Organization of evening classes.
Director of Services of Vocational Guidance.	Briefing. Guidance of soldiers wishing to take CNTE courses (Tele-Education).
Director of FPA centre.	Visit to Centre. Informative talk. Evening classes.
Director of agricultural high school.	Briefing. Evening classes.

Military Authority
Company Commander
(continued)

Person to Contact   Type of Contact

Head of Centre of Tele-Education
60 bld. du Lycée
Vanves

Director   of   Regional   Centre
of   Teaching   Documentation   Correspondence courses
of Lyon   of the CNTE
47 rue de Lassale, Lyons   (Tele-Education).

Director   of   Regional   Centre
of   Teaching   Documentation
Toulouse
3 rue Roquelaine, Toulouse

Director of ANIFRMO   Courses preparatory
3 bld. Kellerman   to FPA.
Paris 13ème

Director of Agricultural   Agricultural
Services for Department.   correspondence courses.

Division of Pupils

It is clearly important to understand properly the educational levels of candidates and all the possibilities offered by
the ministries in the way of education. It is a complicated and

delicate task in which goodwill cannot make up for lack of experience. It seems thus unreasonable to leave it to the officiers-conseil alone, who are ill-prepared for this sort of work.

The solution will be different for different candidates.

1. For illiterates and semi-illiterates the problem is simple; they have been detected at call-up with the help of the tests of general education of the Recruiting Service.

2. Young men wishing to learn a trade should be advised by the Services of Vocational Guidance in regions where they exist. Those wishing to take an FPA course should take a psycho-technical examination at the regional centre of ANIFRMO.

3. The case of young men who wish to complete their general education and sit an examination higher than that of the Certificate of Primary Studies (elementary certificate, certificate of studies in the first cycle, baccalaureat, certificate of agents in technology, commerce or industry, a technical certificate, etc.) is more complicated. The information given by the Recruiting Service does not provide a precise determination of scholastic level. Moreover, the level of knowledge attained by those concerned at school or high school is not necessarily the same as that as the time of recruitment.

Candidates for correspondence courses from the Centre National de Télé-Education would be most usefully directed to the Service of Professional and Scholastic Guidance. (The Guidance officers can travel if the numbers warrant their journey.)

When the courses required take place outside, in a college or high school, the soldiers' knowledge can be tested by an examination organized on the initiative of the person in charge of the course.

After this preparation candidates will be classified by type of education: correspondence courses, evening classes, courses preparatory to FPA, sessions of agricultural information, and within the first two by levels.

Practical Organization

Will be concerned with:

1. Accommodation.
2. The search for teachers and supervisors.
3. Enrolment.
4. Finance.

Accommodation

Company Commanders should use to the fullest extent the possibilities offered outside the company (colleges, schools), which will avoid the problems of heating and lighting and ensure that courses are held in rooms which are suitable.

However, in certain isolated companies or outside France, instruction must be given within the company, using to the maximum all the company's resources.

In any case, lecture rooms must be provided for internal courses (preparatory courses for the FPA, agricultural clubs).

In addition, one room serving as a study must be open to the soldiers, students of CNTE, and all those who wish to work outside the class time, in conditions and at times fixed by the Company Commander.

Teachers

To run the courses, recourse must be had, whenever possible, to civilian teachers from the different ministries. Only the job of hearing homework will be done by soldiers. However, where it is impossible to find civilian teachers, courses will be run by military teachers.

Military teachers will be chosen from among volunteers, members of the Education Corps or, failing them, holders of the baccalaureat or certificates of higher education.

Military assistant teachers in charge of commenting on the FPA preparatory courses will be trained in the methods for teaching adults by a week's course at the National Institute for Vocational Training. Because of the extra tasks thus imposed on military teachers and assistant teachers, compensation (exceptional privileges) may be given them on the initiative of the Company Commander.

Enrolment

Enrolment is the responsibility of officers and will be carried out in liaison with the representatives of civilian ministries.

The hope of encouraging and helping deserving pupils, and not devaluing instruction given in the armed forces, has resulted in the fixing, in agreement with the representatives of the ministries, a probationary period of three months at the end of which a pupil may be struck off the list if the head of the institution or man in charge of the course considers his work or application to work is unsatisfactory. However, because of the exigencies of military duty, the opinion of the Company Commander will be sought and taken into consideration.

Finance

Equipping the lecture-rooms, buying books, registration of conscripts for correspondence courses, travelling, cost money. The experience of the first companies to start general or technical education courses has shown that an appropriation of 52 francs per pupil is necessary. Initial funds for setting up the courses will also be granted. These funds, the allocation of which by the Minister of Armed Forces will be the subject of a special directive, will be placed at the disposition of Company Commanders by the Regional Commanders.

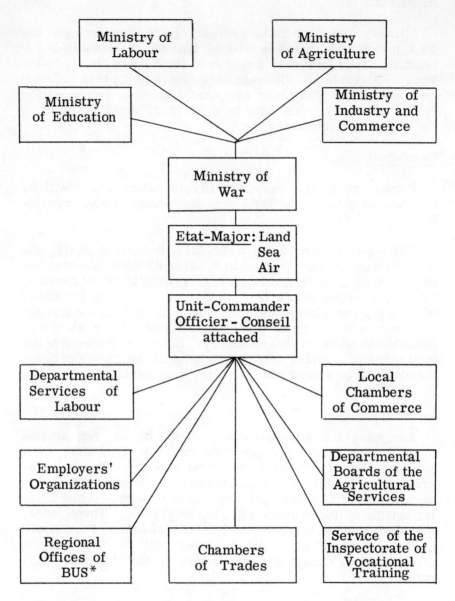

Organization of Vocational Training in the Army

*The Bureau Universitaire de Statistiques provides information on all questions relating to further education and vocational careers.

EMERGENCY ACTION IN CASES OF NATURAL DISASTER

(excerpt from the 29th Report of the Administrative Committee on Co-ordination, United Nations Economic and Social Council, Document E/3886, 5 May 1964)

127. In its twenty-eighth report (E/3765), the ACC suggested that the ECOSOC might wish to draw the attention of member Governments to the delays and difficulties caused by the absence of national co-ordinating machinery to help in determining the degree and character of the relief required and in making ad hoc arrangements to give unified direction to relief operations.

128. Notwithstanding the handicaps resulting in certain cases from the absence of such national co-ordinating machinery, the arrangements for exchange of information between the Secretary-General and the executive heads of the interested international organizations of the United Nations system have worked in a reasonably satisfactory manner in such recent disasters as the earthquake in Skoplje, Yugoslavia, the volcanic eruption at Bali, Indonesia, the earthquake at Barce, Libya, floods in Morocco, and the devastation caused by Hurricane Flora in a number of Caribbean countries.

129. The Council has requested the Secretary-General "to take the lead in establishing, in conjunction with the specialized agencies and the League of Red Cross Societies, appropriate arrangements for assistance in cases of national disaster" (E/3816, page 39).

130. In conformity with this request consideration has been given to possible measures which might be adopted separately, but not in isolation, in the following fields:

(i) arrangements for the exchange of information within the United Nations systems at Headquarters and at the country level;

(ii) consultation and contact with non-governmental organizations, in particular the League of Red Cross Societies.

In each case separate consideration is called for in regard to:

(a) immediate relief to cope with hunger, disease, lack of shelter, clothing, sanitary arrangements, etc.;

(b) long-term rehabilitation and reconstruction to restore normal conditions of living.

The former calls for the utmost speed, the latter for comprehensive and mutual adjustment. It is recognized that any co-ordination arrangement must avoid procedures likely to affect the flexibility of operations of agencies concerned to provide as speedily as possible help to those desperately in need.

131. The Secretary-General proposes to strengthen existing arrangements in New York and Geneva by the designation of officers in each place to maintain the necessary contacts. These two officers will, so far as possible, serve as a point of information on action being planned or taken.

132. At the country level it is important for the United Nations system to designate a "focal point" for the exchange of information on the plans and activities of the Governments and of the various agencies (inter-governmental and voluntary). The officer occupying the national "focal point" should normally be the Resident Representative of the Technical Assistance Board and the Special Fund. Local representatives of the international organizations as well as special officers sent out by those organizations (individually or jointly) to assess the scale of relief needed and to arrange for its provision and distribution would keep in close touch with the "focal point" officer.

133. In disasters where the relief required is predominantly the concern of one agency, the representative of that agency might, by common agreement, be regarded as the "focal point" representing all members of the United Nations system which might have only a marginal interest in the relief and reconstruction involved. In special cases it might be necessary to appoint a special representative or make other ad hoc arrangements.

134. The role of the Red Cross--particularly the League of Red Cross Societies and the International Red Cross--which is particularly equipped to provide certain types of immediate

relief, needs no emphasis. While existing arrangements between the Red Cross and certain individual organizations are working satisfactorily and effectively, tentative discussions have already taken place with the object of developing closer co-operation in certain respects. The Secretary-General will continue to keep the League of Red Cross Societies informed of any appeals he may receive which appear to require emergency assistance, and will also exchange information on the aid planned and provided. The ACC is conscious of the importance of voluntary national organizations capable of undertaking relief programmes. In countries where no such organizations exist, there would seem to be a great advantage if national Red Cross or Red Crescent Societies could be established.

135. In cases of natural disasters Governments themselves often directly offer aid to the affected countries. There are special fields in which donor Governments can often be particularly helpful--e.g. the loan of helicopters, landing craft from some nearby location, the provision of shipping space to carry supplies, the loan of motor transport within the devastated country to distribute supplies, the assignment of technical personnel. Government missions, as well as international organizations, having transport in a country, intended for other purposes, could deploy it temporarily for relief purposes. It is hoped that such possibilities will be reported to the United Nations "focal point" in the country involved.

136. Apart from the over-all arrangements for immediate relief outlined above, rehabilitation efforts are being pursued within the normal procedure for co-operation and co-ordination. As an example, the United Nations is actively studying emergency and reconstructive activities in the field of housing, building, and planning following natural disasters. In those activities, ILO, FAO, WHO, UNESCO as well as UNICEF and the WFP are participating at the technical level. In other fields also similar co-operation exists among agencies.

137. In its twenty-eighth report (E/3765), the ACC proposed the collection and collation of information regarding the type of assistance and the conditions governing its provision which organizations comprising the United Nations system are in a position to provide. Such a document is being prepared and it is proposed to make it widely available in due course to all international bodies, Ministries and Departments of Governments, and voluntary organizations.

RESETTLEMENT OF EX-SERVICEMEN

(Extracts from a circular by the Director-General
Resettlement to all Resettlement Officers,
24th May 1965)

EMPLOYMENT OF EX-SERVICEMEN

Procedure for Registration with Employment
Exchanges and Its Renewal

National Employment Service

Ex-servicemen should know that there is an organization called "The National Employment Service" which is entrusted with the task of providing employment through its various branches known as "Employment Exchanges." These Employment Exchanges are spread all over the country. The Employment Service is a FREE service. No fee is levied on employment seekers who seek the assistance of the Employment Exchanges.

Registration - Ex-Servicemen

To avail of the facilities provided by the National Employment Service, ex-servicemen desirous of employment should make it a point that they get their names registered at any single Employment Exchange nearest to their residence.

Registration for employment assistance can be done either in person or by post by filling in forms obtainable free from the Employment Exchange at which it is desired to be registered.

273

Registration - Serving Personnel

Servicemen (but not ex-servicemen) are eligible to get themselves registered for employment assistance at any single Employment Exchange in or outside their normal place of residence, not excluding the Exchange nearest to where they are serving, six months or less before their actual release.

Re-Registration - Essential

If an ex-serviceman is not provided employment within three months of his registration, he must then get his registration renewed; otherwise he would forfeit his claim for employment assistance through an Employment Exchange. He can re-apply for registration, but in that case he would have lost his place in the queue. Renewal of registration can be done in person or by post. There is also no objection to renewal of registration by proxy provided the proxy bears a written authorization from the applicant concerned. To facilitate renewal of registration, three renewal cards are attached to the registration form which is given to the person registering. The period covered by the initial registration as well as the period of each renewal is three months; thus with the three cards a person can cover a period of one year.

Assistance by Recruiting Officers

Recruiting Officers have instructions to assist ex-servicemen residing in their areas of jurisdiction in the matter of renewal of their registration cards. They are required to examine the registration cards of unemployed ex-servicemen as and when they come in contact with them and collect such cards which need renewal and forward them to the Employment Exchanges concerned so that the names of unemployed ex-servicemen are always borne on the live registers of the Employment Exchanges.

In addition, the Recruiting Officers are required to maintain close liaison with the Employment Exchanges in their areas with a view to help ex-servicemen in their placements in civil jobs.

Concessions Applicable to Ex-Servicemen for Employment in General Government Vacancies

Priority

Ex-servicemen, including reservists, are accorded Priority III by Employment Exchanges in the matter of submission against Central Government vacancies other than those which are required to be filled through a competitive test conducted by the Union Public Service Commission. In regard to the priority for employment of ex-servicemen in State Government vacancies, ex-servicemen are advised to contact the District Soldiers', Sailors', and Airmen's Boards. They vary from State to State; efforts are being made to make them uniform.

Preference for Certain Appointments

By virtue of their training and experience, ex-servicemen are specially suitable to certain posts which require proficiency in the use of arms, e.g., posts in the Police, Excise, Forests, Home Guards, Watch & Ward of the Railways, State Transport Services, and Armed Constabulary and similar other posts for which military training is a qualification. Instructions have been issued to Employment Exchanges that, other things being equal, ex-servicemen should be given preference over others as candidates for these posts.

Defence Establishments - Recruitment for

Orders have also been issued to all Defence Establishments that, while notifying vacancies to Employment Exchanges, they should ask them to sponsor ex-servicemen candidates to the extent of at least 50 per cent.

Relaxation in Upper Age Limit for Employment

For appointments made otherwise than on the basis of open competitive tests held by the Union Public Service Commission, the period of service in the Armed Forces is deducted from the candidate's actual age and if the resultant age does not exceed the prescribed maximum age for the post applied for by more than three years, he is deemed to satisfy the condition in respect of the upper age limit and would therefore be eligible if his age so computed is within the prescribed age.

Military Pensioners and Reservists

There is no specific upper age limit for civil employment in the case of military pensioners and reservists. Such ex-servicemen who retire before the age of superannuation are eligible for civil appointments if their age at the time of such re-employment is below the normal age of superannuation for the post in which it is proposed to re-employ them.

Service Educational Certificates and Their Equivalent

The Government of India has recognized the following Service Certificates as equivalent to Matriculation or High School Examination of a recognized Indian University for employment under the Central Government:

Indian Army Special Certificate of Education (also recognized by State Governments).

Higher Educational Test of the Indian Navy.

Indian Air Force Educational Test for Re-classification to leading Air Craftsmen in respect of only such non-Matriculate candidates who were recruited to the Royal Indian Air Force during the war.

Equation of Services Trades vis-à-vis Civil Trades

The experience gained by servicemen and the skills attained by them in various Services trades have not yet been recognized for purpose of civil employment. It has now been decided that the skills attained by servicemen in various Services trades be assessed and equated with the corresponding civil occupations. A board of officers has recently been appointed for the purpose by the Ministry of Defence to work with the Directorate General of Employment and Training, Government of India. As soon as the task of equation of Services trades with civil trades is finalized, due publicity will be given.

Employment of Ex-Servicemen and Their Wives
as Primary School Teachers in Villages

As it is considered that a good number of ex-servicemen
will be suitable and willing for employment as primary school
teachers in the villages, where there is a great shortage of
teachers, the Ministry of Defence, Government of India, has
approached the Chief Secretaries of all State Governments vide
their letter dated March 12, 1965, to issue instructions to their
subordinate departments/offices for ex-servicemen's appointments in Government primary schools in rural areas.   In the
same letter request has also been made for similar jobs for the
wives of ex-servicemen where considered suitable.

SPECIAL FUND FOR THE RECONSTRUCTION
AND REHABILITATION OF EX-SERVICEMEN

This was constituted with Rs. 50 million (U.S. $ 10 million)
from the National Defence Fund and an initial contribution of
Rs. 10 million from the Central Government.

Its objects are:

To award stipends to ex-servicemen for technical, manage-
rial, vocational, or agricultural training at recognized training institutions.

To sanction grants or loans to cooperative societies or
other associations of ex-servicemen for schemes and projects
of resettlement, e.g., horticulture, animal husbandry, industry, transport, etc.

To sanction scholarships and grants to dependents of ex-
servicemen for studies in technical, vocational, or agricultural
education.

To sanction expenditure on special collective measures for
the maintenance of old and destitute ex-servicemen or their
widows.

To grant loans to individual ex-servicemen for starting industries or business undertakings.

The fund is administered by a Central Committee which includes the Defence Minister, the Secretary of the Ministry of Defence, the three Service Chiefs, two ex-service officers nominated by the Central Government, and the Director-General of Resettlement.

It is distributed as follows:

1. Eighty per cent of the contribution from the NDF and from the Central Government is reserved for distribution to the States (and/or Union Territories) on the basis of the number of men in the Armed Services.

2. The State (or Territory) receives this share only if its Government (or Administration) contributes an equal share within three months.

3. The balance of the fund, including sums available for want of a matching grant under (2) may be spent on the management of the fund and in furtherance of its objects under the directions of the Central Managing Committee.

APPENDIX G PAKISTAN

PART I - NOTE ON MILITARY CIVIC PROJECTS

Indus Valley Road Project

The Gilgit Agency and adjoining states of Hunza and Nagar are at present connected with West Pakistan by a land route (jeepable) through Kaghan Valley, which passes over Babusar Pass at an altitude of 13,600 feet. This route is open for traffic for only three to four months in the summer and remains snow-bound during the remaining part of the year. All the supplies have to be airlifted, causing an exorbitant increase in the prices. In 1949, the Pakistan Government decided to explore the possibilities of constructing a snow-free land route that would be open throughout the year and would not only help in social and economic progress of this backward area, but also attract tourists to this area of exotic natural beauty.

A survey was carried out by the Public Works Department, and it was estimated that an all-weather road from Karora (Swat State) to Gilgit via Chilas (239 miles) would cost Rs. 65 million (U.S. $13.7 million). The project was considered a number of times but could not be undertaken due to lack of funds and resources.

At the end of 1958 it was finally decided to take on the project with the help of the Corps of Engineers of the Pakistan Army, who have the skill, experience, and resources necessary for such tasks. A major portion of the road from Karora to Chilas (158 miles) that traversed unexplored mountainous territory was entrusted to the Army Engineers. The remaining portion, Chilas to Gilgit (91 miles), where a jeep track already existed, was assigned to the Public Works Department. Using Army resources the estimated cost of the road (fit for three-ton vehicles) was reduced to Rs. 33 million (U.S. $6.9 million).

279

The Army Engineers started work in January, 1959. Tackling their portion from both ends (Karora and Chilas), they have completed 117 miles of road, largely by blasting through rock. A number of bridges and rest houses have also been constructed. Work on the main bridge (400-foot span) over the Rivers Indus and Kamila will be started shortly. The project was scheduled to be completed by the end of 1965.

Irrigation and Water Supply Schemes at Quetta

A number of schemes for the augmentation of water supply for Quetta Valley have been proposed from time to time. Some of the dams constructed or being constructed are described below:

Flood Control Reservoir at Wali Tangi

This dam is sixteen miles upstream of the Urak weir and was considered a most difficult project. Pakistan Army Engineers completed this difficult project in the short period of just over a year and at the low cost of Rs. 692,000 compared with earlier estimates of Rs. 3,500,000. This dam was opened on November 22, 1961.

Sra Khula Dam

A concrete dam, 50 feet high and 20 feet long; has a catchment area of 23 square miles. Its outlet channel to Hanna Lake is 172,000 feet. This dam was completed in under four months at a cost of Rs. 300,000.

Kach Dam

When completed, this dam will be 50 feet high and 180 feet long. Its catchment area is 28 square miles. It is estimated to cost Rs. 380,000.

Drainage Work in Ghulam Mohammad Barrage Area

Ministry of Fuel, Power, and Natural Resources requested Ministry of Defence for help in execution of the "Crash Drainage Plan" to reclaim waterlogged land in the neighbourhood of the Ghulam Mohammad Barrage. The Army Engineers were asked to construct a 50-foot wide, 7-foot deep drain from Tando Mohd Khan to the Arabian Sea, a distance of approximately twelve miles. Troops were moved by special trains in the second week of April, 1960, and completed the job in eight and a half weeks.

Azad Pattan Bridge

The old suspension bridge at Azad Pattan, with the passage of time, outlived its usefulness. This bridge provides an important commercial link for a very large portion of Azad Kashmir Territory, which it serves. On the request of the Azad Kashmir Government, Army Engineers constructed a Class 40 suspension bridge at a cost of two-thirds of a million rupees in the short span of sixteen months. Crossing the River Jhelum, which flows through a deep gorge, involved building up substantial approaches.

Flood Relief

Floods are a regular threat to life and property in this subcontinent during monsoons. Army Engineers have invariably been called up in aid of civil administration. They exhibited great courage and devotion in controlling the floods and evacuation of persons from affected areas. Their efforts in rehabilitation of communication and control of diseases after the devastation of floods have always been highly appreciated.

Fire Fighting

Army Engineers have gone another step forward in helping the civil administration to fight against fire at various occasions.

PART II - POST WAR SERVICES
RECONSTRUCTION FUND

WELFARE ACTIVITIES

The PWSR Fund provides the following benefits to its beneficiaries:

Educational Stipends

General

Stipends--of which 25 per cent are reserved for girls-- range from Rs. 10 to Rs. 50 per month for day scholars and from Rs. 15 to Rs. 100 per month for boarders, for all classes--both pre-matric and post-matric, technical courses, etc. We encourage students to take science and technical subjects and award stipends for Arts courses only in the case of students who passed their previous university examinations in the 1st Class and to girls.

Selections

Selections for pre-matric awards are made on a district basis by a representative committee presided over by the Deputy Commissioner/President, District Armed Services Board of the area, and on which Naval HQ, Air HQ, the District Education authorities, the District Armed Services Board, and an ex-JCO are represented.   Selections for post-matric awards are made on a regional basis, roughly corresponding to the old provinces of West Pakistan, by committees presided over by the local GOC's and on which again, the Director of Public Instruction, the West Pakistan Armed Services Board, Naval HQ, Air HQ, an ex-officer and an ex-JCO are represented.

Military College at Jhelum

The PWSR Fund of West Pakistan also awards a stipend of Rs. 20 each to fifty students of the Military College at Jhelum. Selections for these awards are made by the Director of Army

Education. The Fund has recently also agreed to finance the preliminary academic education at the Military College of up to twenty "Y" Cadets.

Non-Academic Training Facilities

Vocational Training

There are six Government vocational training centres in the country, with a total of 2,008 seats, of which 25 per cent, or 502, are reserved for ex-servicemen. Each trainee at these centres gets a Government stipend of Rs. 15 per month and the Fund awards a stipend of Rs. 40 each to ex-servicemen trainees, so that they can have a total income of Rs. 55 per month each during their training. The procedure for the admission of ex-servicemen trainees is very simple. An ex-serviceman has only to report to his nearest vocational training centre and produce his discharge certificate. When the principal of the centre is satisfied that he is an ex-serviceman, he gives him an aptitude test and tells him what line he thinks he is best fitted for. If the man agrees to take the training in that line, he is admitted straightaway, and his papers are sent by the principal to the Fund for sanction of his stipend. But though we have provided for 300 ex-servicemen trainees, we have never been able to get more than 274 to take advantage of this training as detailed below:

1960-61	183
1961-62	272
1962-63	274
1963-64	241
1964-65	261

The grant for this training during the financial year 1964-65 was Rs. 115,000.

Pre-Release Training

The PWSR Fund of West Pakistan has also arranged for the pre-release training of sixty OR's at a time at the Fauji textile mill for a period of six months.

Masonry Training at the Engineers Centre at Risalpur

The PWSR Fund of West Pakistan has arranged for the training of thirty OR's at a time in masonry at the Engineers Centre at Risalpur for a period of six months. The cost of this training in 1964-65 was Rs. 2,260.

Pakistan Veterans Land Settlement Training Centre, Nukerji

The Fund has set up a land settlement training centre at Nukerji, where ex-servicemen and their children are trained in the latest methods of agriculture and animal husbandry. Only those trainees are taken as have land of their own. The intention is not so much to train them to be able to take up employment after their training as to enable them to put their own land to the best possible use.

The cost of the centre in 1964-65 was Rs. 96,080. This centre has closed and arrangements are being made to train these persons at the Agricultural University at Lyallput.

Officers' Training in Business Administration at Karachi

The Fund has arranged for the training of officers in business administration at the National Institute of Business Administration at Karachi. The Institute has arranged a special course to meet the requirements of our officers.

The cost of this training in 1964-65 was Rs. 20,000.

Medical Facilities

TB Beds in Military Hospitals

The Fund provides facilities for the treatment of TB patients among ex-servicemen and their families. For this purpose, the Fund has had 280 beds reserved in military hospitals all over the country. Patients are normally treated at the military hospitals nearest to their homes, and Army recruiting officers maintain lists of the patients in each military hospital in his area. A patient wishing to gain admission fills in an application form and sends it to his local District Armed Services Board for verification of his eligibility. The application is then sent to the Army recruiting officer, who sends him to the nearest military hospital as a vacancy occurs. If there is a vacancy in the nearest military hospital to the applicant's home, the recruiting officer sends the patient there and notifies the hospital. If there is no such vacancy, but there are vacancies in another military hospital in his area, the recruiting officer approaches the ADMS of the area, who may authorize the admission of the patient there. At these military hospitals, routine treatment is given for TB.

Government TB Sanatorium - Dadar

The Fund has also built three wards at the Government TB Sanatorium at Dadar with beds for twenty-two male patients and eight female patients.

Veterans Hospital for Chest Diseases

The Fund has set up the Veterans Hospital for Chest Diseases at Rawalpindi, where provision has been made for giving surgical and other specialized treatment to TB patients. When a patient in one of the military hospitals needs surgical or specialized treatment, he is transferred to the VHCD for treatment.

The VHCD was originally intended to have 250 beds and we have so far only completed the first phase, providing for all the technical and administrative facilities and beds for 52 patients. But we have found that we are unlikely to get even this number of patients who will need the surgical and other specialized treatment provided there. The VHCD is at present the only institution where such treatment is available in Pakistan, and we have therefore offered facilities there to the Civil Government for civilian patients on mutually acceptable terms. The Fund is also considering other ways of utilizing the facilities at the VHCD to the best advantage.

Rehabilitation Centre for Disabled Veterans - Lahore

The Fund maintains the Rehabilitation Centre for Disabled Veterans at Lahore, where paraplegics and other seriously disabled ex-servicemen are rehabilitated and given vocational training so that they can become useful members of society. There are facilities at the centre for sixty inmates, but we have never had more than thirty-five. The policy of the Fund is to train these inmates in a trade and to encourage them to go out and stand on their own legs. But they have so far been reluctant to go--understandably, because it will not be easy for them to get the domestic facilities they get at the centre elsewhere.

It has recently been suggested that the PWSR Fund should take over the Artificial Limb Centre, which is at present a Defence Unit, and help to modernize it with external assistance, which has been promised. This will enable the Rehabilitation Centre for Disabled Veterans to be expanded into a self-sufficient organization, and the proposal is under consideration.

Rest Houses

The Fund maintains rest houses at the District Headquarters of certain Districts for the convenience of ex-servicemen of the rural areas who have occasion to visit the Headquarters of the District for official and other purposes. The rest houses are administered by the Pakistan Armed Services Board, but the Fund finances them. The object is to provide such ex-servicemen with the sort of living facilities at the District Headquarters that they had become accustomed to in the Army at a nominal cost. The Fund has buildings at Rawalpindi and Jhelum which are used as rest houses and it has hired buildings elsewhere. The policy of the Fund is not to construct any more buildings, but to hire suitable ones wherever a demand for a rest house is established.

The expenditure on rest houses during the year 1964-65 was Rs. 17,000.

PART III - EXCERPTS FROM PAKISTAN ARMED SERVICES BOARD ANNUAL REPORT 1964-65

(Extracts from the Minutes of a Meeting Held in the
Office of the Home Secretary on 6-8-1964 to
Consider the Report of the Committee for
Reorganization of Employment Exchanges)

The Secretary, Pakistan Armed Services Board, gave a résumé of the case which led to the setting up of the Employment Exchanges. Following World War II, it was the intention of the Government that Employment Exchanges should be able to settle, within a target date of five years, the demobilized personnel in civil life by finding suitable employment for them and arranging for their technical and vocational training. This had happened in other countries where the armed forces personnel had to be demobilized after World War II. But the Employment Exchanges in West Pakistan had not shown that much interest in the rehabilitation of the ex-servicemen. Since Independence, 500,000 servicemen have been demobilized and according to the Government instructions each one of them was to be registered at the Employment Exchanges and provided with employment in civil life, but the Employment Exchanges in West Pakistan have hardly registered 45,000 ex-servicemen and provided employment to a still lesser number.

The Home Secretary asked the representative of the Labour Department why the rest of the ex-servicemen could not be registered at the Employment Exchanges. He explained that the Employment Exchanges register all ex-servicemen who notify to the Employment Exchanges their desire to be registered. As all the ex-servicemen do not notify the Employment Exchanges, all of them are not registered. Home Secretary observed that all the three Armed Services should invariably send a copy of Form X-26 to the Employment Exchanges, who should register all the demobilized persons, irrespective of the fact whether such persons signify their intention to be registered or not.

As to the question why all registered ex-servicemen could not be employed, the Joint Director of Labour explained that there were several reasons for it, some of which are as follows:

1. The ex-servicemen are mostly unskilled and therefore their field of employment is limited.

2. Many of them do not adjust themselves to their new environments as quickly as other younger job-seekers do.

3. They are concentrated in certain specific regions and are reluctant to move to distant areas.

The meeting decided to ask Government to increase the percentage of reserved vacancies for ex-servicemen in the regions where there is a greater concentration of them.

Secretary, PASB, pointed out that adequate facilities were not provided to the ex-servicemen for post-release training, though this was one of the main functions of the Employment Exchanges. The Joint Director, Labour, explained that a number of training centres had been established in important towns where 25 per cent of available seats are reserved for ex-servicemen or their sons and dependents. If this number was considered inadequate, the Labour Department could increase the percentage to 50 provided the reserved seats were taken up by ex-servicemen themselves and not their dependents. It was decided to recommend the following steps to improve the post-release training of ex-servicemen:

1. A report on the working of the training centres and the facilities available in them should be prepared periodically and circulated to all units in the three Armed Services. This should be done on a quarterly basis. The list of officers/offices to whom these reports should be addressed may be supplied by the Secretary, PASB, to the Labour Department (Manpower) within a month.

2. Reservation of vacancies in the training centres should be suitably increased for regions where there is a larger concentration of ex-servicemen.

3. The Employment Exchanges should intimate the anticipated fields of employment in which ex-servicemen
   can be absorbed to the Armed Services so that they can
   adjust the pre-release training of the ex-servicemen
   to make them suitable for such jobs. Greater stress
   should be laid on pre-release training, as the ex-
   servicemen find it difficult to adjust themselves to
   post-release training in quite new and different environments.

4. The equipment and standard of training in post-release
   training centres should be made more attractive to the
   trainees.

5. Five per cent of the seats in Polytechnic Institutes
   should be reserved for ex-servicemen subject to such
   conditions as the Education Department may prescribe
   for the purpose.

Secretary, PASB, pointed out that the Committee in its
report has recommended that special cells should be set up in
the Employment Exchanges to assist the ex-servicemen in finding employment and that these cells should be headed by ex-
servicemen. He suggested that these cells should be entirely
manned by ex-servicemen and that they should issue a bulletin
on the lines of the one issued by the Labour Ministry in the
United Kingdom. Home Secretary enquired whether the Labour
Department had any objection to these suggestions. Labour
Department's representative stated that the cells could be
headed by ex-servicemen, but it would not be feasible to man
them entirely with ex-servicemen. As regards the issue of a
bulletin, he said that it could be considered by the Department.
It was decided that the proposal to issue a bulletin explaining
the performance of Employment Exchanges and training centres
vis-à-vis ex-servicemen should be favourably examined by the
Labour Department.

Secretary, PASB, observed that it was provided in the
report that where there are no Employment Exchanges, the
Armed Services Boards should register the ex-servicemen.
He suggested that the staff required for the purpose should be
provided by the Employment Exchanges but should be entirely
under the control of the DASB's. Home Secretary, however,
was of the view that while technical and operational control

would rest with the Employment Exchanges, disciplinary control should rest with the Secretary, DASB's.

There was a general discussion on the working of the Employment Exchanges and the following recommendations were made for improving their working:

1. Registration and job-placement of ex-servicemen should be explicitly recorded as the major duty of Employment Exchanges.

2. The Labour Department should open new branches of Employment Exchanges where there is concentration of ex-servicemen.

3. There should be greater coordination and cooperation between the Services HQ's and Employment Exchanges.

4. The Employment Exchanges should notify in advance the likely number and nature of vacancies in consultation with various employers.

5. In cases where Employment Exchanges cannot provide suitable candidates to the employers, non-availability certificates should be sent to the employer within twenty-one days of the receipt of the demand, and after that the employers should be at liberty to fill the vacancies directly.

6. While issuing Introductory Cards to the candidates the Employment Exchanges should ensure that prescribed percentage of vacancies should go to the ex-servicemen. Any failure in this behalf should be properly accounted for.

7. Separate lists of disabled ex-servicemen should be kept and they should be provided with sheltered employment. The statistics maintained by the Employment Exchanges should make a separate mention of disabled ex-servicemen.

It was decided that the Report of the Committee for Re-organization of Employment Exchanges should be accepted subject to the observations made above.

W. E. Cir. 8/34
Dated 18. 2. 1965

To

THE MANAGERS OF ALL EMPLOYMENT EXCHANGES
IN WEST PAKISTAN
(for necessary action)
Government of West Pakistan
Directorate of Labour Welfare
(Manpower and Employment Wing)

Subject: SPECIAL REPORTS - DEVELOPMENT OF NEW
INDUSTRIES AND OTHER ESTABLISHMENTS

From time to time new industrial units and other establishments being established in different places substantially add to
the aggregate employment of the area. Every new establishment means a firm demand in certain specific occupations on
the manpower resources of the locality. Frequently the new
managements have to face embarrassment on account of non-
availability of suitable workers in certain categories. In order
to be able to keep abreast of the happenings and keep knowledge
of the employment structure of the area up to date, it is incum-
bent on the Managers of Employment Exchanges to keep very
close track of all the new factories and other establishments,
and expansion, shrinkage, or closing down of the existing ones,
as the case may be. Unless the Managers of Employment Exchanges keep their knowledge up to date they are likely to find
themselves unable to meet the manpower demands of the area
in an adequate manner.

It would be appropriate to open new Employers' Cards immediately for new establishments and amend the existing ones
as necessary. Whenever an Exchange Manager gets information on the prospect of a new factory or establishment in his
area, he is expected to contact the controlling management at
the earliest opportunity and obtain details with respect to the
likely time of going into operation, the employment structure,
and the size of total employment. This information should be
checked with the managements at reasonable intervals to dis-
cover any changes in their plans that may have been made.

A report on setting up of new establishments or closing down of the existing ones should be submitted separately for every single case. For the present, only those establishments that have a prospect of employing 100 or more persons should be reported. A variation which is less than 25 may not be reported.

It is appreciated that in some cases Managers of Employment Exchanges may not be able to remain up to date with this aspect of work on account of limitations on their resources but the Managers are expected to give this work a high priority and submit the reports on new establishments, etc. in purposeful manner as far as they can go. The keenness of the Officers is likely to be judged by the size and quality of their performance on this item.

An Annual Report will be submitted by all the Employment Exchanges in the proforma given in Appendix III. In this report the total number of reports submitted during the year will be enumerated. This report will be submitted by all the Employment Exchanges on the 30th of June every year.

When discussing Employment Trends in the Monthly Narrative Reports, the over-all situation with respect to industries in operation within the area should be discussed as indicated in Circular 8/13. The necessity of confirming to the pattern as given in Appendix to the above-mentioned Circular cannot be over-emphasized. The Managers, Employment Exchanges, remain personally responsible for making sure that discussion on Employment Trends in future Monthly Narrative Reports is in the correct form.

Discussion on different industries in Employment Trends should be objective, i. e. it should contain material indicating the anticipated or planned expansion or shrinkage on an over-all basis. The effect of these changes on different occupations should be assessed specifically. In Part IV of Employment Trends, any likely rearrangement or pronounced shortage expected as a result of the current local trends and a probable action calculated to meet the additional demands should be discussed.

* * * * *

W.E. Circ. 7/31
Dated   26.11.64

To

THE MANAGERS OF ALL EMPLOYMENT EXCHANGES
IN WEST PAKISTAN
(for necessary   action)
Government of West Pakistan
Directorate of Labour Welfare
(Manpower and Employment Wing)

Subject: REHABILITATION OF EX-SERVICEMEN IN CIVIL
POSTS

The Government of West Pakistan under their orders have
made reservation of 50 per cent of new vacancies in Class IV
and 25 per cent at the Junior-most level of Class III for ex-
servicemen. Orders have also been issued for relaxation of
age limit and educational qualifications (Appendix I). Autonomous bodies in West Pakistan have also been ordered to
follow the same policy (Appendix II).

Orders of the Central Government relating to the reservation of Class IV vacancies and Class III posts of staff car drivers
and relaxation of age limit are reproduced in Appendix III.

Under the existing orders, all the vacancies expected to be
of longer than three months' duration have to be notified by the
Government establishments and autonomous bodies to the Employment Exchanges and appointments may only be made from
amongst the applicants submitted by the Employment Exchanges. It has been found that in a large number of cases the
employers do not specify any reservation for ex-servicemen.

Although the Employment Exchanges do not have authority
to enforce the ex-servicemen quota in new appointments, it is
a matter of very great importance for the Employment Exchanges, and no effort is to be spared to make sure that ex-
servicemen not only get their full share but are considered
for appointment against the remaining open vacancies also.

The Employment Exchanges, when making submission against vacancies notified by Government establishment/semi-Government and autonomous bodies, shall include a suitable number of ex-servicemen, even where no reservation for ex-servicemen has been notified. The Managers of Employment Exchanges will personally remain responsible to ensure that the employers always have a reasonable number of ex-servicemen under consideration.

Whenever vacancies are received from a Government employer, or autonomous bodies, the Manager, when giving a direction as to the total number of persons to be submitted, should clearly indicate the minimum number of ex-servicemen to be included therein. When making selection for submission of ex-servicemen, the qualifications and age as prescribed by the employer may be modified in view of the Government orders. This relaxation should be intimated to the employers also.

If for any reasons suitable ex-servicemen cannot be found, the Employment Exchange Manager should carefully review the case himself, and: (1) consider circulating the vacancies to other Employment Exchanges within the region or the area to which the candidate should belong, according to the regional quota rules in force from time to time; or (2) relax the direction as to the submission of ex-servicemen to the extent it is considered necessary.

Before a vacancy of ex-servicemen quota can be filled by a non-ex-serviceman, a non-availability certificate has to be issued by the Employment Exchanges to the employer. The Employment Exchanges shall issue the certificate only when it has become impossible for them to find suitable ex-servicemen, and these certificates shall be issued specifically for each notification of vacancies. A copy of this certificate along with a copy of the vacancy notification letter, etc., and statement showing the efforts made by the Manager as well as the reasons for non-availability shall be submitted to the Director, Labour Welfare (Manpower and Employment Wing).

All instances where it has not been possible to submit the required number of ex-servicemen should also be reported in a special report every month which may also include the cases of non-availability certificates.

* * * * *

UNITED KINGDOM MANPOWER FORECASTING

(The Ministry of Labour's Manpower Research Unit, set up in 1963, is concerned with this problem. The following are extracts from two of its publications reproduced with the permission of Her Britannic Majesty's Stationery Office. Firstly, "Manpower Studies No. 1--The Pattern of the Future.")

It is important to recognize the limitations of forecasts. They represent no more than a careful assessment of probabilities based on the best evidence at present available, both statistical and non-statistical. Even when the main trends have been discerned--and this is complicated, especially in the case of manufacturing industry, by the intrusion of cyclical factors--their translation into quantitative terms at particular dates must be a hazardous operation. Moreover, the method used for the employment forecasts, which consists essentially of projecting past employment trends, modified as necessary in the light of known plans and likely future developments, represents no more than a first approach to the problem. Other methods are being explored which may later lead to some revision of the present forecasts.

The aim is to give a broad assessment of the main trends in employment. While this is a necessary first step in the process of manpower planning, it is no more than a first step. Technological progress is constantly altering the occupational structure of the labour force and creating demands for new types of skill. It is vital to get as clear a picture as possible of such changes, which may well be more marked in the future than in the past. Changes in the numbers and proportions of workers engaged in any particular sector of employment depend in the main upon economic and technological factors--changes in the levels of demand for various goods and services and in foreign trade, and changes in methods of production or in the actual nature of the product. Such factors are not independent of one another, nor can they be wholly divorced from demographic and other social considerations. In this complex of interacting conditions, forecasting becomes very much more hazardous than in the relatively simple field of broad population changes, and mathematical precision is not be be expected, even in the short term.

The methods used in the present study consist essentially of extrapolation from past employment trends, modified in the light of known plans and informed opinion as to likely future developments. Such methods should give a reasonably good guide to trends over the next five years. This is sufficiently far ahead for most practical purposes which require forecasts with some degree of precision, though for some purposes a broader view of the more distant future is also useful. In forecasting over a five year period, account can be taken of recent or immediately foreseen developments and their probable rate of spread through the economy. Within such a period, it is unlikely that any development as yet completely unforeseen would have a major impact on employment. This does not hold for the longer term.

Method and Assumptions Used to Forecast the Future Working Population

Forecasts of the future working population of Great Britain and of the United Kingdom are made annually by the Ministry of Labour, in consultation with other Government Departments. They are based on available statistical information relating to past years and an assessment of demographic, social, and economic trends in the medium-term future.

Method of Forecasting

The forecasts published in October, 1963, and used in this report were based on (a) forecasts of the mid-year total population, prepared by the Government Actuary's Department and published for selected years in the April, 1963, issue of the Monthly Digest of Statistics and (b) assumed relationships (termed "activity rates") for most age-sex groups between the number in the working population and the number in the total population at mid-year.

The Nature of the Forecasts

There are many variable factors influencing the size of the working population about which assumptions have to be made. There are substantial inward and outward movements both among regular full-time workers (e.g. on leaving school or college, migration, permanent and temporary retirement, disablement, and death) and among part-time, seasonal and occasional workers, particularly students during vacations and week-ends, married women, and older workers. These movements are associated to some extent with the pressure of demand for labour, as well as demographic, educational, and social changes. Forecasts of the size of the working population, even in the short term, cannot have the same degree of reliability as those of the total population, in view of the additional variable factors about which assumptions have to be made. The forecasts are consequently only intended to indicate how the size and age-sex structure of the working population may change on the assumptions made. If developments occur which invalidate these assumptions, the future working population could well differ substantially from the forecasts.

General Assumptions

As regards the total population forecasts used in 1963, the principal assumptions were that (a) net immigration into the United Kingdom was 60,000 persons in the year from mid-1962 to mid-1963 and would fall in the longer term to a notional 20,000 per year; (b) the average age of women on marriage would continue to fall; and (c) death rates would decline steadily, with rates of decline becoming smaller with age.

As regards the working population forecasts, the main assumptions were that (a) there would be full employment with a high pressure of demand for labour; (b) the proportion of young persons aged fifteen to twenty-four in full-time education would rise progressively; (c) the activity rate for married women aged twenty to twenty-four would continue to fall and the rates for married women aged thirty to sixty-four would continue to rise; and (d) the activity rate for persons aged sixty-five and over, other than married women, would decline gradually.

Limitations of the Forecasts

The assumption about the level of demand for labour is particularly important. The working population is smaller during periods of reduced pressure of demand; there are then more withdrawals from the working population as marginal workers stop working, retirements are advanced and emigration increases; the numbers entering or re-entering the working population fall, e.g. immigrants, married women.   Although the effects of some of these changes may only be temporary, some may persist for several years.   For example, if during a recession the age of retirement is advanced, many of those retiring will not re-enter the working population when economic conditions improve.   Changes in migration also have long-term effects.

The pressure of demand for labour in the period 1961 to 1963 was lower than that assumed in the forecasts.   The gain from migration was also lower. These are probably the main reasons why the calculated "forecast" of the working population at mid-1963 was higher by 159,000 males and 56,000 females than the subsequent published estimate for mid-June, 1963, based on the count of National Insurance cards exchanged in the June-August quarter of 1963.

Method Used to Forecast Future
Levels of Employment

The method of forecasting levels of employment in particular sectors consisted of two stages: the calculation of purely statistical projections of past trends; and the modification of the future levels so obtained in the light of informed opinion as to known plans and other developments likely to influence the trend.

Statistical Projections

Two methods of statistical projection were used. First, a simple projection to 1968 was made of the time trend of the last decade, calculated by fitting a straight line to the annual estimates of employees in employment over the period 1953-62. Secondly, the same data, over the period 1948-63 were used to prepare alternative projections for 1968 by a more complex method which adapts itself to alterations in the slope or level of the trend.

These calculations were carried out by computer. The basic data were the mid-year figures of employees in employment for Great Britain, derived from the annual exchange of insurance cards and related data, by minimum list headings of the Standard Industrial Classification (SIC). In order to overcome the changes of classification introduced in 1959, it was necessary to group a number of headings together in several instances. This meant substantial loss of detail, for the earlier period, in the engineering and vehicles groups. Males and females were taken separately in those cases (about half the total number of series) in which females formed a substantial share of employment, or where past trends were clearly divergent as between males and females. Independent projections were made by both methods of the series for each Order total of the SIC (taking Orders VI and IX together), males and females separately.

Neither method of prediction took account of data other than past employment series and it was not expected that the adaptive method would necessarily give better results for any given series. It was hoped, however--as proved to be the case-- that a systematic comparison of the two results would draw attention to cases of unusual difficulty, and incidentally provide some useful insights into the extent to which the results of forecasting depend upon the particular method used.

Modification of Projections

At the second stage the figures so obtained for each minimum list heading or group of headings were scrutinized and, where necessary modified in the light of all other relevant information available, both quantitative and qualitative. This included such information as was readily available about production and productivity trends, including technological developments. To a considerable extent this was a process of judgement, in which informed opinion was consulted, especially with regard to the possibility that major economic or technological changes might be in prospect for the industry before 1968, whose effects were not yet reflected in the recorded employment data.

This stage was undertaken in consultation with other Government Departments and with the National Economic Development Office. Extensive use was made of information about actual plans and likely developments supplied by firms and organizations to these Departments, to the National Economic Development Office and to the Unit itself in the course of its special studies of manpower in the metal manufacturing, metal using and construction industries, and of the effect of computers on office employment.

The modifications were substantial in a few cases, but in general they did not much alter the broad pattern of employment indicated by the trend extrapolations. A similar process of judgement was applied to the Order total projections in the light of the modified forecasts for the constituent series. An adjustment was then made to relate these forecasts for Great Britain to figures for the United Kingdom, on the assumption that Northern Ireland trends were similar.

Finally, since these forecasts had been prepared independently of the forecasts of the total working population, their total had to be checked for consistency with it. Because they refer to employees in employment only, deductions were first made from the total working population to exclude all other groups (that is, H.M. Forces, employers, self-employed, and registered unemployed). After this adjustment had been made, the two totals were found to differ only slightly, and an excess in

the total of the employment forecasts of less than half of one
per cent was corrected by an adjustment distributed propor-
tionately among them.

Interpretation of the Forecasts

The resulting forecasts represent an assessment of the way
in which the estimated future level of employment is likely to
be distributed between different sectors, on the basis of past
trends, employers' present plans, and informed opinion as to
likely future developments. The study was not concerned with
the precise assumptions as to the rate of growth of the economy
as a whole, or the pattern of demand within it, which might
underlie these plans or opinions. The method thus differs from
that used by the National Economic Development Office in their
industrial enquiries. In addition to information about current
plans, the Office sought information as to what manpower re-
quirements--among other economic variables--would be on the
basis of a common assumption of an average annual rate of
growth in gross domestic product between 1961-66 of 4 per
cent.

The pattern of employment as between broad sectors for 1968
resulting from the present study is in fact much in line with
that for 1966 set out in the NEDC reports, but as their objectives and methods were different neither can be regarded as
confirming the results of the other.

Alternative Methods

The method of employment forecasting used for this report
was adopted as a first approach to the problem. Being comparatively simple and requiring only readily available data, it
has enabled this assessment of broad trends to be carried out
reasonably quickly. An alternative approach is to treat future
levels of employment as functions of estimated or assumed
levels of output and projected trends of output per man. Such
an approach has the advantage of enabling employment forecasts

to be given on the basis of alternative assumptions about the future level of economic activity. Some work has already been done on these lines both in this country and abroad, particularly in the U.S.A., but progress has been somewhat hampered by lack of appropriate data, especially as regards productivity. The possibilities of such alternative methods are being further explored.

(A second report: "Manpower Studies No. 2--The Metal Industries," discusses occupational trends in the metal manufacturing and metal using industries. It is the result of an enquiry amongst individual firms. The following are extracts from it):

Of primary importance in any attempt to seek a better balance in the future between the supply of and demand for skill is an improvement in the efficiency of training arrangements of all kinds. With this in view, Training Boards are being set up for a number of important industries. In order to carry out their functions efficiently, the Boards will need to have the fullest information which can be obtained about future requirements for skilled manpower in their industries.

During the next ten years, the impact of technological change will affect the demand for different types of skill and the content of particular occupations, not least in the metal manufacturing and metal using industries, which together form a large and important sector of the economy.

For all these reasons, it is important to get as clear and accurate a picture as possible of the occupational structure of these industries and of the trends which have been affecting it and which are likely to do so in the foreseeable future.   Is automation and technological innovation the dominant factor in determining changes in the numbers of people employed in the industries? Will automation mean that fewer unskilled workers be required in future? Are skilled workers needing to become more skilled? If so, is the trend towards greater specialization or towards competence in a wider range of skills? Is the need for particular skills declining (or perhaps disappearing) either because the job itself is required less or because production processes are reducing or breaking up its skilled content? Which skills are likely to be in increased demand in the years ahead?   These and other questions of a similar nature have to be answered if the industries' labour force is to be adequate for the needs of an expanding economy and equipped to meet the challenge of change.

...It was recognized that for many employers the request to provide forecasts would raise problems of a new and often formidable kind; for this reason the enquiry was conceived as an exploratory study only and the results should be interpreted accordingly.   Little was known in advance about the extent to which manpower forecasting over a period as long as five years is already undertaken in some firms, or about the practical problems of ensuring the uniformity of method and assumptions between one firm and another on which a fuller statistical enquiry would need to be based.

The fact that the enquiry breaks new ground in this respect is a pointer both to its main value and to its principal limitations. It was expected, as proved to be the case, that a first exploration of the problems by the participating firms and the Manpower Research Unit would prepare the way for an improvement in the present methods of forecasting. At the same time the reliability of the results, as a guide to the future as the firms themselves see it, must inevitably reflect the limitations inherent in a first attempt by many of them to look ahead over a five year period.

The Method of Enquiry

The enquiry was addressed to more than 300 large and medium-sized firms in the metal manufacturing and metal using industries throughout Great Britain, each of which was asked to complete a questionnaire showing details of its labour force in 1958 and 1963 under various categories and occupations, together with an estimate, under the same headings, of its labour force in 1968. Though there were, of course, marked cyclical fluctuations in manufacturing industry generally between 1958 and 1963, those years occupied points in the cycle which can be taken as a reasonable basis for comparison. In addition, a number of non-statistical questions were asked about developments that had affected or might affect the firm's labour force:

training arrangements; the extent of manpower forecasting by firms; estimates of longer-term trends and so on. A copy of the questionnaire used is reproduced below (see p.308) which also draws attention to a number of points that need to be borne in mind in considering the results of the enquiry.

The selection of firms for the enquiry, which was made in consultation with the Ministry's Regional Controllers and with other Government Departments, was deliberately biased towards the larger and more technically advanced firms because it was felt that these were the ones most likely to be able to attempt realistic forecasts and to provide useful indications of future trends in their industries. No attempt was made to obtain a uniform coverage of the different industries or to secure a statistically valid sample.

Participation in the enquiry was entirely voluntary and an undertaking was given to firms that any information that they provided would be treated in strict confidence and would not be published in an attributable form.

In most cases, firms that had been approached were visited by officers of the Ministry to provide any necessary background and, where appropriate, to clarify or supplement the written replies. These visits proved a most valuable source of qualitative information.

Many of the questions asked in the enquiry were of a general nature and it would clearly be wrong to assume that the absence of specific replies to some of these necessarily meant that they were not applicable to the particular firm; on the other hand, where comments were made this might itself be an indication of exceptional circumstances. For instance, firms were asked whether particular sections of their existing labour force were under or over staffed and whether the increases forecast could be met from their existing resources (including their own training programmes). Where reductions in numbers were forecast they were asked to say whether there was likely to be redundancy. Very few figures were given in reply to these questions, but it is clear that this should not be taken as implying the expected absence of either shortages or surpluses. Many firms said they had considerable difficulty in estimating their future needs and few attempted to go further.

Assumptions Used by Firms in
Making Forecasts

The firms participating in the enquiry were asked to base their forecasts on their own assumptions about the future and to say what these were. It was felt that individual firms were in the best position to assess the many factors which would affect the size and composition of their labour force. Accordingly, the results of the enquiry, so far as they relate to the future, are based on a variety of assumptions. Generally, however, it is clear that participating firms made assumptions based on their own experience of the past and on their own expectations; and for the most part these are of continued growth in which they will share, not only at home but generally overseas as well. There was, however, relatively little indication that firms had been excessively optimistic by, for instance, assuming a higher share of a limited market.

Some assumptions related to Government policy, ranging from direct support in the defence field to the absence of fiscal measures that might adversely affect trade.

Participating Firms

The participating firms had a total labour force, in mid-1963, of 1,183,000, or 27.3 per cent of the total in the industries covered.

The degree of cooperation obtained can be seen from the fact that of 308 firms approached, 262, or 85 per cent, provided reports in time for inclusion. Some of these firms had only one establishment.   Others had more than one and some of these provided separate reports for each establishment. Thus in the end 307 reports that were suitable for use were received from 262 firms.

The question inevitably arises how far, if at all, the forecasts and comments made in the report can be taken as a measure of future requirements in the industries concerned. Firms were asked whether they themselves considered their position to be typical of their industry, and this point was also explored in discussions with industrial organizations and others. The main result was to confirm the view that a good deal of allowance should be made for the fact that the enquiry was addressed predominantly to larger firms, since smaller ones are apt to differ not only in the structure of their labour force but also in the extent to which they are influenced by technological change...

Generally speaking, the participating firms have tended to grow faster than their industry or decline more slowly.

(Under the heading "Summary of Results" the report continues:)

The Main Factor Influencing the Demand for Labour

Production. The general view of participating firms was that over-all changes in employment were dictated primarily by changes in the volume or range of production, deriving in turn from changes in product demand. In some industries, the influence of demand was especially strong: in machine tools, for example, special mention was made of the effects of cyclical fluctuations in manufacturing investment and the bunching of orders; in shipbuilding, of the effects of the depression of world freight rates and the expansion of world shipbuilding capacity; in aircraft, of the effects of particular orders. Over practically the whole field, however, firms were subject to specific factors affecting demand. It was widely indicated that increases in employment would not keep pace with increases in output, though firms made few specific comparisons of rates of increase of references to productivity levels. In many cases, expansion of production was expected to accrue from investment already made and modernization schemes completed or nearing completion.

Organization. Production and organizational factors were interwoven and the effect of each was not always easily distin-

guishable; but organizational change did not emerge as a major
influence on levels of employment. On the whole, the effects
of changes in structure seem to have tended to even out, though
the selection of participating firms, the attempt to compare the
position over the recent past within each firm, and the choice
of dates all inhibit more precise assessment of the effects of
this sort of change.

Other forms of organizational change (better layout, programming, etc.) were not seen as particularly notable, though
they did appear to affect mechanical engineering rather than
other industries. Reference was made to the use of work study
and other management aids to efficiency which cumulatively
were capable of exerting a significant influence on the use of
labour.

Technological change. In the view of participating firms generally, the main effects of technological change have been partially to offset increases in employment derived from expansion of demand, thus permitting increases in the volume of production without proportionate increases in manpower, and to
bring under review traditional elements of occupational skills
(more particularly in relation to existing divisions between
skilled operatives on the one hand and semi-skilled workers
and technicians on the other). These effects were expected to
continue. In the field of automation, fairly extensive use of
computers was reported, for production control and design as
well as for administration; many firms referred to the introduction of automatic machines or automatically controlled
machine tools; the importance of automatic instrumentation
was emphasized, particularly in relation to metal manufacture;
the possibilities and implications of automatic or semi-
automatic assembly were emphasized, especially in the electrical engineering field. Though there was less emphasis generally on the introduction of further mechanization, a good
deal of reference was made to the developing use of conveyors
and of mechanical handling methods generally. There was also
a substantial volume of comment on the use of new materials,
both plastics and metals, and on other changes in techniques.

Questionnaire Used in the Enquiry

MINISTRY OF LABOUR

Enquiry into Future Requirements for Skilled Labour
in the Metal Manufacturing and Metal Using Industries

Introductory Note

The objects of this enquiry are:

(a) to obtain as detailed a picture as possible of the probable
size and occupational distribution of firms' manpower
requirements, particularly in the skilled crafts, in five
years' time, compared with the position five years ago
and now;

(b) to assess how far any increases in the numbers of skilled
craftsmen will be met by firms' own training programmes
and how far any decreases may give rise to redundancy;

(c) to find out the reasons for any changes;

(d) to obtain wherever possible a broad indication of likely
developments in manpower requirements beyond five
years.

This questionnaire consists accordingly of two sections of equal
importance:

Section A asks you to set out in summary form such figures
as can be provided under the headings and classifications
shown. Where precise figures are not available, estimates--
in the form of proportions of the total labour force or percentage changes--would be welcome. If any particular
heading or classification causes difficulty, you are asked to
give the nearest available figures, if any, and to indicate the
extent of the difference in your reply to Section B.

Section B poses some questions designed to bring out the reasons and assumptions behind the figures given in Section A and to obtain your views on the wider issues. If you need more space than is available on the form, please use a separate sheet. Copies of any available memoranda, reports, etc. relevant to this enquiry would be welcome.

NOTES ON SECTION A

1. The figures for May, 1963, should if possible relate to the last pay week for which pay had been computed by 18th May, 1963; this was the date used for the recent enquiry under the Statistics of Trade Act into the occupations of employees in manufacturing industry. If these figures were influenced by abnormal conditions please indicate the extent of this in reply to Question 1 in Section B.

   The figures for 1958 should be those for the comparable pay week in that year, if available. If no figures for 1958 are available, please give estimates, e.g., as a percentage of numbers currently employed. If the changes in the labour force since 1958 are due to changes in the structure of the firm, please give relevant details in reply to Question 1 of Section B.

2. Part-time workers (normally those working 30 hours per week or less) should be included throughout. If their number is significant, please show it in brackets after any figure in which it is included.

3. These include all apprentices and others undergoing systematic training within the firm. A description of training arrangements is asked for in Question 4 of Section B.

4. Please indicate the extent to which the numbers employed exceed (+) or fall below (-) real requirements.

5. If the number estimated to be employed in 1968 is less than the number currently employed, please indicate if possible the number (+) likely to be declared redundant over the five

SECTION A	May, 1958 (See Note 2)		May, 1963
Name and . . . . address . . . . of firm . . . . M.L.H.	Number employed (Note 2)	Apprentices etc. included in col. (ii) (Note 3)	Number employed (Note 2)
(i)	(ii)	(iii)	(iv)
I. Total employed: (a) Males . . . . . . (b) Females			
II. Broad occupational categories: (a) Administrative, technical and clerical workers . . . . (b) Skilled operatives engaged on production or maintenance (including persons being trained) (See Note 6) (c) Other employees. .			
III. Details of certain occupations: (a) Qualified scientists,) professional engineers) and other technologists) (b) Technicians other) than draughtsmen (See) * Note 7) . . . .) (c) Draughtsmen (not) including tracers) . . .) (d) . . . .) (e) etc. . . . .) **			

* Included in II (a) above
** Main crafts included in II (b) above (See Note 8)

(See Note 1)		May, 1968		
Apprentices etc. included in col.(iv) (Note 3)	Surplus or shortage (+or -) (Note 4)	Estimated number employed (Note 2)	Apprentices etc. included in col.(vii) (Note 3)	Surplus or shortage(+or-) from available resources (Note 5)
(v)	(vi)	(vii)	(viii)	(ix)

years (i.e., over and above the normal wastage and any number likely to be found other jobs within the firm). Any such estimate will be regarded as tentative and for the purpose of this enquiry only, and will be treated in the strictest confidence.

If the number to be employed in 1968 is greater than the number currently employed, please indicate (-) the extent, if any, to which your existing resources together with your training programme (less net wastage) are likely to fall short of requirements, i.e., the number of trained people you hope to recruit over the five years from outside.

6. This should include all operatives (and apprentices or other trainees) on skilled work, i.e., work for which an apprenticeship is normally served. Operatives on semi-skilled work should be included in II (c).

7. A suggested description of technicians is attached. (Not included in this study.) If your own classification differs materially from this, please indicate the extent of the difference in reply to Question 1 of Section B.

8. Please give the required information for each of the crafts listed that is employed, or expected to be employed, by the firm. This list is the same as that used for the enquiry into the occupations of employees in manufacturing industry.

   Crafts in which only a small number is employed can be ignored unless they are of particular importance (e.g., toolroom crafts). If there are large numbers in a miscellaneous category (e.g., welders), please specify the particular crafts included.

SECTION B

Name and address of firm . . . .
. . . .

1. Please indicate any special difficulties encountered in completing Section A, such as difficulties of classification, changes in the structure of the firm within the past five years, etc.

2. Please give the reasons for any substantial changes in man-power requirements experienced over the past five years or expected over the next five years; in particular, please indicate how far they are due to changes in the scale or range of production and how far due to technological change.

3. Please indicate any major economic assumptions on which your forecasts are based, concerning either the national economy or your industry as a whole, e.g., the growth of demand at home and abroad, and the level of investment likely to be required.

4. Please describe briefly your present training arrangements and any development of them envisaged in relation to your forecasts, whether as regards apprenticeship or other training for young people, or as regards adaptation of existing skills.

5. Is it the practice of your firm to make forecasts of its man-power requirements some years ahead? If so, with what frequency and in how much detail?

6. Looking ahead 10 to 15 years, what general trends do you expect to see in the occupational structure of your labour force, particularly among craftsmen?

7. How far would you say your manpower position and fore-casts are typical of other firms in your industry or of firms in other industries employing similar types of labour?

8. Please add any general comments you may have that are relevant to the purpose of the enquiry.

RECOGNITION OF ARMY TRADESMEN
AND TRADESWOMEN BY TRADE UNIONS

Numerous agreements have been made between the armed services and individual trade unions whereby recognition is accorded to service training and experience. They are reached following correspondence between the two parties. Sometimes, in addition, the trade union sends an official to examine the technical standard reached by the service tradesman before agreeing to recognize the trade.

Below are summarized agreements made between the Ministry of Defence (Army) and certain trade unions.

Schedule 1

Mechanical Engineering Trades

Agreement with the Amalgamated Engineering Union

Conditions of Eligibility

Skilled membership

Tradesmen in the trades listed in Section A below who: (a) received their trade training at Army trade training establishments; (b) have completed a minimum of five years' training and experience in their trade, including boys' service; and (c) have attained the required classification.

Semi-skilled membership

Tradesmen with less than five years' training and experience in the trades listed in Section A and those listed in Section B can be accepted only for semi-skilled membership.

The trade union's rules provide for a man with five years' experience at the trade to be transferred subsequently to the skilled section of the union provided he satisfies his branch of the union as to his qualifications.

Section A
Skilled Section

Aircraft Technician (Airframes and Engines)
Artificer (Aircraft) (Airframes and Engines)
Artificer (Gun)
Artificer (Instruments, A.A.)
Artificer (Instruments, Field)
Artificer (Vehicle)
Carriage and Wagon Repairer
Draughtsman (Mechanical)
Engine Fitter (I.C. and Pumps)
Engine Fitter (Plant)
Engine Fitter (Steam)
Farrier
Fitter
Fitter, Gun
Fitter (Locomotive)
Fitter, Machinist
Fitter (Railway Signals)

Instrument Mechanic (Surgical)
Artificer (Weapon)
Clerk of Works (Mechanical)
Armourer
Blacksmith
Boilermaker
Machinist (Metal)
Marine Engineer
Petroleum Fitter
Plumber and Pipefitter
Refrigeration Mechanic
Sheet Metal Worker
Shipwright
Toolmaker
Turner
Vehicle Mechanic
Welder

Classification (where applicable): Classes I and II

Section B
Semi-skilled Section

Saw Doctor

Classification: Classes I and II

Schedule 2

Lithographic Printing Trades

Agreement with the Amalgamated Society
of Lithographic Printers

Conditions of Eligibility

Tradesmen who have been classified as Class I or II in the trades listed below are recognized as eligible for direct admission as skilled men on probation for twelve months. Normally men should have been employed at their trade for six years but other cases will be given individual attention.

Lithographic Helio Worker
Lithographer (Machine Minder)
Photo-printer (Photo Mechanical) (Lithographic Plate Maker)
Storeman Survey (with Lithographic Plate Graining experience)
Survey Print Technician

Schedule 3

Leather Workers and Allied Trades

Conditions of Eligibility

Tradesmen and tradeswomen in the trades listed below are eligible for skilled membership of the societies shown, provided they have reached the minimum trade classification. They should have served for a period of at least three years in the specified trade.

Amalgamated Society of Leather Workers and Kindred Trades.

National Union of Leather Workers and Allied Trades.

Coachtrimmer	Class III
Equipment Repairer	Class III
Saddler and Harness Maker	Class III
Shoemaker	Class III
Textile Refitter	Class III

Schedule 4

Metal Working Trades

Agreement with the Associated Blacksmiths' Forge and Smithy Workers' Society

Conditions of Eligibility

Tradesmen in the trades listed below are eligible for membership provided they have: (a) passed the Class III or higher trade test; and (b) completed a minimum of five years' training and experience in the trade: blacksmith, farrier, welder.

Schedule 5

Dental Technicians

Conditions of Eligibility

Dental Technicians are eligible for membership of the Associated Dental Technicians' Sections of the societies listed below provided they have: (a) successfully passed a course of training at the Depot and Training Establishment, RADC; (b) been classified as a Dental Technician, Class II or higher; and (c) completed a total of not less than five years' training and experience in the trade.

Society of Goldsmiths, Jewellers, and Kindred Trades.

Union of Shop, Distributive, and Allied Workers.

Schedule 6

Draughtsmen

Agreement with the Draughtsmen's and Allied Technicians' Association

Conditions of Eligibility

Draughtsmen (Mechanical) and Draughtsmen (Railway and Port Construction) are recognized as qualified to become members or associate members provided they fulfil the following conditions:

Full members: (a) have passed the Class I trade test; (b) be at least twenty-five years of age; (c) be employed at the trade at the time of application for membership; and (d) have had eight years' engineering experience, at least three years of which have been in a drawing office.

Senior associate members: (a) have passed the Class II trade test; (b) be at least twenty-one years of age; (c) be employed at the trade at the time of application for membership; and (d) have had at least three years' engineering experience of which one year must have been in a drawing office.

Junior associate members: (a) have passed the Class II trade test; and (b) be employed as a draughtsman. Junior associate members who attain the age and experience of senior associate membership must at once transfer to that class.

THE HEARTS AND MINDS CAMPAIGN

(Extracts from the Pamphlet Issued to All British Troops in Brunei)

The winning of the Hearts and Minds of the peoples of Sarawak and Sabah is of great importance, perhaps even greater importance, than the successful conduct of ground and air operations against the enemy.

Success will only be gained through the combined efforts and contributions of the Civil Governments, the Police Forces and the Armed Forces.

The Contribution of the Armed Forces. The people among whom you live and work consider you to be representative of their Government.

The greatest contribution that you can make to the winning of this campaign is in your daily contact with the civilian population.

You must treat all Malaysians whom you meet as friends and with good will. A confident, firm and friendly attitude will help greatly. A smile and a greeting to those whom you meet, especially in their own language, serves to break the ice.

You must not tolerate any misconduct or ill-discipline in your units. A single act of misconduct or ill-discipline cancels out the effects of much good behaviour.

Some "Do's" and "Don'ts" for ops in Malaysian Borneo:

Some "Do's"

Cooperate closely with the Police and Government.

Give help in making foot paths and bridges.

Give help with boating and river problems.

Render first aid to civilians in need of it.

Evacuate critically ill civilians by air and arrange for their return when cured.

Help in flood relief and putting out fires.

Pass urgent messages over service radio nets.

Deliver letters to and from remote areas.

Treat civilian leaders with due respect.

Help and advise on rural development.

Demonstrate equipment and weapons to civilians.

Play games with locals and share hospitality.

Conduct evening education classes in Malay.

Learn to speak the local language.

Publicize the Police Reward Scheme.

Assist Government officers to get about their areas.

Distribute Government publications.

Help in driving wild animals off padi crops.

Help in the killing of vermin.

Take an interest in local affairs.

Treat the civilians you meet as equals.

Respect the women of the country.

Some "Don'ts"

Don't give offence by ignoring local customs or conventions.

Don't bathe or wash in the nude.

Don't shout at civilians. They hate that.

Don't interfere in religious affairs.

Don't take anything without paying for it.

Finally

Do give all the help that you can which does not interfere with your military tasks.

Do go out of your way to find out what the local problems are and try to solve them. If you cannot, then ask advice from your superiors.

UNITED STATES FOREIGN ASSISTANCE ACT

SECTION 505

(1965 Amendments are underlined)

Sec. 505.   UTILIZATION OF ASSISTANCE

(a) Military assistance to any country shall be furnished solely for internal security, for legitimate self-defense, to permit the recipient country to participate in regional or collective arrangements or measures consistent with the Charter of the United Nations, or otherwise to permit the recipient country to participate in collective measures requested by the United Nations for the purpose of maintaining or restoring international peace and security, or for the purpose of assisting foreign military forces in less developed friendly countries (or the voluntary efforts of personnel of the Armed Forces of the United States in such countries) to construct public works and engage in other activities helpful to the economic and social development of such friendly countries. It is the sense of the Congress that such foreign military forces should not be maintained or established solely for civic action activities and that such civic action activities not significantly detract from the capability of the military forces to perform their military missions and be coordinated with and form part of the total economic and social development effort.

(b) Except (1) to the extent necessary to fulfill prior commitments, or (2) for civic action assistance, or (3) to the extent that the President finds, with respect to any Latin American country, that the furnishing of military assistance under this Act is necessary to safeguard the security of the United States or to safeguard the security of a country associated with the United States in the Alliance for Progress against overthrow of a duly constituted government, and so informs the Congress, no further military assistance under any provision of this Act shall be furnished to any Latin American country.

ABOUT THE AUTHOR

Hugh Hanning is Assistant Foreign Editor on the Statist, a journal of world affairs, industry, and investment published weekly in London. Concurrently, he is a consultant on African armies to the Institute for Strategic Studies. His long interest in military operations was supplemented by service in the Royal Naval Volunteer Reserve in World War II. He has also been a defence correspondent for the Observer and the Independent Television News, and a diplomatic correspondent for the Glasgow Herald.

Mr. Hanning has published two books about the United Nations and has contributed to Foreign Affairs and Brassey's Annual. He received an Honours Degree from University College, Oxford.